# JOHNNY DEPP

## Recent Titles in Greenwood Biographies

# JOHNNY DEPP

## A Biography

Michael Blitz and Louise Krasniewicz

GREENWOOD BIOGRAPHIES

GREENWOOD PRESS
WESTPORT, CONN. LONDON

**Library of Congress Cataloging-in-Publication Data**

Blitz, Michael.
Johnny Depp : a biography / Michael Blitz and Louise Krasniewicz.
     p. cm. — (Greenwood biographies, ISSN 1540–4900)
  Includes bibliographical references and index.
  ISBN–13: 978–0–313–34300–1 (alk. paper)
  1. Depp, Johnny. 2. Motion picture actors and actresses—United States—Biography.
I. Krasniewicz, Louise, 1952– II. Title.

  PN2287.D39B58  2008
  791.4302'8092—dc22      2007034936

British Library Cataloguing in Publication Data is available.

Library of Congress Catalog Card Number: 2007034936

ISBN–13: 978–0–313–34300–1
ISSN: 1540–4900

First published in 2008

Greenwood Press, 88 Post Road West, Westport, CT 06881
An imprint of Greenwood Publishing Group, Inc.
www.greenwood.com

Printed in the United States of America

The paper used in this book complies with the
Permanent Paper Standard issued by the National
Information Standards Organization (Z39.48–1984).

10  9  8  7  6  5  4  3  2  1

# CONTENTS

CONTENTS

*Photo essay follows page 65*

# SERIES FOREWORD

In response to high school and public library needs, Greenwood developed this distinguished series of full-length biographies specifically for student use. Prepared by field experts and professionals, these engaging biographies are tailored for high school students who need challenging yet accessible biographies. Ideal for secondary school assignments, the length, format and subject areas are designed to meet educators' requirements and students' interests.

Greenwood offers an extensive selection of biographies spanning all curriculum-related subject areas including social studies, the sciences, literature and the arts, history, and politics, as well as popular culture, covering public figures and famous personalities from all time periods and backgrounds, both historic and contemporary, who have made an impact on American and/or world culture. Greenwood biographies are chosen based on comprehensive feedback from librarians and educators. Consideration is given to both curriculum relevance and inherent interest. The result is an intriguing mix of the well known and the unexpected, the saints and sinners from long-ago history and contemporary pop culture. Readers will find a wide array of subject choices from fascinating crime figures like Al Capone to inspiring pioneers like Margaret Mead, from the greatest minds of our time like Stephen Hawking to the most amazing success stories of our day like J. K. Rowling.

While the emphasis is on fact, not glorification, the books are meant to be fun to read. Each volume provides in-depth information about the subject's life from birth through childhood, the teen years, and adulthood. A thorough account relates family background and education, traces personal and professional influences, and explores struggles, accomplishments, and contributions. A timeline highlights the most significant life events against a historical perspective. Bibliographies supplement the reference value of each volume.

# INTRODUCTION: "I, JOHN"

Until his spectacular success as Jack Sparrow in the *Pirates of the Caribbean* film franchise, Johnny Depp probably did not strike most adults as a major figure in American culture. Although he now commands one of the highest salaries in Hollywood, has acted in more than 35 feature films since 1984, and starred in a hit television program in the early 1990s, he has never offered the kind of easy categorization that cultural icons demand. He is not a political figure like Susan Sarandon or Tim Robbins, or an intellectual leading man like Gregory Peck or George Clooney. He has not crossed over into political office like Arnold Schwarzenegger or Jesse "The Body" Ventura, or become involved in charity work like U2 singer Bono. And he certainly does not get involved in the issues of the suffering third world like Angelina Jolie and Brad Pitt.

But what he does do, besides drive girls and women and even some men into a veritable frenzy, is provide the culture with a concrete example of one of its favorite stories. From his early days of teen rock-and-roll bands through his drug-saturated 20s and law-breaking 30s, and dragging along a lifelong reputation as the devoted lover of famous and beautiful women, Depp has always presented a bad-boy image. He was such a stereotype of the young, immature male star that it was sometimes hard to keep his story apart from the sordid goings-on of similar bad boys like Charlie Sheen or Robert Downey Jr.

But then something happened, not just in the film roles he was playing, but in the life he was publicly and proudly professing to embrace. Not an embarrassing immersion in ecstatic religion like Tom Cruise's or a sudden awakening to a problem with alcohol like Mel Gibson's, Depp's transformation was simple and all-American. He found a woman to love and had children who, he says, gave him life and ended the illusion he had been living.

The transgressions of his early life, then, come to be seen not as a typical and foolish Hollywood soap opera, but as the backstory for a beautiful and compelling tale of redemption. We as a culture forgive and forget the most outrageous behaviors if the famous protagonist changes course, turns over a new leaf, or transforms into a more normal person. Redemption is generally not religious but moral in the sense that the person stops drinking or doing drugs or partying, or discovers a new respect for women.

But if that were all, if Johnny Depp's recent transformation was merely the result of getting older, getting wiser, finding the joys of kids and family, and settling into a house in the country (albeit a foreign country), his personal story would not be enough to earn him more than a cursory biography. What sets him apart from the numerous actors in the Brat Pack generation, however, are his remarkable screen portrayals of challenging, quirky, and compelling characters. What he has given the culture is a new and unique set of heroes and antiheroes, memorable characters who compel us to pay attention to him and his story. Although none of his roles by themselves, except for Captain Jack Sparrow and perhaps Edward Scissorhands or Willie Wonka, warrants an elevation to iconic status, together his 35 or so roles reveal an approach to acting and storytelling that can be a model for understanding what movie stories are supposed to do for us and why we take the stars in them seriously.

Before Jack Sparrow sauntered onto the big screen and changed Johnny Depp's fate and fortunes in *Pirates of the Caribbean*, the actor was best known to movie buffs as the onscreen alter ego of American director Tim Burton. To fans of the eccentric and bold Burton, Depp was the perfect personification of Burton's tortured outsider, the man who is so brilliant or so different that he will never fit into society and will never have a normal life. Was Depp expressing Burton's view of life when he played Edward Scissorhands as a sweet but asocial adolescent, or Ichabod Crane as a young man obsessed with the certainty of science but blind to the ways of the community of Sleepy Hollow, or Willy Wonka as the bizarre chocolate factory recluse? Or is there something of Johnny Depp in these characters, too, something that Tim Burton was able to tease out better than other directors?

Perhaps the most economical description of Johnny Depp's life in cinema comes from the Internet Movie Database (IMDb): "Frequently plays freakishly eccentric outcasts whose oddities are misunderstood by society, and have a usually flamboyant appearance and mannerism."[1] As Depp explained back in 2001, "It fascinates me how damaged individuals survive in this life, what is hiding behind their facade...there is not one person who isn't damaged. Me not the least."[2]

But can we learn anything about an actor from the performances he presents in a movie? We cannot assume the character he gives the audience has anything to do with his offscreen life, after all, since this is supposed to be acting. Depp has come to be thought of as one of the best actors of his generation and has earned two best actor Oscar nominations in recent years. That is an easy way to categorize him. It is much more difficult to capture Depp's identity beyond his movies.

He's adored by fans for his offbeat, antiestablishment, anti-Hollywood approach to his own stardom. He's hot. He's cool. David Letterman called him "the coolest guy we've ever had on the program," to which Dave's sidekick Paul Schaeffer added, "Can't get much cooler." When the studio audience went wild over his coolness, Depp reacted as though surprised, "Ha ha. Wow! That's amazing!"[3] Yet, according to Depp, the image of the ultracool star is not really accurate. "It's a misunderstanding that I am a cool guy," he told one interviewer in 1998. "I'm a little shy man who feels pain very easily. Not only physical...but also psychologically. Because of one stupid remark I can get completely confused. Or if they say to me: 'Johnny you totally messed up that scene,' it knocks me out."[4]

While it may be hard to imagine anyone telling Depp that he "totally messed up," it is not so hard to understand his desire for everyone "to think that I'm a hard worker, that I've got talent."[5] As his story will show, he is a hard worker, and he does have talent. He also has a way of appearing to be a bit startled by his success and fame, and more than a little cynical about it. "I'm paid insane amounts of money to make different faces and tell lies pretending to be someone else."[6] Recently, *Forbes* magazine named Depp number six among this year's top "power players," and he was number one in earnings for the year, taking in over $92 million. As one reporter put it succinctly: "Not bad for a pirate."[7]

Depp's has been a remarkable career, from his first foray into acting in 1984 to the *Pirates of the Caribbean* series that has made not only Johnny Depp but also Jack Sparrow household names. For Depp, playing Jack Sparrow has been "the most fun I have ever had playing a character. It's a character that can essentially do anything and get away with it."[8] For audiences around the world, it is a character that provides endless opportunities to think about the important things in life: love, hate, trust, betrayal, order and rules, disorder, freedom, and death. Not bad for some giddy movies about pirates.

Musician, actor, lover, father, club owner, hard drinker, drug user, chain smoker...Depp's done it all. As he told James Lipton of *Inside the Actors Studio*, his least favorite word is *no*. Of course, Depp's answers to questions about his life do not necessarily reveal much beyond a momentary desire to make an impression on his audience. In that interview with Lipton, we learn that the best piece of advice anyone ever gave him came from his mother, who told him how to deal with a school bully. "'The kid's bugging you. He puts his hands on you, you pick up the nearest rock, or whatever you can get your hands on, and you lay him out.' And I did! And I felt better. And it worked."[9]

We find out other facts in the same, sometimes silly interview: "breathing" turns him on, and "not breathing" turns him off; he loves the sound of his daughter's voice and hates the sound of a vacuum cleaner; if he was not an actor he would like to be a writer; he would "absolutely NOT" like to be the President of the United States; and what he would most like to hear upon his arrival in heaven is a voice saying, "Wow!"[10]

Perhaps a trained psychologist would be interested in these, but for the rest of us, Depp's responses do not tell us much about what drives him to take on such a wide variety of fascinating film roles, what has driven him to so many extremes throughout his life, what he wants from family life, and why we care about all this. For those answers, we must look at the broad spectrum not only of what he has said, but what he has done and been since his birth in 1963 and what it means for us as an audience to his life and work.

"I know exactly what I want," he said in 2006. "Everything. Calm, peace, tranquility, freedom, fun, happiness."[11] Often considered the quintessential outsider, Johnny Depp has fascinated his fans for more than two decades. His ability to fascinate extends beyond being a teen idol or a movie star, however, and his outsider status is what enables him to make larger contributions to the cultural imagination. His work and his life provide us with glimpses into the powerful world outside of reality, into arenas where carefully presenting the stories of our culture has real value as well as consequences.

The tale of redemption Depp's life draws from is not his alone but one embraced by a culture that seems hungry for his creative contributions and illusions. If he has found a way to leave the illusory life of Hollywood stardom behind and embrace a simpler set of goals, he has nevertheless provided us with the screen illusions that enrich all our lives, especially in the wildly popular character of Jack Sparrow. This is a biography of Johnny Depp and inevitably his popular character Jack Sparrow, but it is also is a story of our culture at this moment and why we want to embrace the pirate's redemption.

A note on the chapter titles: Long before he acted, Johnny Depp was a musician, and music has remained an enduring passion for him. In keeping with his love of music, each chapter title is the name of a song—not about or by Depp specifically, but about guys named Johnny from various sources in American lore. An extensive list of "Johnny Songs" can be found in a delightful website at http://www.johnnysongs.net/. Clips of these title songs can be found in an iMix at iTunes at http://phobos.apple.com/Web Objects/MZStore.woa/wa/viewIMix?id=258489626&s=143441.

## NOTES

1. "Biography for Johnny Depp," IMDb.com, http://www.imdb.com/name/nm0000136/bio (accessed September 1, 2006).

2. Johnny Depp, interview with Ab Van Ieperon. *Vrij Nederland*, May 19, 2001 (The Netherlands), http://www.johnnydeppfan.com/interviews/vrij.htm (accessed March 18, 2007).

3. Johnny Depp, interview with David Letterman, November 1999, http://www.johnnydeppfan.com/interviews/letterman.htm (accessed June 2, 2007).

4. Johnny Depp, interview with "Joepie," 1998, http://www.johnnydeppfan.com/interviews/jeopie.htm (accessed August 13, 2007).

5. Ibid.

6. "Cot Death—The Fear That Haunts Johnny Depp," *News World*, June 1999, http://www.johnnydeppfan.com/interviews/newsworld.htm (accessed June 1, 2007).

7. Erin Carlson, "Oprah Tops Forbes' List of Power Players," June 14, 2007, http://news.yahoo.com/s/ap/20070614/ap_en_ce/forbes_celebrity100 (accessed June 14, 2007).

8. "Johnny Knows Jack!" *Disney Adventures – Ultimate Pirates Fan Guide*, June/July 2007, 30

9. Johnny Depp, interview with James Lipton, *Inside the Actors Studio*, Bravo, September 8, 2002, transcript by Heather, http://www.johnnydeppfan.com/interviews/ias.htm.

10. Ibid.

11. "Johnny Depp: From Hellraiser to Family Man," *The Independent*, September 21, 2006, http://education.independent.co.uk/magazines/article1703706.ece (accessed May 19, 2007).

# TIMELINE: SIGNIFICANT EVENTS IN THE LIFE OF JOHNNY DEPP

| | |
|---|---|
| **1963** | John Christopher Depp II born on June 9 |
| **1976** | At age 13, Johnny Depp claims to have lost his virginity |
| **1978** | John Depp Sr. and Betty Sue Depp divorce |
| **1983** | Moves to Los Angeles with his band The Kids, who subsequently change their name to Six Gun Method |
| | Works as a telemarketer |
| | Marries and divorces Lori Anne Allison, who introduces him to Nicolas Cage, who steers him to his first acting job |
| **1984** | Plays Glen Lantz in *A Nightmare on Elm Street* |
| **1985** | Plays Jack in *Private Resort* |
| | Plays Lionel Viland in a single episode of ABC television's *Lady Blue* |
| **1986** | Depp's band breaks up |
| | Plays Donnie Fleischer in the TV movie *Slow Burn* |
| | Plays Private Gator Lerner in *Platoon* |
| | Begins to take acting classes at the Loft Studio |
| | Begins dating actress Sherilyn Fenn |
| **1987** | Appears in the first episode of *21 Jump Street* on April 12 |
| | Plays Detective Tom Hanson in the TV series *21 Jump Street* from 1987–90 |
| **1988** | Relationship with Sherilyn Fenn ends |
| | Has his mother's name, Betty Sue, tattooed inside a heart on his left bicep |
| **1989** | Relationship with actress Jennifer Grey begins and ends |
| | Begins dating Winona Ryder in late 1989 |

**1990**    Appears in Concrete Blonde's music video "Joey"
          Plays Wade "Cry-Baby" Walker in *Cry-Baby*
          Plays Edward in *Edward Scissorhands*
          Depp and Winona announce their engagement on February 26
          Receives a Golden Globe nomination for best actor in a comedy/
          musical for *Edward Scissorhands*
          Plays in *Freddy's Dead: The Final Nightmare* (lists himself in the
          credits as Oprah Noodlemantra)
**1991**    Appears in Tom Petty's music video "Into the Great Wide
          Open"
**1992**    Appears in the Lemonheads' music video "It's a Shame about
          Ray"
**1993**    Purchases a 29-room mansion in Hollywood Hills, alleged to
          have once belonged to Bela Lugosi
          Plays Axel Blackmar in *Arizona Dream*
          Plays Sam in *Benny & Joon*
          Plays Gilbert Grape in *What's Eating Gilbert Grape*
          Buys the Viper Room
          Depp and Winona Ryder announce their engagement is off on
          June 21
          Plays Ed Wood in *Ed Wood* (released in late 1994)
          Receives Golden Globe nomination for best actor in a comedy/
          musical for *Ed Wood*
**1994**    Receives Golden Globe nomination for best actor in a comedy/
          musical for *Benny & Joon*
          Receives MTV nomination for best comedic performance and
          best on-screen duo with Mary Stuart Masterson for *Benny &
          Joon*
          Meets Kate Moss in January
          Appears in Shane McGowan's music video "That's Woman's
          Got Me Drinking"
**1995**    Plays Don Juan in *Don Juan DeMarco*
          Plays William Blake in *Dead Man*
          Johnny participates in the *United States of Poetry* program for
          PBS
          Plays Gene Watson in *Nick of Time*
          Named by *Empire* magazine (issue #1) as one of the 100 sexiest
          stars in film history
          *Divine Rapture* begins filming in July, but production ends on the
          16th as the funding fell apart

**1996**     Chosen by *People* magazine as one of the 50 most beautiful people in the world

Wins the London Critic Circle Film Award's actor of the year for his work in *Ed Wood* and *Don Juan DeMarco*

Plays the slide guitar for Oasis's song "Fade In-Out" on the *Be Here Now* album

Films *Cannes Man* (released 2002)

**1997**     Plays Donnie Brasco/Joseph D. "Joe" Pistone in *Donnie Brasco*

Plays Raphael in *The Brave*, which he also co-writes (with D. P. Depp) and directs

Ranked 67th in *Empire* magazine's (October 1997) top 100 movie stars of all time list

**1998**     Plays Raoul Duke in *Fear and Loathing in Las Vegas*

Plays William Blake and Himself in *L.A. Without a Map*

Relationship with model Kate Moss disintegrates

Narrates "Top Secret—National Security Agency, Scotland Yard, and The Mossad"

Meets Vanessa Paradis in Paris while filming *The Ninth Gate*

Begins relationship with Vanessa Paradis (mother of Jack John III and Lily-Rose)

**1999**     Plays Dean Corso in *The Ninth Gate*

Plays Commander Spencer Armacost in *The Astronaut's Wife*

Plays Ichabod Crane in *Sleepy Hollow*

Receives Golden Satellite Awards nomination for best actor in a comedy/musical for *Sleepy Hollow*

Receives Academy of Science Fiction, Fantasy & Horror Films nomination for best actor for *Sleepy Hollow*

Wins the Blockbuster Entertainment Awards for favorite actor—horror for *Sleepy Hollow*

Lily-Rose Melodie Depp born in Paris, France on May 27

Plays Jack Kerouac in the documentary film *The Source*

Receives his star on the Hollywood Walk of Fame on November 16 (Tim Burton and Martin Landau appear as guest speakers)

Wins the French César Award for his body of work

Appears in the "Red Nose" special episode of *The Vicar of Dibley*

**2000**     Appears in the final episode of BBC comedy *The Fast Show*

Plays Cesar in *The Man Who Cried*

Plays Lieutenant Victor in *Before Night Falls*

Plays Roux in *Chocolat*

**2001**    Nominated for best actor by the Academy of Science Fiction, Fantasy & Horror Films

Directs music videos for Vanessa Paradis—"Portant" and "Que fait la vie?"

Plays George Jung in *Blow*

Plays Inspector Frederick Abberline in *From Hell*

**2002**    Jack John Christopher Depp III born in Paris, France on April 9

Appears as himself in documentary entitled *Lost in La Mancha*

**2003**    Plays Jack Sparrow in *Pirates of the Caribbean: The Curse of the Black Pearl*

Plays Sands in *Once Upon a Time in Mexico*

*People* magazine names Depp the sexiest man alive

**2003 / 2004**    Along with costars, director, and producers, receives multiple nominations for *Pirates of the Caribbean*

Receives Academy Award nomination for best actor in a motion picture

Receives Screen Actors Guild nomination for best actor

Receives British Academy of Film and Television Arts (BAFTA) nomination for best actor

Receives Golden Globes nomination for best actor in a musical/comedy

Receives Golden Satellite nomination for best actor in a comedy/musical

Receives Online Film Critics Society nomination for best actor

Film wins Broadcast Film Critics Association Award for best family film—live action

Film wins People's Choice Award for favorite motion picture

Film receives Golden Satellite nomination for best motion picture in a comedy/musical

Film receives Golden Satellite nomination for Geoffrey Rush as best supporting actor in a comedy/musical

**2004**    Plays Mort Rainey in *Secret Window*

Plays L'inconnu in *Ils se marièrent et eurent beaucoup d'enfants* (*And They Lived Happily Ever After*)

Plays Sir James Matthew Barrie in *Finding Neverland*

Plays Rochester in *The Libertine*

Receives his first nomination for an Academy Award for *Pirates of the Caribbean* (loses to Sean Penn)

Receives the SAG Award for outstanding performance by a male actor for *Pirates of the Caribbean* (Award was accepted by

Renee Zellweger because Depp was not present for the awards
ceremony)
VH1 ranks Depp fifth among the 100 "hottest hotties" in the
world

2005    Plays Willy Wonka in *Charlie and the Chocolate Factory*
Voices Victor van Dort in *Corpse Bride*
*TV Guide* (January 2005) ranks Depp fourth on their list of the
25 greatest teen idols
*Premiere* magazine ranks Depp 47th on a list of the greatest movie
stars of all time in their "Stars in Our Constellation" feature
Although unable to attend, Depp is awarded the Gary Cooper
Spirit of Montana Award at the 2005 HatcH Audiovisual Arts
Festival in Bozeman, Montana, where he is honored for his out-
standing career and his role as a mentor and inspiration to young
and aspiring artists

2006    Provides voice for PC and Playstation 2 game *Pirates of the Caribbean: The Legend of Jack Sparrow*
Plays Jack Sparrow in *Pirates of the Caribbean: Dead Man's Chest*
*Premiere* magazine ranks Depp's performance in *Edward Scissorhands* 22nd on the list for the 100 greatest performances of all
time (In that same year, *Premiere* ranked Depp's performance in
Pirates of the Caribbean: The Curse of the Black Pearl 79th on
that same list)
Johnny Depp is ranked first in the best Hollywood signers 2006
list by *Autograph Collector* magazine (May)

2007    Plays Jack Sparrow in *Pirates of the Caribbean: At World's End*
Cast in the lead role of Tim Burton's *Sweeney Todd* (the sixth
collaboration between Depp and Burton)
Cast as Paul Kemp in Hunter S. Thompson's *The Rum Diary*
(tentative release date: 2008)
Cast as Lindsay in Mira Nair's *Shantaram* (tentative release date:
2008)
Cast in *Sin City 2* and *Sin City 3*, scheduled for release in 2008

# Chapter 1

# "JOHNNY, COME HOME": BEGINNINGS

If you stood on the corner, say, of Frederica Street and West 4th Street in Owensboro, Kentucky, on June 9, 1963, and inhaled deeply, you might take in the aroma of mouth-watering barbecue. Owensboro proclaimed itself the Barbecue Capital of the USA, and barbecue season meant welcoming tourists into town to mingle with the locals as they enjoyed fire-cooked specialties and friendly conversation. On that day in June, Owensboro welcomed John Christopher Depp II to their town and to the world. John Depp Sr. was a civil engineer, and his wife, Betty Sue, was a waitress at one of the local coffee shops. Young John came along to join his sister Christine, his half-sister Debbie, and half-brother Danny. Danny and Debbie were Betty Sue's children from her first marriage; both were later adopted by John Depp Sr. and took his last name.[1] Before long, John Depp II became just plain Johnny, and the Depp family commenced bestowing a variety of nicknames upon him: Johnny Dip, Dippity Do, and Deppity Dog,[2] to name a few. One of Depp's earliest memories of his childhood was of "catching lightning bugs. Beautiful, fascinating bugs. There was a little girl who lived next door who had a brace on her leg. We used to play on the swing set, and the night the astronauts landed on the moon, her father came out and looked up and said, in all serious-ness, 'When man sets foot on the face of the moon, the moon will turn to blood.' I was shocked. I remember thinking, Geez, I'm six and that's a little deep for me. I stayed up watching the moon. It was a big relief when it didn't change."[3]

But let's take a few steps back. Johnny Depp is one of those superstars whose story has, in some sense, many beginnings. Those stories are rooted in the people and places that came together to make Johnny Depp one of the most famous actors of a generation.

## GRANDPARENTS

Just as the young Johnny had his nicknames, so too did one of his favorite family members: his maternal grandfather, known affectionately as Pawpaw. On his mother's side, his grandparents were Walter "Pawpaw" and Bessie Wells, who owned a tobacco farm in Frankfort, Kentucky. John Depp Sr.'s parents, Oren and Violet "Maddie" Depp, described by one biographer as middle class, lived in a somewhat wealthier area near Frederica Street in Owensboro.[4]

Depp's grandfather Pawpaw was near and dear to the young Johnny. "I remember picking tobacco with my grandfather back in Kentucky. ... We were inseparable, me and Pawpaw. He died when I was seven, and that was a real big thing for me. But somehow I believe that he's around. I believe in ghosts. I hope I'm a ghost someday. I think I'd have more energy. But I'm sure my Pawpaw is around—guiding, watching. I have close calls sometimes. I think, Jesus Christ! How did I get out of that? I've just got a feeling that it's Pawpaw."[5]

Since Pawpaw's death, Depp claims that he continues to feel his grandfather's spirit within him.[6] Depp has said, "I have got Cherokee blood running through my veins"[7] partly as a way to explain this. His great-grandmother Minnie was, by all of Depp's accounts, a Cherokee, as was Depp's maternal grandfather, so his Native American roots seem to run deep. Yet being a Cherokee and having Cherokee blood are not necessarily the same thing. The Cherokee Nation,[8] which has been a recognized entity since the 1700s, has established a way to identify who is Cherokee and who is not but the process is contentious and complicated by politics, issues of race, and concepts of cultural identity.[9]

Unlike some tribes, the Cherokee have not until recently relied on a specific "blood quantum," that is, the percentage of Native American blood or relatives you can claim. Instead, it has involved meeting a more specific requirement: being able to provide documents that show you are the ancestor of someone who was enrolled in the Cherokee Nation between 1899 and 1906 and resided in Indian Territory (Oklahoma).[10] The blood quantum of these ancestors ranged from 0 to 100 percent. Yet even within these guidelines the Cherokee Nation has disagreements about who should be considered Cherokee today and who gets to decide this. There is also a struggle to reconcile people who have

Cherokee blood but have no interest in the cultural heritage, and those who may have little blood but are committed to preserving and promoting the traditional culture. But even more serious are attempts to exclude "Black Cherokee" or former black slaves called Freedmen who were on the tribal rolls.[11]

Except for his work on the movie *The Brave* (1997), Depp has exhibited little understanding of the complexity of his heritage and instead participates in discussions of it as the source of his good looks. According to one of Depp's biographers, Pawpaw "had the same haunting good looks, sharp cheekbones, and sculpted visage"[12] that helped to make Depp a heartthrob to millions of teenage girls and women and the envy of a whole lot of men. In an interview Johnny Depp did with director John Waters, the two joked about Depp's inherited facial structure:

JW:  Where is the Indian in your family?
JD:  It's on my mom's side, mostly.
JW:  I still think you should marry Raquel Welch and I'll sell the children, because she's part Indian too, and you could have the kids with the best cheekbones in America. And we could sell 'em to rich yuppies.
JD:  We could start a cheekbone-implant business.[13]

With Pawpaw, young Johnny would pick tobacco in the Kentucky fields, exchanging grandfather-to-grandson wisdom and banter. When Pawpaw died—Johnny was seven years old—it was the first deep loss in the youngster's life and it left him with a combination of grief and awareness that, at least in this case, the dead continue to reside in some ways within us.

## JOHN DEPP

The elder John Depp was a civil engineer, a somewhat fancy-sounding title for someone responsible for the planning, construction, and maintenance of public works, such as roads, water supplies, sewers, and even traffic controls. It may not have paid a high salary—"we weren't particularly overflowing with money,"[14] as Depp once put it—but between John's salary and Betty Sue's tips for waiting tables, the Depp household managed. Both John Depp and Betty Sue had volatile tempers; they fought frequently, though the fights were limited to shouting matches and cold shoulders. But there is evidence that Betty Sue could hold her own in these verbal battles.

## BETTY SUE

Betty Sue Wells' first marriage resulted in two children: Dan and Debbie. Her second marriage, to John Depp Sr., resulted in two more children: Christie, and then Johnny (Dan and Debbie took on the last name of Depp as well.) The end of her first marriage left Betty Sue "a broken-hearted victim just waiting to happen,"[15] which may explain her willingness to step into another marriage that was to prove so volatile. She may have been unlucky in love, but she was not a meek and fragile woman. She swore, gambled, and smoked—hardly the picture of frailty. Still, it was by most appearances a typical marriage and a typical working-class suburban family. While her husband, John, worked for the town, Betty Sue toiled as a waitress, earning modest tips. The Depps owned a small house in a small suburban town, and lived the life that resembled those of tens of thousands of families in the post–Korean War era.

The late 1960s and early 1970s saw a great deal of social transformation—and turmoil—in the United States and abroad: the war in Vietnam, student uprisings at U.S. universities (including the 1970 protest at Kent State University in Ohio where unarmed students were shot and killed by the National Guard), the emergence of rock 'n' roll music as the dominant musical style for teens at home and in Europe, prison uprisings (most notably in Attica State Prison in 1971, where prisoners' demands for more humane conditions went unheeded, escalated to violence, and ultimately prompted the use of overwhelming force by the New York State Troopers who had been ordered by the Governor to retake the prison), the assassinations of President John F. Kennedy in 1963, Robert Kennedy and the Reverend Martin Luther King Jr. in 1968, and the Watergate scandal and the corruption of the federal government in the early 1970s.

The restlessness of the nation paralleled Betty Sue's own restlessness; "My mother had this wanderlust, she always liked to be moving around," Depp explained.[16] The young Depp was quickly aware of the limitations of small-town life after the family moved from Kentucky to Miramar, Florida: "All we had was a school, a drugstore, and a pizza joint. I was really frustrated and wanted to get out of there so bad. Everybody knew everybody. It was suffocating."[17]

The family moved to Miramar when Depp was seven years old, and then they moved "at least another 30 times in 10 years,"[18] a number that may not be logically possible but that suggests a definite uncertainty and lack of roots in those years. "We moved like gypsies. From the time I was five until my teens we lived in 30 or 40 different houses. That probably has a lot to do with my transient life now. But it's how I was raised so I thought there was nothing abnormal about it. Wherever the family is, that's home. We lived in apartments, on a farm, in a motel. Then we rented a house, and one night we moved from there to the house next door. I remember carrying my clothes across the yard and thinking, this is weird, but it's an easy move."[19] While in retrospect he makes it seem more or less routine to move so frequently, it was a source of puzzlement for the young boy. "I asked my mom why [we moved so much]. I never did understand her explanation."[20]

When she and John Depp divorced, according to Depp, "my mother was deeply hurt and sick physically and emotionally."[21] As Depp put it, "Her life as she had known it for 20 years was over. Her partner, her husband, her best friend, her lover, had just left her. I felt crushed that he had left, but when you're faced with something like that, it's amazing how much abuse the human mind and heart can take. You just get past what you need to get past."[22] Depp had to work out the emotional aftermath for himself. "When my parents split up was when I think I realized these are the most important people in my life, and you know, I'd die for these people. I was 15, and it just sort of happened. You just deal with it, but there's no escaping the hurt. I mean, it definitely hurts, man."[23] But the hurt did not stop Depp from turning an attentive eye toward helping his mother cope with this dramatic change in family life.

After the divorce, Depp and his sister Christie opted to live with their mother, as did his brother Dan. Debbie, his half-sister, chose to live with John Sr. in Hallandale, Florida. Although Johnny was the youngest of the Depp children, he ended up having to grow up quickly. He was responsible for going to his father's office to make sure his father had written out the check for child support.

Depp grew even closer to his mother, referring to her as "the greatest lady in the world," his "best friend, coolest thing."[24] On May 31, 1988, Depp immortalized his love for his mother by having her name tattooed inside a red heart on his bicep.

## CHRISTIE, DEBBIE, AND DANNY

Christie, two years Johnny's senior, became his manager and advisor, and his brother Dan "D. P." Depp, nine years older, became part of Johnny's production company and would later co-write a screenplay with him. It was Dan who first introduced his brother to the variety of rock music that was to become Johnny's passion. Debbie, seven years older than Johnny, chose to stay out of the limelight. When Johnny was 17 years old, his sister Christie had a baby, Megan, and he found the experience both wonderful and nerve wracking. "I was terrified about it because I had read a long article on crib death." Depp worried that Megan might mysteriously stop breathing, so "every night I would sneak into the room where she was sleeping and put my hand in her crib, holding her little finger, and sleep on the floor next to the crib just to make sure she would be all right."[25] A dozen or so years later, Depp included his niece in a photo shoot he did with *Vogue* magazine.

## "FARTS WILL ALWAYS BE FUNNY"[26]

By his own accounts, Depp's youth was a bit off-kilter: "Growing up, I had a sneaking suspicion that it was OK to be different, but there's this fear—nobody wants to be considered crazy or weird...so they do their best to hide their individuality."[27] It's easy to imagine that Johnny Depp was a young boy unlike any others because his grown-up persona is considered so eccentric and complex, especially among his Hollywood peers. He once made the connection between the grown man and the child: "There are certain elements of boyhood we can't escape. And farts will always be funny."[28]

But in at least some ways, Depp's early childhood was similar to that of tens of thousands of youngsters throughout the United States. He never felt quite comfortable in school, and he rebelled a good deal, but he had a few close friends, watched the occasional episode of Captain Kangaroo,[29] and he pursued his main interest—music—with a passion that distinguished him as a boy with a good deal of maturity. According to Depp, "My parents always said, I was a weird kid. Most of all because I always did everything twice. Honest. For instance, if I drank a glass of Cola, I would put the glass down, take it in my hand again, raise it to my mouth and drink. And that did not only happen with a few things—I really repeated everything I did."[30]

He and his friends had wild times, doing things that in hindsight were obviously reckless, dangerous, foolish, and even stupid. He recalls having carved his initials in his arm with a penknife at the age of 12. "Yeah, it was probably some early form of tattoo for me. It was anger and unhappiness and a form of self-loathing."[31] But Johnny Depp had a remarkable ability to pull the plug on his risky behaviors when they put him too close to losing his vision of becoming a successful musician and performer. Besides, as he has said, "it wasn't like I was some malicious kid who wanted to kick some old lady in the shin,"[32] he was just another curious, vulnerable, and bored young teen living around a place—Miami—that had no shortage of drugs and petty crime to tempt him.

## WHAT *EVEL* LURKS . . .

Like most kids, young Johnny Depp was enchanted by some of the people and programs—real or fictional—popularized by television. One such program was the 1960s TV comedy *Hogan's Heroes*. The show appealed to Depp's ongoing fascination with the events of World War II. Premiering in 1965 and playing until 1971, *Hogan's Heroes* was a campy, utterly fictionalized representation of American and British prisoners of war in a Nazi POW camp. Hogan and his men, presumably captured by the Germans, were actually more like secret agents whose mission was to sabotage the Nazi war effort. Depp loved to dream up his own episodes of *Hogan's Heroes*, and according to at least one biographer, he used to dig tunnels in his backyard, emulating the secret tunneling that Hogan's men had done to hide their activities from their German captors.[33] Adding to the satisfaction he derived from these tunnel digs was the thrill of wondering whether the newly dug passageways would suddenly cave in on him.

Jack the Ripper was another of Depp's childhood fascinations. "Ever since I was nine, and I saw a TV special on Jack the Ripper . . . I was fascinated by this unsolved case."[34] Jack the Ripper was the name given to the unknown killer of a number of prostitutes in the East End of London in 1888. By the time he was 15 years old, Depp had read 10 books on the notorious murderer. Perhaps it was the fact that the Ripper murders were never solved. Or perhaps it was the variety of stories that grew up around the case—for example, letters to police allegedly written by the Ripper (generally believed to have been hoaxes) and a diary supposedly written by the Ripper (though discovered actually to have been written by James Maybrick, who was himself on trial for murder in 1889).[35] That the Ripper was given the name Jack makes Depp's interest in him somewhat ironic; it is the name of his most famous movie character, Jack Sparrow, and the nickname of his own young son, John Christopher "Jack" Depp III.

Johnny Depp's admiration was reserved for those individuals who somehow eclipsed the ordinary in more creative ways. An extreme example was another of Depp's childhood heroes, the stunt motorcyclist, Robert Craig "Evel" Knievel. Here was a pop-culture star of a different kind. In 1965 Knievel began his daredevil career when he formed a troupe called Evel Knievel's Motorcycle Daredevils. The group would tour around the country, performing stunts such as riding through walls of fire and jumping over live rattlesnakes and mountain lions. In one famous stunt, Evel Knievel would have himself towed at 200 miles an hour behind dragster racecars while holding on to a parachute. In 1966 he began touring alone, taking care of all the details of his stunts himself. He drove the truck holding his motorcycles, he built the ramps, and he did a remarkable job of self-promotion of his increasingly daring stunts. On New Years Day 1968, he jumped 151 feet across the fountains in front of Caesar's Palace in Las Vegas. He made the jump but botched the landing and was so seriously hurt that he spent the next 30 days hospitalized in a coma. When he was sufficiently recovered, he immediately began planning even more daring, death-defying jumps, including a plan to jump the Grand Canyon.

Something about Evel Knievel's willingness to put his life on the line for every stunt, and his passion for every detail of every stunt and event, made him especially appealing to young Johnny Depp. So compelling a figure was the motorcyclist that Depp identified with him. Recognizing his attraction to Knievel's passion but with an appropriate sense of humor about the particulars of the daredevil's chosen profession he recalled, "I wanted to be Evel Knievel, but I was going to change my name to Awful Knawful."[36]

Wanting to be someone, or something, that reflected his intensity, Depp also fantasized about being a great martial artist like Bruce Lee (Depp is a Green belt in karate) or a celebrated basketball showman. "I wanted to be the first white Harlem Globetrotter. I could spin the basketball on my finger and I could make it go through my arms."[37] Even more than becoming a Globetrotter, Depp wanted to be Barnabas Collins (originally played by Jonathan Frid and then later by Ben Cross) from the 1966–1971 TV series *Dark Shadows*. A "self-loathing yet sympathetic 175-year-old vampire,"[38] Barnabas Collins "was a huge obsession of mine . . . so much that I found a ring, it was probably one of my mother's rings, and I wore it on this finger, and I tried to comb my hair like Barnabas Collins, and I was trying to figure out how I could get fangs. It really had a heavy impact on me, a heavy influence on me."[39] The appeal of Barnabas Collins seemed to be his vulnerability, despite his monstrous behavior. Indeed, his nature was described as "less a monster and more a tortured gothic hero,"[40] a quality that quite obviously intrigued Depp. His own Edward Scissorhands might have been a relative of Barnabas'—grotesque in appearance, tortured by nature, and somehow sympathetic and even alluring to others.

It is interesting to note that Johnny Depp did not try to be *like* these favorite characters; he wanted to *be* them. These young obsessions motivated Depp to do more than simply dream; he worked and practiced—whether with a basketball or karate katas—to inch closer to the desire of the moment. But whereas life as a daredevil, Globetrotter, or martial arts star never got past his imagination, life as a musician became a reality—at least a Johnny Depp–style reality.

# NOTES

1. "Johnny Depp: the Complete Chronicle of a Hollywood Legend" in *Life Story* magazine. ed. Karen L. Williams, March, 2007, 8.

2. Nick Johnstone, *Johnny Depp: the Illustrated Biography*. (London: Carlton Books), 2006, 9.

3. Johnny Depp, interview with Kevin Cook, *Playboy*, January 1996, http://www.johnnydeppfan.com/interviews/playboy.htm.

4. Denis Meikle, *Johnny Depp: A Kind of Illusion*. 2Rev Ed. (Surrey, England: Reynolds & Hearn) 2007, 21.

5. Kevin Sessums, "Johnny Be Good," *Vanity Fair*, February 1997, http://www.johnnydeppfan.com/interviews/vanifair.htm.

6. Meikle, *Johnny Depp: A Kind of Illusion*, 9.

7. Johnny Depp, interview with *Jeopie*, 1998, http://www.johnnydeppfan.com/interviews/interviews.htm.

8. As defined on their website: "The Cherokee Nation is the federally recognized government of the Cherokee people." http://www.cherokee.org/home.aspx?section=government; there is another band that represents Cherokee in Oklahoma—the United Keetoowah Band of Cherokee Indians; there is also an eastern band of Cherokee Indians.

9. See the work of anthropologist Circe Sturm on Cherokee identity: *Blood Politics: Race, Culture and Identity in the Cherokee Nation of Oklahoma*, Berkeley: University of California Press, 2002, 2–4.

10. Cherokee Nation News, http://www.cherokee.org/home.aspx?section=services&service=Registration&ID=8sRG9ZCF7PE.

11. Marilyn Vann, "Q and A from the Freedmen Perspective," *Cherokee Phoenix*, October 2006, 32.

12. Nigel Goodall, *The Secret World of Johnny Depp*. (London: Blake Publishing Co.), 2006. (Also published as *What's Eating Johnny Depp: An Intimate Biography*, 2004), p.19.

13. Johnny Depp, interview with John Waters, *Interview*, April 1999, http://www.johnnydeppfan.com/interviews/interviewmagapril90.htm.

14. Johnny Depp, interview with Anwar Brett, http://www.bbc.co.uk/filmms/2005/07/25/johnny_depp_chocolate_factory_interview.shtml.

15. Goodall, *The Secret World*, 26.

16. The Johnny Depp Resource, http://deppdownloads.com/info/biography.html.

17. Johnny Depp, interview with Cindy Pearlman, *Seventeen*, October 1994, http://www.johnnydeppfan.com/interviews/17.htm.

18. *Life Story*, 12.

19. Johnny Depp, interview with Kevin Cook, *Playboy*, January 1996, http://www.johnnydeppfan.com/interviews/playboy.htm.

20. Johnny Depp, interview with Bonnie Churchill, *The Christian Science Monitor*, October 19, 2001, http://www.csmonitor.com/2001/1019/p18s1-alip.html.

21. Goodall, 27.

22. Johnny Depp, interview with Kevin Cook, *Playboy*, January 1996, http://www.johnnydeppfan.com/interviews/playboy.htm.

23. Johnny Depp, interview with *US* magazine, June 26, 1989, http://www.johnnydeppfan.com/interviews/us1989.htm.

24. Goodall, 27.

25. Christopher Heard, *Depp*. (Toronto: ECW Press), 2001, 9.

26. "Johnny Depp Quotes," DeppImpact.com, www.deppimpact.com/quotes.html (accessed March 12, 2007).

27. "Johnny Depp: From Hellraiser to Family Man," http://education.independent.co.uk/magazines/article1703706.ece (accessed April 10, 2007).

28. EW.com Summer Movie Guide 2007, www.ew.com/ew/gallery/0,,20035285_20035355_20039648_9,00.html.

29. Johnny Depp, interview with Anwar Brett, http://www.bbc.co.uk/filmms/2005/07/25/johnny_depp_chocolate_factory_interview.shtml.

30. Johnny Depp, interview with Pauline Haldane, *Hit* magazine, 1993, http://www.johnnydeppfan.com/interviews/hit1993.htm.

31. Johnny Depp, interview with Steve Goldman, *Empire*, June 1997, http://www.johnnydeppfan.com/interviews/empire0697.htm.

32. Goodall, 29.

33. Goodall, 24.

34. "Actor Turns New Page as the Family Man," Johnny Depp, interview with Bonnie Churchill, *The Christian Science Monitor*, October 19, 2001, http://www.csmonitor.com/2001/1019/p18s1-alip.html.

35. Casebook: Jack the Ripper, http://www.casebook.org/ (this website describes itself as "the world's largest repository of Ripper-related information").

36. *Life Story*, 13.

37. *Life Story*, 13.

38. "Barnabas Collins," http://www.answers.com/topic/barnabas-collins.

39. Johnny Depp, interview with Jeffrey M. Anderson, http://www.commbustiblecelluoid.com/intdepp.shhtml.

40. "Dark Shadows," The Museum of Broadcast Communications, http://www.museum.tv/archives/etv/D/htmlD/darkshadows/darkshadows.htm.

# Chapter 2

# "JOHNNY GUITAR": ROCK 'N' ROLL . . . AND ON THE ROCKS

By his own account, by the age of 14, Johnny Depp had done "every kind of drug there was."[1] You might say his drug use began with a kiss—or more precisely, with his introduction to the music of Kiss, one of the hottest rock bands of the 1970s and known for bizarre costumes, makeup, and a heavy-handed guitar sound that appealed to Depp. His older brother, D. P., had introduced the younger Depp to rock 'n' roll when the two shared a room in their home in Miramar, Florida. D. P. would crank up the volume on his stereo, playing songs from Bob Dylan, Van Morrison, and Kiss.[2] Two years earlier, Depp had fallen in love with a musical instrument that would become a life's companion to him.

## THE FIRES OF MUSIC

"I was 12 when my mom bought me a $25 electric guitar. I had an uncle who was a preacher, and his family had a gospel singing group. He played guitar in church, and I used to watch him. I became obsessed with the guitar. I locked myself in my bedroom for the better part of a year and taught myself chords. I'd try to learn things off records."[3] His uncle's rock band was called The Gospel Sunlighters, and at 12 years old, Depp thought "they were the greatest thing in the world."[4] Music may have been the greatest saving grace in Johnny Depp's life. While still a wild child, music became a focus for the young rebel, and by age 13 he had formed his first rock band. "It was called Flame and it was terrible," Depp told a reporter some years later.[5]

Flame turned out to be an ironic choice given a nearly tragic incident that took place when Depp was around 12 years old. While hanging out with some friends and trying to be as outrageous as Gene Simmons, the lead vocalist from Kiss, Depp recalls that he "put a t-shirt on the end of a broom handle, soaked it in gasoline and lit it. Then I put gasoline in my mouth and breathed fire like Simmons. Only it set my face on fire…"[6] According to one version of the story, Depp's quick-thinking friend Bones jumped on him and put the flame out with his hands.[7] Nearly 20 years later, Depp would show his gratitude for Bones's heroism by drawing on Bones's personality for his portrayal of Gilbert in *What's Eating Gilbert Grape* (1993). Fortunately, Depp's facial burns were mostly superficial and left no scars. But he felt compelled to lie to his mother and told her that some fireworks had gone off in his face. It was not the last time Johnny Depp would do something vaguely self-destructive, though lying to his mother was something he was reluctant to repeat. "I wasn't the best kid in the world, but I wasn't an ax murderer, either."[8]

No, he was no ax murderer, but he was obsessed with his "ax"—a slang word for electric guitar. With the formation of the first of his many bands, Depp saw himself as a musician first and a middle school student a distant second. He would bring his guitar to school, cut most of his classes, and hang out in the music practice room, continuing to teach himself chord after chord, song after song. Incredibly, at age 13, Johnny Depp and Flame began playing stage shows in local clubs. As an underage boy, barely a teenager, Depp had to sneak into the clubs or pass himself off as older to be permitted to play. It was during this time that Depp lost his virginity to a young girl who liked to hang around to hear Flame play.[9] That moment, where very early sexuality combined with a life around the adult club scene, may have been the catalyst for behaviors that by Depp's own admission were the result of hanging around "with bad crowds."[10] According to one biographer, it was after Depp's encounter with that first "girlfriend" that he and his friends ran wild.[11] "I hung around with bad crowds.…We used to break and enter places. We'd break into the school and destroy a room or something. I used to steal things from stores."[12]

## TIME OF RECKONING

It was the kind of time where a young man could easily slip off into oblivion, ruin his life, and become one of too many lost adolescents in the chaos of the American counterculture. For Johnny Depp, it was instead a time of reckoning, of taking stock of his own desires and the events in his life. To mark these milestones in a manner consistent with his eccentric nature, he started to cut his own skin, beginning with his own initials. This behavior evidently continued into his 20s. In a 1993 *Details* magazine interview Depp explained his self-cutting: "My body is a journal in a way. It's like what sailors used to do, where every tattoo meant something, a specific time in your life when you make a mark on yourself, whether you do it yourself with a knife or with a professional tattoo artist."[13] Of course, he made those remarks at age 30—with the wisdom of hindsight. At the time, he was a confused and curious young man who felt compelled to try things even when his reasons were not clear.

One year Depp tried out for the high school football team, perhaps intending to please his hard-to-please father. He hated the experience and quit, only to be talked into rejoining the team not once but twice[14] before he finally rejected school sports for good. It was more appealing to be part of the rock 'n' roll crowd, and to be a rebel rocker who, to many, seemed hell-bent on crashing. But while his friends were increasing their drug use and drinking and diminishing their chances for a fulfilling life, Johnny Depp took a giant step back and away from that lifestyle, although it was someone else's turmoil that caused this reevaluation. In 1978, when he was 15 years old, Depp's parents announced that they were separating.

Depp dropped out of school for good when he was 16. "I'd found myself at the end of my rope as far as school was concerned; there seemed no particular reason for me to stay. The teachers didn't want to teach, and I didn't want to learn—from them."[15] Surprisingly, his family did not give him much grief for it. In fact, they were supportive, unlike family friends and other people. Ironically, when he was asked in 1988 at age 25 if he had any advice for young teens, he said, "My advice would be to stay in school, because I didn't and it was kind of a mistake. It was a stupid thing to do, dropping out. So my advice would be to learn as much as you can, and when you get out of school, continue to learn as much as you can. Just try and always do the right thing. Follow your instincts. Learn, make mistakes, and learn even more from your mistakes."[16]

One thing Depp did to keep his mind active and sharp was to read—at least after his brother, D. P., introduced him to an author whose work would prove to be "life changing" to him. "Keep in mind that in all my years of elementary school, junior high and high school, possibly the only things I'd read up to that point were a biography of Knute Rockne, some stuff on Evel Knievel and books about WWII"[17] (and presumably the Jack the Ripper books he mentioned elsewhere). In Jack Kerouac's train-of-thought book, *On the Road*, Depp found "great inspiration for a train-of-thought existence"[18] that appealed deeply to him. He began to read the works of other Beat Generation writers: Gregory Corso, Neal Cassady,

William Burroughs, and Allen Ginsberg. "I dove into their world full on and sponged up as much as I possibly could of their works.... The riches I was able to walk away with from those heroes, teachers and mentors is not available in any school that I've ever heard of."[19]

Depp was determined to pursue his education "from living life, getting out there in the world, seeing and doing and moving amongst the other vagabonds."[20] His instincts told him that he was a rock musician and that he should pursue music rather than formal education. "Music has always been my first love. I use music in my work because it's the fastest way to an emotional place."[21] With his band Flame, Depp played to small crowds along the Florida nightclub circuit, but since he was too young to be permitted into these drinking establishments, the clubs would have to sneak him in and then he would have to leave after playing a set with the band. "That's how I made a living on about $25 a night."[22]

Sometimes the band did better, earning a couple thousand dollars, a good-sized sum in 1979, considering how young the band was and how local their appeal. By then, the band had changed its name to The Kids, and they were performing covers of famous groups like Talking Heads and U2. While they may have called themselves "Kids," Depp and his friends were living the lives of young adults on the fringes of society. One of his close friends, Sal Jenco, had decided to move away from his broken home. Without much money and with no particular place to go, Sal decided to move into his car, a 1967 Chevrolet Impala. In a show of loyalty and friendship, Depp decided to move into the Impala with Sal, the two of them getting by on stolen sandwiches and drinks. It was not much of a life, but Johnny Depp just knew that music was going to be his way out of obscurity.

## ON THE ROAD

When Depp was 18 years old, The Kids played a couple of shows where they opened for Iggy Pop, sometimes called the Godfather of Punk. Iggy Pop had played with a band, The Stooges, throughout the 1960s and early 1970s, and he and the band were notorious for their live performances; sometimes Iggy Pop might leap off the stage, expose his genitals, and even rub raw meat on his chest. On more than one occasion, while on stage, he cut himself with broken bottles. It is not hard to imagine why his style of music and performance—particularly songs like "Real Wild Child"—appealed to the young rebel, Johnny Depp. At least one other connection between the 18-year-old Depp and 34-year-old Iggy was that both were hard-drinking and drug-taking rockers. Depp recalls that after the show, for some reason, "I started screaming and yelling at [Iggy Pop]...I don't know why, because I always idolized him."

As Depp found out years later when he and Iggy appeared together in the John Waters film *Cry-Baby* (1990), Iggy Pop had not been perturbed by the teen Depp's outburst. He told Depp, "I was probably in the same condition as you."[23] Worth noting, once again, is that Depp found deeply compelling yet another eccentric, countercultural figure in Iggy Pop. The pattern was undeniable. From Evel Knievel to Barnabas Collins to Jack the Ripper, Johnny Depp had set his sights on a fascinating constellation of "stars" whose relative strangeness and personal torments would fuel his own characterizations as his career took shape.

One of the ways in which Depp and his bandmates emulated their punk-rock heroes was by performing in various kinds of makeup to give them a more memorable look on stage. The Kids had a makeup artist by the name of Lori Anne Allison. Lori's sister, Suzanne, was dating another member of The Kids, Bruce Witkin,[24] and she was evidently instrumental in bringing her sister Lori and Depp together. After the briefest of courtships, the two married on December 20, 1983; Lori was 25, and Depp was 20 years old. Now a husband and a self-styled professional musician, Depp moved with Lori to Los Angeles, as he said, "to try our luck. We figured we were great in Florida, we'd be even better in California."[25] It was not that far-fetched an idea. Los Angeles seemed to be producing a slew of successful bands, and expectations were high that Lori and Depp, along with the rest of The Kids, could make a big name for themselves on the West Coast. After all, he and the band had talent; Depp had been practicing his guitar playing obsessively for over seven years by that point. He was newly married and committed to making a life as a musician.

## A BREAK...AND A BREAKUP

But things did not work out so well in Los Angeles for Depp's newly named band, Six Gun Method. "We were always pretty much broke," he remembers.[26] The band scraped together some money to travel to Hollywood, where they were convinced there was room for one more rock band. Again, they discovered that getting shows in Hollywood was almost futile. They did play a few shows, and shared a stage with bands like the Bus Boys and with Billy Idol, a rising punk star who enjoyed a fair amount of fame, and for Depp, "It actually turned out to be kind of fun."[27] But the money was running so low the band members had to get side jobs. Depp tried telemarketing, selling advertisements and then personalized pens over the phone. While the job was "horrible," according to Depp, in retrospect he saw it as his "first acting job."[28] He used his phone-sale opportunities to develop vocal characters with various fake names. Mostly he knew he was just killing time until he could make, or catch, a break.

That break came, ironically, at the same time as a breakup. Depp and Lori had faced the disappointment of seeing The Kids fail to make it in the music world. They had survived the move from Florida to California, and they had even found moments of enjoyment in day-to-day life in Hollywood. But the two also knew that their feelings for each other were simply not strong enough to sustain a marriage. Two years after their wedding, Depp and Lori decided to end their marriage. But before they did, Lori provided him with what would prove to be a life-changing opportunity. She had gotten to know a young actor named Nicolas Cage whose movie, *Rumble Fish*, and whose family connection to celebrated director Francis Ford Coppola (Cage is his nephew) had placed him firmly in the limelight. Lori suggested to Depp that he "might earn some extra money as an actor."[29] The rest, we might say, is history. But what a history!

## A NEW LIFE IN "DEATH"

Cage took a liking to Depp immediately—the two became drinking buddies—and enlisted his agent to help Depp get an audition for a part in a movie directed by Wes Craven, who had already developed a cult following for horror movies like The Hills Have Eyes (1977) and Swamp Thing (1982), and for television movies like Stranger in Our House (1978). Craven had written the screenplay for a film whose theme had grown out of a strange phenomenon he had read about. Long fascinated by dreams and the role they play in the unconscious, Craven had come across a remarkable story about immigrants from Laos who had died, apparently as a result of horrific nightmares. Evidently hundreds of Laotians—particularly those known as the Hmong—had died from a disorder that is now known as SUNDS, the Sudden Unexpected Nocturnal Death Syndrome. The first such death was reported in 1977, and at the time of Craven's interest in these cases, researchers could not determine "what it is that is killing these seemingly healthy people in their sleep."[30] This idea—grim and tragic as it was—fascinated Wes Craven, appealing to his ongoing interest in dreams and dreamers and his love of producing cinematic horror.

Craven's new movie took as a point of departure the idea of dreams that kill and created a character who would, himself, become a symbol of horror in popular culture: Freddy Krueger, the man-monster with the mangled face and razor-blade fingernails. Craven cast Heather Langenkamp in the roll of survivor Nancy, but he needed to find an actor for the role of Glen, Nancy's boyfriend. There were not a lot of notes toward a description of Glen's "type," but the little there was suggested something of a stereotypical, football jersey–wearing high school jock. When confronted with the possibility of an intruder in the Elm Street house, he had lines like, "I'm going to punch out your ugly lights whoever you are."[31] Glen's most memorable moment in the film was to be "unceremoniously sucked into his bed by Freddy Krueger,"[32] swallowed up and then ground into a bloody pulp of guts and flesh that are then belched out and upward onto the ceiling. Or, as one writer put it, Glen "goes out in a blaze of blood."[33]

When Nic Cage's agent managed to get Depp an audition with Craven, it could easily have been a rotten experience. For one thing, Depp had no confidence in his ability to act. In a 1987 interview, he recalled that, "I told the agent that I had no acting background, not even a drama class in high school—that I had done nothing and knew nothing."[34] Depp was definitely not the type Craven had been seeking for the part of Glen Lantz. As Depp put it, "I was this little scrawny pale little guy with long dark hair starched to death with five-day-old hairspray"[35]—hardly the stereotype of a macho jock! He considered the whole experience of auditioning and then, later, acting in the film, as a "trial-by-fire sort of thing....I'd never acted before. I'd never done school plays. Nothing. The fact that it was totally new to me was a tremendous challenge."[36]

In a more conventional life story, this is the part where Depp would go in to that audition and nail it—impressing the director and cast members alike. However, not only was he the wrong physical type, he did not quite fit in to the ensemble cast. In fact, he might not have been cast at all if not for Wes Craven's daughter. She had come to the auditions to read lines for the actors. When Depp finished his audition and left the room, Craven's daughter told her father that Depp was sexy and fascinating. Craven was evidently impressed by his daughter's reaction; he cast the young Johnny Depp in the role that would mean the beginning and the end for him. It was the beginning of a film career, but the end of Six Gun Method, his band. He could not keep up with the demands of on-set movie requirements and music rehearsals and performances. Acting was suddenly paying his bills; music was not. He did not stop loving music or playing his guitar, but with his customary intensity, he had turned his attention in a new direction.

This would be the place, in a customary biography, to say that a star was born. But little about Johnny Depp's life follows conventional storylines. His unexpected experience as an actor meant that he could now think about his next acting choice. He had the support of Wes Craven, who had been happy with the box office results of *Nightmare on Elm Street*, and although his most dramatic movie moment so far had been his death, he had shown that he had at least some ability as an actor. So, the thing to do was to find a new movie project, one that would satisfy his desire for challenges and offbeat work, not to mention something that would provide a paycheck. His pick, unfortunately, was not one he would look back on with much nostalgia.

## FIRST JACK

Twenty-two year old Depp took a part in the thoroughly forgettable movie entitled *Private Resort* (1985). Depp and his costar, the young Rob Morrow (for whom this film was his movie debut), played teenagers—not the last time a director would cast Depp as a younger teen—who spend a weekend at a resort trying, of course, to get girls. Depp's character, Jack—a name that would figure most significantly in his movie career and private life—and Morrow's Ben spend the movie chasing women and getting on the bad side of a bad guy named Maestro whose wife they believe is trying to seduce them. Depp showed off a comic side, careening from bedroom to bedroom and making amusing faces directly into the camera. But that was not all that the camera saw. At various points in the film, both Depp's Jack and Morrow's Ben are caught in the nude (mostly posterior views). While not particularly revealing by today's standards, those brief moments of nudity made *Private Resort* a kind of collector's item for Depp fans. However, it did little to advance Depp's film career, in spite of its fairly professional production values. He would rarely discuss the movie in subsequent years. Still, it may have been during the filming of *Private Resort* that he realized he could carve out a profession from acting. Where to go next? What to do?

In October of 1985, Depp landed a small role as Lionel Viland in a single episode of *Lady Blue*, an ABC television series starring Danny Aiello and Ron Dean that was canceled the following year. His next role was once again as a character younger than his real years, a wealthy teenage boy and kidnap victim named Donnie Fleischer in the made-for-cable movie *Slow Burn*. (Interestingly, and ironically, both *Private Resort* and *Slow Burn* were set in South Florida at a location quite close to Miramar—the very place Depp had been looking to escape!) Donnie ends up murdered and, it turns out, not the son after all. The reviews of the movie were almost universally negative, and Depp's role was, once again, rather forgettable. As one critic noted, "Johnny Depp is very young in this one and has an awful 80's haircut. He chews gum and tosses a soccer ball around for about 5 minutes and that is all we get to see of him."[37] Actually, we see more of him than that, but mainly as a bloody pulp of a body—a slightly tamer reprise of his demise in *Elm Street*. And while his character and the film were not destined for much glory, he was able somehow to show executive producer Joel Schumacher that there was something about him worth discovering.

Schumacher, who would later direct such hits as *St. Elmo's Fire* (1985), *Falling Down* (1993), *Batman Forever* (1995), *Batman and Robin* (1997), and *Phone Booth* (2002), saw in Johnny Depp a hint of the qualities that would become Depp's trademarks. "He had that demeanor, like James Dean...he was a very cool guy without putting much effort into being cool. He seemed to have an attitude that he was applying himself but that an acting career really didn't matter to him all that much, yet you could see it in his face that he was well read, well prepared, and giving the job every due diligence."[38] Such a comparison to James Dean meant that Depp had been noticed for his seriousness and his commitment to the project. But he himself was not overly fond of the analogy. "Everybody compares everyone to James Dean these days,"[39] he has said. Already in his dawning acting career, he wanted to be known for his own persona. He landed another short-term (one episode) role in 1987, in another ABC television series entitled *Hotel*. Not surprisingly, Depp was once again cast as a teenager. Soon, however, he would find himself working with truly A-list movie stars, with a top-of-the-line director, in a film destined to be a blockbuster.

## DRAFTED!

Oliver Stone was scary to the young Depp. The powerful and intense director, screenwriter, and producer of films like *Midnight Express* (1978), *Conan the Barbarian* (1982), *Scarface* (1983), *Salvador* (1986), *Wallstreet* (1987), *Born on the Fourth of July* (1989), *JFK* (1991), *Natural Born Killers* (1994), and *World Trade Center* (2006) was well known and increasingly controversial. But Depp's fear of Stone's considerable clout did not stop Depp from hungering for a part in Stone's current project at the time—a Vietnam war movie to be entitled *Platoon* (1986). Stone had circulated throughout Hollywood a description of what he was going to expect of his actors; they would be put through a slightly abbreviated version of military basic and combat training in the jungles of the Philippines. The training would be realistic, exhausting, no nonsense, and relentless. Most actors passed on the project.

Thirty performers became Stone's elite, chosen group; Johnny Depp was one of them. The film would star Charlie Sheen, Willem Dafoe, and Tom Berenger, and would include other soon-to-be-big names like Forest

Whitaker and Kevin Dillon. Oliver Stone himself would make an appearance as a major, as well. Depp's character, Private Gator Lerner, would be 23 years old, his actual age for once. Lerner was his platoon's interpreter, able to speak fluent Vietnamese. Stone was determined to make a movie that told the truth about the experience of the Vietnam War from soldiers' perspectives, and Depp was excited and nervous to participate. "Looking back, it is easily the toughest...thing I have ever had to do, ever."[40]

From an uncle who was a Vietnam veteran, Depp learned a little of what it had been like for young soldiers arriving in the thick of war in Southeast Asia. From Stone, he learned that the boot camp experience in Manila would be more rigorous preparation than he had ever experienced for an acting role. From his fellow actors, he learned the meaning of teamwork for the two weeks of combat training. "You put thirty guys in the jungle and leave them there to stay together for two weeks, just like a real platoon, and you build a real tightness. It's almost like a family. We became a military unit—a platoon."[41]

It would be nice to be able to say that Depp emerged from the training, from the rehearsals, and from the filming and editing as a superstar and a major player in Oliver Stone's acting ensembles. But it would not be true. Depp's character Gator Lerner is killed halfway through the movie and apparently many of Depp's better scenes and bits of dialogue were dropped on the cutting room floor during the editing process. Audiences never saw much character development from him. However, for a young actor it was an important experience. "Though my part in *Platoon* was relatively small, it was obviously a huge break," Depp says. "We knew that we were doing something that would be critically acclaimed, but nobody could foresee the magnitude of it."[42]

## WILLING TO GIVE, SORT OF

It was no secret to Depp that if he wanted to continue acting, he was going to have to get a lot better at it and give a lot more *to* it. He had begun more serious training by training with well-known acting coach Peggy Feury at the Loft Studio in Beverly Hills. He read books about acting methodology, and poured himself into the craft of acting. "After I saw how bad I was in my first couple of jobs, I decided I'd better do something about it," he said in a 1990 interview.[43] Not only was he doing something about his work, he was doing something about his love life, too. An actress who was also studying at the Loft Studio, Sherilyn Fenn, found herself playing opposite Depp in a short film for the American Film Institute, entitled *Dummies*.[44] Sherilyn, who would later star in David Lynch's imaginative television show *Twin Peaks*, was attracted to Depp, and that suited him just fine; he was equally attracted to her. The two became an item and continued their acting studies together.

What Johnny Depp was *not* attracting was employment. In the days, weeks, and months following his experience in *Platoon*, he was discovering yet again that acting jobs were not falling at his feet. His fallback option was music, and he took up with a Florida-based band called Rock City Angels. He was once again strumming his guitar and making the music he loved. Maybe this was the right path for him after all. Or maybe not. He could not make $45,000 a week playing his guitar. Of course, no one was paying him that much to act, either. At least not yet.

## NOTES

1. Johnstone, 13.

2. Johnstone, 10.

3. DeppImpact.com, www.deppimpact.com/quotes.html (accessed February 23, 2007).

4. Mary Kaye Schilling. "Johnny's Really Jumpin'," *Sun Herald*, May 28, 1989, http://interview.johnnydepp-zone2.com/1989_0528SunHerald.html (accessed June 1, 2007).

5. Ibid.

6. Goodall, 23.

7. Heard, 5.

8. DeppImpact.com, www.deppimpact.com/quotes.html (accessed March 3, 2007).

9. Johnstone, 12.

10. DeppImpact.com, www.deppimpact.com/quotes.html (accessed January 29, 2007).

11. Johnstone, 13.

12. "Bad Boy to Role Model," *TV Guide*, January 23, 1988, http://interview. johnnydepp-zone2.com/1988_0123TVGuide.html (accessed May 4, 2007).

13. "All the Tattoos of Johnny Depp," Hub Pages, http://www.mindsay.com/ wiki/Johnny Depp (accessed August 14, 2007). See also, Johnstone, 13.

14. Heard, 7.

15. Johnny Depp. "Kerouac, Ginsberg, the Beats and Other Bastards Who Ruined My Life," in *The Rolling Stone Book of the Beats*. ed. Holly George-Warren, (New York: Hyperion), 1999, 411.

16. Johnny Depp, interview with *Splice*, September 1988, http://www.johnny deppfan.com/interviews/8809splice.htm.

17. Depp 1999, 411; Knute Rockne (1888–1931)was widely regarded as one of college football's greatest coaches, for thirteen years leading his beloved Notre Dame team to many championships, including five undefeated seasons.

18. Depp 1999, 411.

19. Depp 1999, 411; The expression, "Beat Generation" refers to a group of American writers who came to prominence in the 1950s and who were best known for their rejection of the Establishment's rules about social conduct, literary merit, and artistic value.

20. Depp 1999, 411.

21. Johnny Depp, interview with *Rolling Stone*, 1998, 30th Anniversary Special, http://www.johnnydeppfan.com/interviews/rollingstone.htm.

22. Goodall, 34.

23. Goodall, 35.

24. Goodall, 35.

25. *Life Story*, 14.

26. *Life Story*, 14.

27. Goodall, 37.

28. Goodall, 37.

29. *Life Story*, 14.

30. Adler, 54.

31. Script for Wes Craven's "A Nightmare on Elm Street," http://www.hund land.com/scripts/A-Nightmare-on-Elm-Street.htm (accessed May 30, 2007).

32. Ethan Sacks. "Job was Killing Them: Actors Made a Living Dying in Horror Flix," *New York Daily News*, October 29, 2006, 27.

33. Barbara Vancheri. "Depp's Nightmare Returns," *Pittsburgh Post Gazette*, September 1, 2006, C-4.

34. Johnny Depp, interview with Eirik Knutzen, *Toronto Star*, 1987, http://inter view.johnnydepp-zone2.com/1987TorontoStar.html (accessed March 19, 2007).

35. Quoted in Heard, 15.

36. Quoted in Meikle, 45.

37. "User Comments for *Slow Burn*," IMDb.com, http://www.imdb.com/title/ tt0091972/usercomments (accessed May 28, 2007).

38. Quoted in Heard, 23.

39. Quoted in Meikle, 57.

40. Quoted in Heard, 26.

41. Quoted in Meikle, 59.

42. Johnny Depp, interview with Eirik Knutzen, *Toronto Star*, 1987, http://inter view.johnnydepp-zone2.com/1987TorontoStar.html (accessed March 19, 2007).

43. "Johnny Handsome," http://www.johnnydeppfan.com/interviews/ml90.htm (accessed May 30, 2007).

44. "A Fan's Page for Johnny Depp – Filmography," http://www.johnnydeppfan. com/filmography.htm (accessed May 30, 2007).

# Chapter 3

# "HANDSOME JOHNNY": FANS MAKE THE MAN—*21 JUMP STREET* AND STARDOM

About the last thing Johnny Depp was looking to do was a television series. For one thing, it would mean a long-term commitment to a project; for another, it was TV—a far cry from the Hollywood big screen. At that time hit television shows included *ALF* (1986–90), *Cheers* (1982–93), *The Cosby Show* (1984–92), *MacGyver* (1985–92), and the police dramas— *Miami Vice* (1984–89), *Hill Street Blues* (1981–87), and *Cagney and Lacey* (1982–88).

All of these shows had fairly long runs, and Depp was not looking for an extended television stay. On the other hand, he needed a steady income, and at age 23, it was time to seize an opportunity for a regular paycheck. That opportunity came in the form of a brand new weekly series, *Jump Street Chapel*. But it was an opportunity that came close to yielding no results.

If you are wondering why you have never heard of the TV series *Jump Street Chapel*, it is because it never happened. When Depp was asked to read for the part of Officer Tom Hanson, he turned it down. The show was to be about cops who looked young enough to be teens. These youthful detectives would go undercover in local high schools to deal with the teenage criminal element. When the producer Steve Beers failed to land Johnny Depp, the part was offered to another young actor, Jeff Yagher. It took just a few weeks of shooting scripts for Beers and series creator Patrick Hasburgh to see that Yagher was wrong for the part. The show, newly renamed *21 Jump Street*, needed Johnny Depp, and this time Beers was not going to take no for an answer!

Depp's agents were somehow able to persuade him to read the script, and much to everyone's surprise, he finally agreed to take the role, provided that the show not go in the direction of so many standard cop shows. Some have suggested that he wanted his role to provide some kind of positive message for teens, but the more likely reason that Depp was willing to take the role at all was because his agents had assured him that the series was not likely to last even one full season. That and the pay scale of $45,000 per episode[1] provided sufficient motivation for Depp to become a TV show character. If *21 Jump Street* lasted for just six shows, Depp would earn a quarter million dollars.

## SURPRISE HIT

But the show did not last for just six episodes. At the outset, Johnny Depp had been required to sign a five-year contract with Fox, which meant that the show could potentially run for well over 50 to 100 episodes. And last it did, though not without a great deal of turmoil. But at the beginning, when shooting began in 1986, Depp took his first steps into the medium that became his "real schooling in acting."[2] Those first few steps were, as it turned out, giant steps.

From the beginning, *21 Jump Street* producers set out to make a TV show that was hip and cool, with memorable characters played by attractive actors, a catchy musical soundtrack, and fascinating guest stars. The first episode featured the music of Grammy Award–winning rocker Steve Winwood ("Back in the High Life Again," 1986). The stars included Frederic Forrest, an actor for whom Depp had great respect. In that premiere episode, Depp utters a few lines that would prove to be prophetic. Late for a school play rehearsal (recall that he played a detective who looked young enough to be a student and who was undercover in a high school), his excuse is "I got hung up with [celebrity gossip columnist] Rona Barrett. After this, she figures I'm gonna be bigger than Paul Newman."[3] That level of stardom would not come for some time. But Depp's Tom Hanson caught the eyes and hearts of fans almost from the start. The two-hour pilot got good enough ratings to earn a 13-episode contract from Fox. Since the pilot had been a double episode, that left another 11 episodes to shoot—nearly double the six he had been figuring on. It was time for him to move up to Vancouver where the show was being filmed and to engross himself in the rigors of TV acting.

It did not take long for the fresh new talent named Johnny Depp to become a teen idol. *21 Jump Street* was a hit, and Depp's face was making headlines and billboards. Suddenly, the recently underemployed Depp was now a successful and well-paid young working actor. He was also very frustrated. Just a couple of months after he began working on the show, his band, Rock City Angels, signed a recording deal worth over six million dollars! While he co-wrote some of the songs and played with the band, he was not going to get the chance to hit the road with them. He had a show to do. The record, *Young Man's Blues* (Geffen, 1989), did not do particularly well, and the band's tour received lukewarm reviews. It may have been for the best that Depp was stuck in Vancouver making nearly $50,000 per week and racking up invaluable acting experience. Perhaps he took some solace in the fact that the last episode of the first season, entitled "Mean Streets and Pastel Houses," features Tom Hanson playing a punk rocker. At one point, he leaps from the stage into the audience of screaming teens.

By the time the show renewed for a second season—much to Depp's surprise and dread—the young star was receiving quite a bit of fan mail: over 10,000 letters each month according to one source, 10,000 letter a week according to another.[4] Twenty-three years old at the time, he was always surprised—and a little alarmed—at the intensity and volume of the fan mail. "I get mail from very young girls, 13 and 14."[5] Wherever he went, the fans found him, clamored for autographs, begged for handshakes and kisses, and shouted out their love and devotion to America's fresh young heartthrob. The devotion, though, was not mutual. He told an interviewer, "It's the label of teen idol that I hate. It's such an old thing, and it really limits an actor."[6]

Although Depp was less than thrilled with celebrity and frequently discouraged by what he saw as the limited range of television acting, he did his best to speak positively about *21 Jump Street*. In various media interviews he praised the show's socially healthy themes: safe sex, education, avoiding drugs, valuing friendships. Referring to the intelligence of the show's themes, he said, "We've done some strong stuff and the balance has to be between entertainment and public service."[7] He also acknowledged his commitment to the project: "Right now, I'm trying to pump everything I have into *21 Jump Street*, trying to make the most of my biggest break so far."[8]

In keeping with those expressed values, Depp did his best to respond to many of the fan letters himself—"I started off by phoning up the girls who wrote me, but that was expensive"[9]—especially those from desperate young girls who claimed they would kill themselves if he did not answer their letters. For him, this was "the scariest part about this thing called 'celebrity.'"[10] Of course he did not pretend to understand the desperation of this devotion: "I'm just an actor, not a professional psychologist."[11] For such a rookie

TV star to have these kinds of "problems" meant he was truly a working actor—successful, busy, and in demand. It also meant that fans were going to start confusing him with his television persona. He was eager to distinguish himself from his on-screen character, Tom Hanson. "I wasn't a good student like Tom. He's supposed to be clean-cut. I'm a jeans guy. The role and the actor have gotten confused. I've played in bands from the age of 12 or 13 until 23. Hanson doesn't have any street sense. I think most of my knowledge came from the streets…you learn about living in real life, rather than from high school."[12] Evidently, Depp's street smarts were working well for him; his career now had a definite trajectory.

## HELL RAISER

What was not working so well was his relationship with Sherilyn Fenn. Prior to *Jump Street*, Depp's long stint in the Philippines while filming his small role in *Platoon*, along with Fenn's own growing movie success, had put a strain on their relationship. The demands of shooting a television series meant that Depp would be living in Vancouver for nine months each year the series ran. Perhaps hoping to solidify things between them, he invited Sherilyn to move in with him in Vancouver where *Jump Street* was being shot. He would even arrange to get her a guest appearance on the show. (He also invited his mother and stepfather to join them in Vancouver.) And yet, as *Jump Street* moved toward its sophomore season, the romance between Depp and Sherilyn was ending. Despite his job security, it was a difficult and frustrating time for him, and that frustration reached a high point in Vancouver and would mark the unofficial start of his reputation as a temperamental star. At the hotel where he had lived during *Jump Street*'s first season, he got into an altercation with a security guard, ending when Depp spit in the guard's face and was arrested. The one night he spent in a Vancouver jail was enough for the tabloids to latch onto, sparking the media's portrayal of Johnny Depp as a hell raiser. Still, to the public, he remained polite and constructive about his television work. "I'm not trapped," he maintained. "The best thing about the show is that kids learn from it, they're able to see things that go on in their high school and see them objectively. It teaches kids about drugs and safe sex. The worst thing is that some of the scripts we do are not important, they're purely for television."[13]

The producers of *21 Jump Street* were also getting the picture that Johnny Depp was not going to be an easy member of the cast. After a season of trying to live up to not only the teen detective Hanson but also the idolatry of young teens, Depp was fast losing interest in the show and the clamoring of young fans for the image he had created. "I don't want to make a career of taking my shirt off…I'd like to shave off all my hair, even my eyebrows, try it that way. I don't fault the TV stars who do teen magazines. They took hold of their situations, took offers that gave them the big money fast, but they were dead in two years. I don't want that."[14] During the second season, Frederic Forrest was gone (he was written out of the show). Depp was able to secure work for his childhood friend Sal Jenco by having him written into the show as the occasional character called Blowfish.

But the increasingly unhappy Depp would show up to the set in more and more outrageous getups—including rubber bands on his tongue and funny wigs on his head. Still, while he was viewed as an eccentric guy and a bit of a pain in the neck on the set—he is rumored to have set his underwear on fire one day while in a bad mood[15]—he was still expected to fulfill his contract and continue to perform for the series. By the end of the second season, Fox TV had two big hits, *Married with Children* and *21 Jump Street,* and Fox was not about to give up on a revenue producer like *Jump Street* and its star, Johnny Depp.

## JUMPY AT *JUMP STREET*

In many ways, 1988 was an interesting year for Johnny Depp. His hit TV show wrapped up a second season, and his place as an American celebrity phenomenon was secured. At that time, the music scene seemed to be catching up to Depp's own sensibilities. Grunge rock was in, with bands like Pearl Jam and Nirvana leading the way. The grunge look (unwashed-looking torn clothing, dirty-looking hair, Doc Marten shoes or boots) was hot, and Depp—for whom the look had always been his normal attire—fit right in. The Smiths, The Stone Roses, and The Jesus and Mary Chain were a few of the indie (independent label) bands of the day, and their music and lyrics spoke to young people like Johnny Depp who saw themselves as somehow disconnected from the demands of traditional rules and regulations. There was also Michael Jackson, coming off the staggering success of his *Thriller* (1982) album—one of the best-selling albums ever— following it with his giant hit album, *Bad* (1987), and then a record-breaking solo world tour in 1988, the year in which he wrote his first autobiography. And, in a country that would one day be home to Johnny Depp, a 14-year-old girl named Vanessa Paradis—a child singing star—launched a hit record of her own entitled *Joe le Taxi*.[16] An ocean and 11 years separated Depp and Vanessa…but only for another decade. But more on that later!

Back on the set for the third season of *21 Jump Street*, the producers were not taking any chances on the anchor for their show. They brought on a new character, Booker, played by Richard Grieco who was, himself, an interesting, intense actor. It did not take long for Booker to become *Booker*—an entirely new TV series spun off of *Jump Street*. Whenever Booker made an appearance on *Jump Street*, Depp's Tom Hanson appeared less frequently in the show. Still, he could not escape the series entirely, and his contractual obligations seemed to be keeping him from pursuing more interesting and fulfilling acting projects. As his energies for the show waned, so did the ratings. On July 16, 1990, Johnny Depp finally won his freedom; he appeared for the last time as "an undercover cop with a pouty demeanor"[17] in his exit episode of *21 Jump Street*. In all, he had appeared in 57 episodes, cementing his public image as the cool, young, and just slightly different detective.

Years later, Depp would describe his *Jump Street* experiences in much more aggressively negative terms. He referred to working on a television series as "assembly-line stuff that, to me, was borderline Fascist." To him, being marketed as a teen idol meant being "shoved down the gullets of America" as a "novelty boy, franchise boy." No longer content to be "plastered, postered, postured, patented, painted, plastic,"[18] Johnny Depp was ready to be discovered, uncovered, and recovered from the mainstream. He and Sherilyn Fenn had split up, and he was now dating Jennifer Grey, star of *Dirty Dancing*. He was also ready to get his own hands much dirtier in the movie business, jumping from the *Street* straight into the Waters— John Waters, to be precise!

## NOTES

1. http://www.hollywoodteenmovies.com/Johnny%20Depp.html (virtually all sources on *21 Jump Street* salaries agree on this figure).

2. Meikle, 89.

3. *21 Jump Street: The Complete First Season* (1987), DVD (2004).

4. See www.cinema.com/articles/311/blow-interview-with-johnny-depp.phtml and http://interview.johnnydepp-zone2.com/1989_09skymagazine.html.

5. Johnny Depp, interview with Jim Baden, *Toronto Star*, 1987, http://interview.johnnydepp-zone2.com/1987_1101TorontoStar.html (accessed March 19, 2007).

6. "Johnny Depp Rocks," YM *Magazine*, March 1988, http://interview.johnnydepp-zone2.com/1988_03YM.html (accessed May 30, 2007).

7. Johnny Depp, interview with Jim Baden, 1987.

8. Johnny Depp, interview with Eirik Knutzen, *Toronto Star*, 1987, http://interview.johnnydepp-zone2.com/1987TorontoStar.html (accessed March 19, 2007).

9. Johnny Depp, interview with Jim Baden, 1987.

10. Stone Wallace. *Johnny Depp: The passionate Rebel* (Alberta, Canada: Icon Press, 2004), 34.

11. Wallace, 34.

12. *Life Story*, 19.

13. "Bad Boy to Role Model," *TV Guide*, January 23, 1988, http://interview.johnnydepp-zone2.com/1988_0123TVGuide.html (accessed May 4, 2007).

14. Johanna Schneller, "Johnny Depp: Girls' Best Friend," *Rolling Stone*, December 1998, http://interview.johnnydepp-zone2.com/1988_12RollingStone.html (accessed May 31, 2007).

15. Rebello 1990, quoted in DeAngelis, Michael. "Gender and Other Transcendences: William Blake as Johnny Depp." In *Ladies and Gentlemen, Boys and Girls: Gender in Film at the End of the Twentieth Century*, ed. Murray Pomerance (Albany State University Press), 2001, p. 295.

16. The translation of the French lyrics are:

> Joe the taxi [cab driver]
> He doesn't go everywhere
> He doesn't work on soda
> His yellow sax
> Knows all of the streets by heart
> All of the little bars
> All of the dark corners
> And the Seine
> And its bridges that shine
> In his car
> Joe's music
> It's the "rumba"
> From old "rock" to "mambo"
> Joe the taxi
> It's his life
> The rum with "mambo"
> Traffic jam
> He's like that
> Joe—Joe—Joe
> In his car
> Joe's music resonates
> It's the "rumba"
> From old "rock" to phony "mambo"
> Go Joe
> Go Joe
> Speed along
> In the night towards the Amazon
> Joe the taxi
> And Xavier Cugat
> Joe the taxi
> And Yma Sumac

Joe—Joe—Joe
Joe the taxi
It's his life
The rum with "mambo"
Traffic jam
Joe the taxi
And the Mariachis
Joe the Taxi
And the "cha-cha-chi"
Go Joe
Speed along
In the night towards the Amazon

Available at http://www.vanessaparadis.info/Mots/lyrics/l_joeletaxi.html (accessed February 24, 2007).

17. Lucy Kaylin. "Johnny in Paradise." *Gentleman's Quarterly* (August, 2003), 92–98.

18. Johnny Depp. "Foreword." In *Burton on Burton*, ed. Mark Salisbury. Revised Edition. (London: Faber and Faber), 1995, ix.

# Chapter 4

# "OH JOHNNY, OH JOHNNY, OH!": JOHNNY WADES IN THE WATERS AND MAKES THE CUT FOR BURTON

Imagine being a young actor in Hollywood and going to work for someone whose biography is entitled *Filthy*[1] and whose reputation is that of an eccentric, cultish Hollywood anomaly. Imagine that your new employer had been an actor in the film *Blood Feast 2: All U Can Eat*. In an understatement that seems funnier the more you learn about him, the Internet Movie Database's mini-bio of John Waters reads, "Growing up in Baltimore in the 1950s, John Waters was not like other children."[2] He is also not like other movie directors. As well known for his flamboyant homosexuality as for such offbeat films as *Mondo Trasho* (1969), *Pink Flamingos* (1972), and *Polyester* (1981), John Waters has created a number of memorable characters and bizarre scenarios.

In 1988, Waters' movie *Hairspray* dabbled a little more in mainstream cinema, starring such celebrities as Sonny Bono, Ricki Lake, and one of Waters' favorite alternative performers, Divine. Born Harris Glen Milstead just after World War II, Divine is described as "Baltimore's most outrageous resident...the international icon of bad taste cinema...the always shocking and highly entertaining transvestite performer."[3] But *Hairspray* made hardly a blip on Hollywood's radar, and Waters felt compelled to try making an even more mainstream film. In 1990, *Cry-Baby* premiered with Universal Studios as its backer. For the lead in this movie, John Waters sought to cast a lead that could fit the tagline: "He's a doll. He's a dreamboat. He's a delinquent."[4] Whose face do you think he found while reading through a bunch of tabloid magazines, and which "dreamboat" do you suppose he contacted for the role?

Johnny Depp played teenager Wade "Cry-Baby" Walker, who falls in love with Allison Vernon-Williams, a rich, conservative girl who decides she wants to be a bad girl when she develops a crush on sensitive tough guy Walker. Depp received a copy of the *Cry-Baby* script and was immediately taken by the story. In his view, *Cry-Baby*'s concept was "like *Grease* on psychedelics."[5] As he said of the film in a 1990 interview with Waters himself, "It makes fun of all that stuff I sort of hate. It makes fun of all the teen-idol stuff. It makes fun of all the screaming girls."[6] In one television interview, Depp explained that he was making fun of his image as a "teen idol," "bad boy," and "young rebel."[7] He explained that he had no control over the image of him that companies were using to sell their products and so *Cry-Baby* was a chance to fight this image.

Many would-be Hollywood advisors warned Depp about the risks of doing a John Waters movie. After all, this was the man who had previously directed a film featuring a 300-pound excrement-eating transvestite! He was told that his reputation would be irreparably damaged, that he would no longer be taken seriously by other directors and producers, and that it was too soon and he was too young to be making movies that parodied the very kind of celebrity he was now enjoying. But Depp had made his typically independent decision to take the part. "I've always admired people like John Waters, who's never compromised," he explained.[8]

Depp would certainly never regret making *Cry-Baby;* it was a time of experimentation for him as an actor and a learning experience for him, too. It was also fun: the actors, director, and producers enjoyed themselves, and, inexplicably, according to Depp, everyone on the set called each other "Mary."[9] Just as significant for him was that he established a close and lasting relationship with John Waters. "He's really smart, and he has a very solid vision of what he wants. We got real close on the movie. He's one of my best friends."[10]

## FROM WATERS TO A MERMAID

In many ways, the part of Wade in *Cry-Baby* would be the rebirthing of Johnny Depp as an actor. The character of Wade Walker was so different than *21 Jump Street*'s Tom Hanson, Depp was able to establish his acting range in a single, if rather strange, movie. One of Depp's costars, Traci Lords, described her experience with Depp this way: "He doesn't act like a star. He's not egotistical, he's not hung up, he's not an idiot. He's just very relaxed, very easy to work with."[11] While *Cry-Baby* was not much of a box-office success in America, it did fairly well in Australia and Europe, and the one million dollars Depp earned for his part was a far cry better than the seven thousand or so he earned for being shredded in *Nightmare on Elm Street*.

And there was another big change in his life. He and girlfriend Jennifer Grey had parted ways after just a few months. In 1989, he had a new girlfriend, the star of hit movies *Beetlejuice* (1988) and *Heathers* (1989): Winona Ryder. Depp was 26 years old; Winona was nine years his junior at age 17. Like her new boyfriend, Winona was a fast-rising star. Born in Winona, Minnesota, she was named Winona Laura Horowitz. Raised on an electricity- and hot-water-free commune by parents who read the poetry of Allen Ginsberg and smoked pot, Winona had lived an alternative lifestyle all her life. In fact, it was her parents who urged her to try acting, and at age 12 she enrolled in the American Conservatory Theater in San Francisco. Three years later, she was cast in the film *Lucas* (1986), directed by David Seltzer. One writer called her "the thinking man's actress for her generation."[12]

It was at the premiere of another of Winona's movies that she first made eye contact with Johnny Depp. The movie was *Great Balls of Fire* (1989), in which Winona played the very-underage child bride of Jerry Lee Lewis (played by Dennis Quaid). Lewis had married his third cousin, Myra Gale Brown, when she was just 13 years old. He was 22...nine years her senior! At that premiere, Depp and Winona merely looked at one another. According to him, "It was a classic glance...like the zoom lenses in *West Side Story*, and everything else gets foggy."[13] Two months later, they began dating. Toward the end of 1989, Depp was making regular flights from Vancouver (where he was still shooting episodes of *21 Jump Street*) to Boston, where Winona was shooting another film, *Mermaids* (1990).

By the time Depp was finished with *Cry-Baby* and deep into the making of *Edward Scissorhands*, he was 26, a millionaire, engaged to Winona whom was also starring in *Edward,* and now sporting his third tattoo: "Winona Forever" was now indelibly etched into his right upper arm, just above the tattoo of the Cherokee Indian chief. "Believe me," he told an interviewer from *Rolling Stone* magazine, "this *Winona Forever* tattoo is not something I took lightly"[14] (that tattoo, it should be noted, has been transformed since Depp and Winona's breakup: it now reads "Wino Forever," a kind of satirical statement on the tattoo's owner).

*Cry-Baby* costar Ricki Lake (who played Depp's constantly pregnant younger sister) had an interesting observation about the young couple: "They're the perfect couple....Physically, they look so similar, it's amazing."[15] It had been Lake who first told Depp about Winona and who had mentioned to Winona that he was available and quite desirable. Depp referred to Lake as his "cupid" which was, he said, "pretty great of her."[16] So smitten were Depp and Winona with one another, she even allowed him to coach her in the art of smoking cigarettes—even though she had not been a smoker.[17] Director Tim Burton called the beautiful couple a "kind of an evil version of Tracy and Hepburn."[18]

Five months into their relationship, they announced their engagement. Depp had every intention of marrying Winona, but he wanted to do so when both had some time off from busy filming schedules. Their engagement was to last over two years, but it would not end in marriage. Many people, events, and situations would cause the two lovers to diverge years later, but at the time, in 1990, Depp avowed that, "there's been nothing ever throughout my twenty-seven years that's comparable to the feeling I have with Winona."[19]

In addition, he had already had an unauthorized biography written about him. In keeping with the rebel persona he had been carefully cultivating since his teen rocker years, Depp told John Waters that he had not even bothered to read the book. "I don't know why anyone would write that. I never read it," he told the doubtful filmmaker, who then asked him how someone could resist reading their own biography. "Why would I read it?" Depp asked, and denied again that he had read the book. Waters pressed him, and finally Depp admitted, "I skimmed it, but I didn't read it. I looked through a couple of different sections and was mortified, and then threw it away"[20] (it turns out he did not really discard it; he gave the copy to none other than John Waters, who claims to have read it thoroughly).

This exchange may reflect another step in the development of Johnny Depp's more fully controlled public image—that of the wildly popular star who affects near-complete disenchantment with his own popularity. As one interviewer for *Movieline* magazine (1990) noted, "Depp does nothing to polish his image; in fact, the day we met, it looked like his hair hadn't been washed anytime recently."[21] Bill Zehme, of *Rolling Stone*, went farther when he wrote that "there is a shadiness to Depp. He looks unattractively unwashed."[22] Even with regard to his growing pile of cash Depp maintained an aloofness: "I never see it. It just goes right to my business manager. So I never really see it."[23]

When it came to his relationship with Winona, despite the obviously public statement that his tattoo made, he often made a point of rejecting fan curiosity about it. He bristled at early rumors that the two had already broken up shortly after becoming engaged. "I hate people who spread rumors. I hate people who pretend to have an idea about our personal lives.

We're together. I love her. It's wonderful. I just wish people didn't want to know so much. I don't ask people in K-Mart how their relationships with their wives and husbands are going."[24] Ironically, the interest fans had—and continue to have—in Depp's love life has always been a direct result of the image he has cultivated, that of the handsome, mysterious, antiestablishment, countercultural, un-Hollywood-like movie star.

Still, he had reason to feel some resentment toward those who started rumors about him and his relationships—especially rumors that were blatantly false. For example, in June of 1990, in an article for *Sky Magazine*, writer Tony Fletcher referred to Depp's Winona Forever tattoo as "a public and permanent declaration of the 26-year-old's love for his pregnant fiancée, actress Winona Ryder." As the magazine's editor had to amend, Fletcher's assumption about Winona's pregnancy "proved false."[25]

## MAKING THE (NEXT) CUT

What was not false at all was the quantum leap in acting ability that Johnny Depp displayed in his role as the star of *Edward Scissorhands* (1990). Director Tim Burton's dark fairy tale featured a scarred, lost, impaired, unfinished android created by The Inventor, played by Vincent Price. The Inventor names his "son" Edward but dies before he can complete him. Edward is left with complicated multiple sets of scissors where his hands should have been. Now alone in his "father's" house, Edward must take care of himself, which he does rather poorly, cutting himself frequently and learning little of the world into which he has been "born." When he is rescued by Peg, a kind cosmetics saleswoman (played by Diane Wiest), Edward is reborn into the real world of people, emotions, and conflicts. Peg's daughter, Kim, is a pretty high school cheerleader with whom Edward, much to his own not-quite-human confusion, falls in love. Kim is played by none other than Winona Ryder.

Depp says of the movie, "*Edward Scissorhands* is about a guy who's sort of an innocent placed into a normal—or what people think is normal—suburban life. It's the story of his dilemma and what he goes through. It's really exciting for me to be doing a movie with my fiancé, with Winona. But to be doing a movie with Tim Burton, and to be doing another movie that's not just your normal everyday, shoot-'em-up, fighting, posing, kissing, gun-toting, law-officer kind of thing...I feel very lucky."[26]

How did Burton find Depp? What first attracted the director's attention to the 27-year-old actor? "I'd seen his television show [*21 Jump Street*], but that's all I knew about him. Then I met him and he reminded me of the old star type that gives you a special feeling....He's one of those people who comes across as both old and young. He's a great character actor in many ways...a leading man. That's what struck me about him from the very beginning."[27] The part about Depp being "both old and young" serves as an intriguing note on the actor's life. In his early acting career, he was cast as a teen even when he was in his 20s. He was able to pull off roles that required a very youthful appearance and an older, wiser, demeanor.

As Edward Scissorhands, he was the creation of an old, dying man who had no time to imbue his son with youth. Instead, Edward is a kind of ageless child, a childlike adult, a character who must be both old and young to be believable. While there were a number of accomplished young male stars for Burton to pick from, his choice of Johnny Depp seemed to guarantee a movie that would be as ageless as the main character. Indeed, Burton's own quick description of *Edward Scissorhands* suggests this timeless quality. "It's not a new story.... It's *Frankenstein*. It's *Phantom of the Opera*. It's *King Kong*."[28] Burton might have added that *Edward* is also the story of *Beauty and the Beast*, *The Ugly Duckling*, and even, in a way, *The Elephant Man*, who both fascinated and frightened the community, stirring such mixed emotions that he was forced to live—and then die—in exile.

The sad on-screen relationship between Edward and Kim became beautifully ironic in that Depp and Winona were engaged as they finished shooting the movie. By the time *Edward Scissorhands* came out in late summer of 1990, the two had been engaged for nearly six months and were, by all accounts, passionately in love. Winona was not quite 19 years old, already a star, and betrothed to the man that millions of women all over the world adored.

That same year, Depp appeared in a music video for the band Concrete Blonde. The song was called "Joey," and was about a woman forgiving her boyfriend for his alcoholism and other addictions. As involved as Depp was becoming in the world of acting, he was never far from his first love, music. He would continue to appear in music videos for years to come, no matter what other projects he took on.

But it was becoming difficult for him to maintain any sense of aloofness from the Hollywood buzz around him. In 1990, he was nominated for a Golden Globe for best actor in a comedy or musical. His co-nominees in the category were Patrick Swayze for *Ghost*, Richard Gere for *Pretty Woman*, Macaulay Culkin for *Home Alone*, and Gerard Depardieu (who won the Golden Globe that year) for *Green Card*. His name was now to be found in the company of well-established, internationally renowned actors whose movies had grossed millions of dollars. Johnny Depp could have taken the leap into the high gloss of pure Hollywood, but in typical

Depp fashion, he had a little project to do—a small part in Wes Craven's *Freddy's Dead: The Final Nightmare*. He plays a teenager on a television show, and is listed in the credits as Oprah Noodlemantra. Once again, he was able to be both old and young, and as 1990 drew to a close, the acting world was wide open for Johnny Depp.

## NOTES

1. Robert Pela, *Filthy: the Weird World of John Waters* (Alyson Books, 2002).

2. "John Waters," IMDb.com, http://www.imdb.com/name/nm0000691/ (accessed May 4, 2007).

3. "Biography for Devine," IMDb.com, http://www.imdb.com/name/nm0001145/bio (accessed May 5, 2007).

4. "Taglines for *Crybaby*," IMDb, http://www.imdb.com/title/tt0099329/taglines (accessed May 20, 2007).

5. Tony Fletcher, "Babyface," *SkyMagazine*, June 1990 at The Johnny Depp Zone Interview Archive, http://interview.johnnydepp-zone2.com/1990_06Sky.html (accessed December 12, 2006).

6. John Waters, "Johnny Depp," *InterviewMagazine*, April 1990, http://interview.johnnydepp-zone2.com/1990_04Interview.html (accessed April 19, 2007).

7. Available at YouTube: http://www.youtube.com/watch?v=HspobrTehDE.

8. Stephen Rebello, "Johnny Handsome," *Movieline*, May 1990, http://interview.johnnydepp-zone2.com/1990_05Movieline.html (accessed April 25, 2007).

9. Christina Kelly, "Johnny Depp from A to Z," *Sassy*, May 1990, http://interview.johnnydepp-zone2.com/1990_05%20Sassy.html (accessed June 1, 2007).

10. Ibid.

11. Tony Fletcher, "Babyface," *SkyMagazine*, June 1990 at The Johnny Depp Zone Interview Archive, http://interview.johnnydepp-zone2.com/1990_06Sky.html (accessed December 12, 2006).

12. Bill Zehme, "Sweet Sensation," *Rolling Stone*, January 10, 1991, http://interview.johnnydepp-zone2.com/1991_01RollingStone.html (accessed June 2, 2007).

13. Ibid.

14. Ibid.

15. Fletcher, "Babyface," June 1990.

16. Fletcher, "Babyface," June 1990.

17. Zehme, "Sweet Sensation," January 10, 1991.

18. Zehme, "Sweet Sensation," January 10, 1991.

19. Zehme, "Sweet Sensation," January 10, 1991.

20. Waters, "Johnny Depp," April 1990.

21. Rebello, "Johnny Handsome," May 1990.

22. Zehme, "Sweet Sensation," January 10, 1991.

23. Waters, "Johnny Depp," April 1990.

24. "Johnny Be Bad," YM, May 1990, http://interview.johnnydepp-zone2.com/1990_05YM.html (accessed June 2, 2007).

25. Fletcher, "Babyface," June 1990.

26. Kelly, "Johnny Depp from A to W," May 1990.

27. *Life Story,* 41.

28. *Life Story,* 41.

# Chapter 5

# "FRANKIE AND JOHNNY": THE GREAT WIDE OPEN—FROM STARDOM TO SUPER-STARDOM

What better way to start the next big phase in his career than for Johnny Depp to appear in Tom Petty's music video "Into the Great Wide Open" in 1991? Tom Petty and the Heartbreakers, a Rock and Roll Hall of Fame band, were white hot in the late 1980s and early 1990s, and their leader, Tom, a Floridian from Gainsville, was a performer after Depp's own fashion. As Petty himself put it, "I'm not exactly a guy who makes new friends easily."[1] More to the point, despite Petty's over-the-top success, he has always been critical of the recording industry in general and of America's gradual loss of independent radio stations that had always been willing to take chances on new music and musicians. Songs like "The Last DJ" (2002) and "Joe" (2002) are prime examples of Petty's disdain for the emergent greed of record-label moguls.

In June of 1992, Depp was working with his brother D. P. Depp on a movie script about which he said, "It's not about the child within. It's basically about good and evil and believing in something."[2] In 1993 and 1994, Depp had not one but three new films under his belt. The first, *Arizona Dream* (1993), gave him his first opportunity to work with a European director, in this case Emir Kusturica. For Depp, Kusturica was a combination of cleverness and complication,[3] a director with a challenging way of running a film shoot. It was an important part of Depp's ongoing film education, and for Depp, his director's talent for showing the innate aloneness of each one of us was deeply appealing. From this shoot Depp picked up ideas for his own film, *The Brave*.

*Benny & Joon*, also released in 1993, paired up Johnny Depp with Mary Stuart Masterson, whose many films include *At Close Range* (1986), *Some*

*Kind of Wonderful* (1987), and *Fried Green Tomatoes* (1991). Once again, with *Benny & Joon*, Depp was drawn to a picture that featured a role in which he is an eccentric, but this time his love interest (Joon), is even more so. Director Jeremiah Chechik explained that he had been look- ing for an actor "who could play a character who is, metaphorically an angel...someone who could achieve a real naïve innocence that would not come off as foolish."[4] That would prove to be quite a challenge, but it was precisely the kind of challenge that Depp was seeking in his film projects. When, at a particularly tender moment in the story, Sam is to tell Joon that he loves her, Depp first tried to surprise everyone on the set, especially the director, when he chose instead to confess to Joon his most intimate secret—that he was a bedwetter. Chechik never included that in the movie, but Depp had proven, in an instant, that he wanted to try things his way. "I wanted to be the first person to say 'I am a bedwetter' in a major motion picture."[5]

As the shooting for the movie was starting, Mary Stuart Masterson and her husband had just separated, and she was, as she put it, in a "hysterical funk."[6] Somehow, though, working with her costar helped her keep things together—as though he really were a guardian angel of sorts. Masterson recalled that "when Johnny walked in, the energy in the room changed. There's something about him, his generosity of spirit."[7] Depp and Mas- terson worked so well together they were nominated for MTV's Award for best on-screen duo. Depp was also nominated for best comedic perfor- mance for *Benny & Joon*.

But in contrast to the easy chemistry between Depp and Masterson, Depp's inner life was weighed down by rumors about Winona. While he was finishing *Benny & Joon*, Winona was filming *Bram Stoker's Dracula* (1992), directed by Francis Ford Coppola. Her costar, Gary Oldman, had recently split from his wife of two years, Uma Thurman. Now there was gossip that Oldman and Winona had had an affair.[8] It turned out to be untrue. What was true, however, was that the 20-year-old Winona was becoming disenchanted with her relationship with her fiancé. Hollywood stars who occupy the spotlight do not get to take care of their personal lives with much privacy, and Depp and Winona both had those spotlights shining on them 24 hours a day. The tabloids kept playing up the rumors of an impending separation, and the rumor mill was working with a full head of steam.

At the same time Depp would find himself in demand for a film role in a story involving another dysfunctional family. Director Lasse Hallström knew Depp was the right man for the part of Gilbert in *What's Eating Gil- bert Grape* (1993), and the film would add another memorable character to Depp's career. Depp plays Gilbert, a young man whose family consists of his two sisters, his retarded brother, and an enormously obese mother. Gilbert's younger brother, Arnie, is an 18-year-old towards whom Gilbert feels both protective and resentful. Arnie is played by Leonardo DiCaprio. His mother has not left the house in years and must be waited on by her children. Her main emotional attachment is to Arnie and her main activity in life is sitting in front of the television, eating, and clicking the TV remote control. The family lives in Endora, Iowa, a town where almost nothing happens. Gilbert is rescued from the profound boredom and sameness of his life by the arrival of Becky, a young woman whose grandmother's van breaks down in Endora. For Gilbert, Becky is a sign that there is life beyond Endora.

## NEW DIRECTIONS

In the real world, Depp said, "I felt bad for the four months we shot. It was a very lonely time."[9] Just as Gilbert Grape had to begin his new journey away from Endora and into uncharted territory, Johnny Depp was about to set out in some new directions as well. On June 21, 1993, less than two weeks after his 30th birthday and exactly four months before Winona's 22nd, Depp and Winona announced the end of their engagement. Although their separation may have been a long time coming, Winona recalls that in the immediate aftermath she was deeply depressed. "I attempted being an alcoholic for two weeks, spending a lot of time in my hotel room, drinking screwdrivers from the mini-bar, smoking cigarettes and listening to Tom Waits."[10] Depp reacted in similar fashion; he was no stranger to cigarettes, drugs, and alcohol. "I just took to poisoning myself, which is really stupid," he told a reporter 10 years later.[11] He obviously survived the self-poisoning, but another fast-rising young star did not, and his tragedy, in late 1993, would add another scar to Depp's life. But first, Depp stepped into yet another movie role; he began shooting for a film entitled *Ed Wood* (1993).

## "I'VE NEVER WORN A BRA BEFORE"

The offer of the starring role in *Ed Wood* came a month before the announced breakup of the two stars. One evening in May, Depp received a call from Tim Burton. Three years earlier, Depp had starred in Burton's *Edward Scissorhands*, and now Burton had a new project underway. Depp had already turned down a number of offers for movies with other directors. Now, Burton wanted Depp to meet him at the Formosa Café at the corner of Formosa Avenue and Santa Monica Boulevard in Hollywood, not far from Depp's apartment. The Formosa Café was one of those "it" places in Hollywood—a place where stars hung out. It was once a railroad car, and became a famous diner whose walls are lined with hundreds of photographs of Hollywood's biggest stars. Every one of these photos was hand delivered and signed by the star. The Café's website describes the place as the "movie biz watering hole, where stars hold meetings over cocktails to discuss their next big picture."[12]

That was precisely what Burton intended to do with Depp. He bought a couple of beers and awaited the arrival of his star. When Depp joined him at the bar, Burton explained that the project was a movie about a man named Ed Wood. Depp did not even know who Ed Wood was, but he had already decided to accept the job if it meant working again with Burton. Ironically, it was a film that *Cry-Baby* director John Waters had earlier hoped to do but could not because of other commitments. Now Depp had a role that would test his training and his experience since he had first worked with Burton, and it would take him far afield from the teen-idol heartthrob image of his past. This was a role in which he could become absorbed and start to move past the loss of Winona Ryder. The first thing he would have to do to prepare for the role was learn everything he could about what it felt like to be a man who wore women's clothes while he made bad Hollywood movies.

Who was Edward D. Wood Jr., and why was Burton so eager to cast Johnny Depp in a movie about the man? At the time, Tim Burton had earned some commercial success as a director, and when he went to Disney with his proposal to do *Ed Wood*, the studio acquiesced; they recognized the value in having Burton among their directorial flock. The story of Ed Wood would be a sympathetic portrait of the man whose "films were canonized as camp, adored for their wide-eyed ineptness, startling continuity gaps, elementary-school acting, irrelevant stock footage."[13] Ed Wood was also noted for wearing women's clothing while he directed. In other words, Wood was an awful director and a strange man and Burton was setting out to make a movie that would make being so bad seem lovable. Author Denis Meikle calls *Ed Wood* "arguably the best film about filmmaking ever made"[14] because it was a portrait of a man, no matter how inept and odd, who loved movies and worked the Hollywood system in order to get them made. The film was, for Depp, "the rocket ship that took me away from that horrible black, bleak time."[15]

While making the movie may have kept some of Depp's personal demons at bay—the loss of his relationship with Winona Ryder, for one thing—another kind of darkness was about to strike, one that could have completely derailed his career. Chuck E. Weiss was the drummer and songwriter for the band Goddamn Liars and a friend of Depp's. As Depp was getting more and more involved in shooting *Ed Wood*, he was also tempted by an opportunity offered by Chuck: to go in as partners in the purchase of a nightclub. Weiss had already picked the place—a rundown club on Sunset Boulevard in Hollywood. For Weiss, the place held fond memories as he had played there every Monday night for over a decade. The owner, Anthony Fox, was looking for someone to bring in cash for renovations, and Weiss knew that Depp would be attracted to the idea of owning the club; it would give Depp a chance to play music with rock 'n' roll friends, and to smoke and drink with musicians. A couple of other Hollywood big shots—Arnold Schwarzenegger and Sylvester Stallone's brother, Frank—were also interested in buying the club, but Depp prevailed and was able to buy 51 percent of the company that owned the club, and renamed it the Viper Room.

Depp's new venture meant a new job for his old friend Sal Jenco, who was hired to manage the Viper Room. Around a month after the club opened, disaster struck. Young star River Phoenix—who had broken into the public eye with his brilliant performance in the movie *Stand By Me* (1986) and then went on to star in *Indiana Jones and the Last Crusade* (1989) and *My Own Private Idaho* (1991)—had become a regular at the Viper Club while filming *Dark Blood*. On October 30, 1993, Phoenix stopped in to spend some time with newfound musician friends. He had evidently taken both cocaine and heroin before arriving at the club, and then shortly after arriving, he took some more. By around 1:45 in the morning on October 31st, River Phoenix had a series of convulsions and seizures just outside the Viper Room door and died of an overdose at age 23.

## LESSON LEARNED?

In a word: no. At this point in the Johnny Depp story, the clichéd version would be that Depp was so shocked and dismayed by the death of River Phoenix (Depp had been at the club at the time) that he swore off drugs and opted for at least a straighter and narrower lifestyle. But we are talking about Johnny Depp here, and nothing like that happened. While Depp regarded Phoenix's death as "devastating" and "an absolute nightmare,"[16] he took a decidedly moody stance in response. Mostly, he was angry at the way the press handled the tragedy. "When River passed away, it happened to be at my club. Now that's very tragic, very sad, but they made it a fiasco of lies to sell magazines. They said he was doing drugs in my club, that I allow people to do drugs in my club. What a ridiculous thought!"[17] Depp closed the club for a couple of weeks, but again his reasons for doing so were mainly, it seems, to allow the media response to quiet down and to "get out of the way so River's fans could bring messages, bring flowers. And I got angry. I made a statement to the press: 'I will not be disrespectful to River's memory. I will not participate in your circus.'"[18]

Depp denied that the Viper Room was a place where celebrities used drugs, and told an interviewer that the media's suggestion to the contrary was "ridiculous and disrespectful to River."[19] When pressed a bit for his emotional reaction to River Phoenix's death, Depp responded, "I shed tears when I heard someone had died. It wasn't until later, four or five in the morning, that they told me it was River....It's so sad to see a young life end. At first...I couldn't go to the club without thinking of it. Later I came to terms with the fact that it had nothing to do with the club. He was here a very short time. It had nothing to do with anything, really, except that what he ingested was bad, and now there is nothing we can do."[20]

What *could* he do, after all? Some thought that Phoenix's death might inspire Depp to curb his own appetites for liquor and drugs. But the many antidrug public service announcements he had made during the *Jump Street* years did little to dissuade him from indulging in a variety of drugs. "If you're talking about drugs, you're talking about America. People die from drug overdoses every single day. You can't say specifically Hollywood or Sunset Boulevard."[21] Depp made little secret of his experience with drugs: "Well...it would be difficult to argue that I was anti drugs. I'm for, ah...being smart about the subject."[22] Depp has admitted to cocaine use—"cocaine is a strange one. A really strange one. I mean, I hated it. You get this synthetic happiness, and then you're just panicking and grinding your teeth"—but has said, to various interviewers, that for the most part he stopped using drugs by 2001 or so. He has added, "I drink, so I still have that form of escape."[23] But in 1993, not even the death of River Phoenix proved much of a detour from living the high life. That's why the making of *Ed Wood* may have been so comforting to Depp. The film gave him a chance not only to act, but to learn a great deal about filmmaking. It also added sufficiently to his bank account so he could buy himself something nice: a mansion.

## THE EARTH MOVES!

As usual, this purchase became part of the lore about Johnny Depp, and many have claimed that the 29-room home in the Hollywood Hills used to belong to famed scary-movie actor Bela Lugosi. However, others have argued persuasively that this is not the case. Laurie Jacobson, in her authoritative history, *Hollywood Haunted,* explains that the so-called castle never belonged to Bela Lugosi. That did not mean that the house lacked an interesting history, however. One of the previous owners had been Hersee Moody Carson, the widow of a multimillionaire. Having had no children of her own, Carson apparently held parties for orphaned children at her home during the 1930s and 1940s. According to Jacobson, Carson's home was, in some circles, known as the Castle of the Fairy Lady.[24] Johnny Depp now owned a fairy castle—fitting for the man whose own life would soon begin to look like a fairy tale.

But Depp's new home was about to have an adventure of its own. Less than three weeks into the new year, on January 17, 1994, California experienced an earthquake that measured 6.7 magnitude on the modified Mercalli scale, according to the Southern California Earthquake Data Center.[25] The Northridge Quake caused an estimated $15 billion in damages. Depp's home was damaged in the earthquake, and he had to move back to the hotel while repairs could be made. But the earth was about to move beneath his feet again, just a couple of weeks later, this time in the form of British supermodel Kate Moss.

In Kate Moss's version, "I met Johnny just after the CFDA [Council of Fashion Designers of America] awards dinner. We all went down to a bar for drinks and he was there. We were together from the second we met."[26] Well into the relationship, Depp told *Playboy* magazine, "I love Kate more than anything. Certainly enough to marry her."[27] This was certainly an interesting turn of events for Johnny Depp. Kate, at age 20, was 10 years younger than her new boyfriend. She was also world famous, fabulously wealthy, and a seasoned six-year veteran of the modeling world. She was one of the star models for Calvin Klein, and her face had been on billboards around the world. If there were two celebrity faces that drew more attention in 1994, it would be hard to find them.

But for a while, the new couple kept as low a profile as they could manage. Depp made a point of saying little about the relationship to interviewers. He told one reporter, "My relationship with my girl [Kate Moss] isn't something I'm going to discuss with anybody, especially a guy with a tape recorder."[28] It was at a Los Angeles club called Smashbox that Depp and Kate made their first public appearance together. It was in February of 1994 at a benefit for the Drug Abuse Resistance Education program (DARE), sponsored by *Vogue* magazine. That outing was doubly significant for Depp. It was at the DARE benefit that he screened a short film he had directed. The film, entitled *Banter,* was essentially an eight-minute public service message warning people about the dangers of drug use. Whether

Depp felt compelled to make this film as a result of what had happened to River Phoenix or for other reasons is anyone's guess. It was hardly the first time Depp had been involved in that kind of public service message. He had made a bunch of antidrug spots years earlier when he was starring in *21 Jump Street*. Perhaps now that he was 30 years old and had seen fellow young stars fall to drug overdoses he felt more directly connected to the message. Of course, Depp's anti–substance abuse message did not stop him from appearing in Shane MacGowan and the Popes' 1994 music video, "That Woman's Got Me Drinking," at the end of which Depp's character is seen slumped over a bar, passed out from booze.

Around a month later, Depp and Kate were photographed vacationing together in St. Bart's, looking every bit the loving couple. Soon after their return to the States, they attended the opening of John Waters' film *Serial Mom* (1994), starring Sam Waterston, more recently the longtime star of television's *Law and Order*. The two also attended the coming-out party for supermodel Naomi Cambell's new autobiography, *Swan*.

## THE LOVER

It may be that Depp was feeling the pressure to get back to moviemaking. *Ed Wood* was not yet released, nor was *Arizona Dream,* and it was time for Depp to get back to work. On top of that, Kate Moss was in demand all over the world and had to maintain a frenetic travel schedule. The pressure seems to have gotten to Johnny Depp; on September 13th, 1994, Depp found himself in handcuffs and on his way to jail after having wrecked his hotel room at The Mark in Manhattan. According to one account, police suspected that Depp had been drunk and fighting with Kate. After a few hours in jail on a criminal mischief charge, Depp was released on condition that he behave himself and repay The Mark nearly $10,000 in damages.[29] It was not Depp's first arrest—he had been arrested several times before for infractions such as speeding, assaulting a hotel security officer, and getting into a heated exchange with a Los Angeles police officer.[30] But this latest skirmish with the law was surely a sign that it was time to channel his energies into a new, constructive project.

By the spring of 1994 he was in a steady romantic relationship, but it was not, evidently, proving to be any more of a stabilizing force than his brief marriage to Lori Allison, his even briefer (months long) engagement to actress Jennifer Grey, his two-year relationship with Sherilyn Fenn, or his three-year relationship and engagement to Winona Ryder. He needed to be inside a new role and get back on track, and as the star who loved women—and the man was adored, worshipped, and desired by millions of women—it was perhaps inevitable that Johnny Depp's next role would be that of the man claiming to be the world's greatest lover. In 1818, poet George Gordon Lord Byron began to compose the work that would be, for many, his greatest: the long satirical poem entitled *Don Juan*. Many authors have written works about the legendary (and fictional) man who was said to be the greatest seducer of women. Byron's poem follows Don Juan from romance to romance, adventure to adventure. Where Byron differs a bit from others in his handling of the Don Juan legend is that his Don Juan seems more seduced than seducer. It is as though women cannot help but fall in love with him and seek to make him their own.

In the movie *Don Juan DeMarco* (1995), screenwriter and director Jeremy Leven cast Johnny Depp to play a young man, John DeMarco. John believes he is actually the great Don Juan and stands atop a building, about to commit suicide over a lost love. Dr. Mickler, a psychiatrist played by Marlon Brando, manages to talk John down by pretending to be a man named Don Octavio de Flores. John/Don Juan then becomes a patient of Dr. Mickler's; the doctor, for his part, must try to help John see through his own delusion. Of course, there is more than enough suggestion in the movie that John might just be the reincarnation of Don Juan. The parallels between Depp's Don Juan and Depp himself may seem fairly obvious.

## THE LESSON

The film gave Depp the opportunity to work with Brando, whose appearance in the film had been one of the conditions Depp had set before accepting the role. Director Leven had commented that as he watched the two men act together, he felt he was witnessing Brando "giving Johnny the room to be the next Marlon Brando. And you know? I think Johnny could handle it."[31] Depp was also able to handle performing with a Spanish accent. His character maintains the accent throughout the film except for one scene in which he speaks in an American accent before a judge. In that moment, John/Don Juan is pretending to confess that he has been having delusions about being Don Juan. He does this to gain release from a mental hospital. The scene is touching and Depp's acting is impressive. Many of the reviews were quite positive about Depp's acting in particular, though one of Depp's biographers claims that *Don Juan DeMarco*, despite Depp's professional performance, "is a dud, a florid, flaccid, pop-psychological panjandrum of a film, full of sound and fury, ultimately signifying nothing of note."[32] But actually, of particular note was Depp's success in arranging for Brando to play a role in the film to begin with. The fact that Brando was eager to appear with Depp was yet another sign of Depp's rising stature in the movie world.

At least one other important lesson came out of making *Don Juan De-Marco*; it gave Depp the experience of working with an inexperienced director, Jeremy Leven. "He was a first-time guy, he was a first-time direc-tor, which is fine. . . . I support that, you know, but he was one of those guys who would not—he refused to admit that he didn't know what he was doing, you know, and he wouldn't take advice from people, you see, he just forged ahead and it was a really awful."[33] Depp was developing a greater sense of control when it came not only to choosing movie roles, but in demanding with which costars he would like to appear. Now he had added some control over the way in which he would accept being di-rected. About Leven, he said, "we hit a point in that film where I actually had . . . to tell the guy, hey, don't . . . you can say action, and cut, and print, if you like, but don't say anything else to me because I wanna kill you, you know, I'd really like to have my hands around your throat—so . . . he didn't bother me any more, just stayed away. He said action, cut, print—wrap, and that was it."[34]

Also still "it" was Kate Moss, who was now earning millions of dollars every time she took on a new modeling job. She and Depp continued to be one of Hollywood's hot couples, though her star was still shining a bit brighter than her famous boyfriend's. When *Ed Wood* opened in late September of 1994, it received high critical marks—especially about its star and its director, Tim Burton—but it never turned into a commercial success. It did, however, solidify Depp's standing in moviedom. There was no doubting that he had proven himself to be talented, intense, and equal to the challenges that virtually any role might offer. He had acted in a variety of films with an eclectic list of directors, and he had established his penchant for playing the role of slightly (or profoundly) off-center characters with deep hearts and memorable looks. It was time to forge ahead with the newfound momentum, time to live it up as a 31-year-old bona fide movie star. How does a man like Johnny Depp make the most of his career's new life? By playing an accountant named after eighteenth-century poet William Blake, in a movie entitled *Dead Man*.

# NOTES

1. "Biography for Tom Petty," IMDb.com, http://www.imdb.com/name/nm0678816/bio (accessed November 19, 2006).

2. William Norwich, "Vogue Men," *Vogue*, June 1992.

3. Christophe d'Yvoirre, "My Way: an Interview of Johnny Depp," *Studio*, January 1992, http://www.johnnydeppfan.com/interviews/studio92.htm (accessed April 26, 2007).

4. *Life Story*, 49.

5. Ibid.

6. Ibid.

7. Ibid.

8. Meikle, 113.

9. Jaime Diamond, "Johnny Depp," JohnnyDeppfan.com, http://www.johnny deppfan.com/interviews/cosmo.htm.

10. "Ryder's 'alcoholism' following Depp split," UGO ActressArchives, http://www.actressarchives.com/news.php?id=1967 (accessed May 12, 2007).

11. "Ed Wood," Depp Impact, http://www.deppimpact.com/edwood.html (accessed August 14, 2007).

12. Formosa Café http://formosacafe.com/ (accessed June 6, 2007).

13. Gary Morris, "It's an Ed Wood World After All," *Bright Lights Film Journal*, http://www.brightlightsfilm.com/16/wood.html (accessed June 1, 2007).

14. Meikle, 132.

15. Diamond, "Johnny Depp," JohnnyDeppfan.com.

16. Elizabeth Vargas, "Transcript: The Buccaneer," *60 Minutes*, September 7, 2003, http://sgp1.paddington.ninemsn.com.au/sixtyminutes/stories/2003_09_07/story_954.asp (accessed June 2, 2007).

17. Kevin Cook, interview with Johnny Depp. *Playboy*, January 1996, http://www.johnnydeppfan.com/interviews/playboy.htm (accessed December 1, 2006).

18. Ibid.

19. Ibid.

20. Ibid.

21. "Johnny Depp Gets Serious," Knight-Ridder Newspapers, 1993, http://www.johnnydeppfan.com/interviews/knightridder93.htm (accessed June 4, 2007).

22. Danny Leigh, "Johnny Be Good," *The Guardian*, May 24, 2001, http://film.guardian.co.uk/interview/interviewpages/0,6737,495635,00.html (accessed May 29, 2007).

23. Ibid.

24. Laurie Jacobson and Marc Wanamaker, Hollywood Haunted (Santa Monica, CA: Angel City Press, 1994), 36.

25. Southern California Earthquake Data Center, http://www.data.scec.org/chrono_index/northreq.html (accessed October 21, 2006).

26. Johnny Depp, interview with Ingrid Sischy, *Interview*, March 1999, http://findarticles.com/p/articles/mi_m1285/is_3_29/ai_54133697/pg_4 (accessed June 1, 2007).

27. Kevin Cook, interview with Johnny Depp. *Playboy*, January 1996, http://www.johnnydeppfan.com/interviews/playboy.htm (accessed December 1, 2006).

28. James Ryan, "Depp Gets Deeper," *Vogue*, September 1994, file:///Users/michaelblitz/Documents/Depp/*INTERVIEWS/A%20Fan's%20Page%

20for%20Johnny%20Depp%20-%20Vogue%201994.webarchive (accessed February 13, 2007).

29. Nadine Brozan, "Chronicle," *New York Times*, September 14, 1994, B-8

30. Shelley Levitt, "Love and Depp," *People,* October 3, 1994, http://www.johnnydeppfan.com/interviews/people.htm (accessed June 1, 2007).

31. *Life Story,* 51.

32. Meikle, 145.

33. Johnny Depp, French television interview with Chiara Mastroianni, November 1998, http://www.johnnydeppfan.com/interviews/chiara.htm (accessed April 11, 2007).

34. Ibid.

# Chapter 6

# "JOHNNY ONE TIME": FROM DEAD MAN TO SPACE MAN

By now, a number of identifiable themes and motifs characterized the movies in which Johnny Depp would appear. He preferred to play characters who were somehow disconnected from the mainstream, romantic in nature, and troubled. He had a clear sense of what he looked for in a director and a movie project, and now he had good reason to expect to be courted by producers and directors for whom he had real respect. In late 1994, Depp was invited by well-respected and award-winning director Jim Jarmusch to star in a film he was planning, entitled *Dead Man* (1995). His movies, *Stranger Than Paradise* (1983) and *Down By Law* (1986), among others, had all won or been nominated for major film awards. Like Depp, Jarmusch was an old rock 'n' roller, having played synthesizers and "oddly tuned guitars" in a band in the 1980s called the Del-Byzanteens.[1] He had also directed a number of music videos for artists such as Neil Young, Tom Waits, Talking Heads, and Big Audio Dynamite.[2] One other interesting connection between Depp and Jarmusch: in 1991, Jarmusch had directed Winona Ryder in *Night on Earth*.

With *Dead Man*, Jarmusch had in mind a deceptively simple story that would allow his actors to plumb the depths of an array of quirky characters. After having played a wide variety of roles, Depp would now step into the life of an accountant who travels west for a new job only to discover there is no job there for him. In short order, Depp's Bill Blake has taken as a lover a former prostitute, Thel, who is shot dead by her ex-fiancé. Blake then shoots the ex-fiancé dead and flees. Unfortunately, he too has been wounded by the bullet, which passed through Thel and struck him in the chest. He is cared for by Nobody, a Native American who must not only help him heal but who becomes an ally. It turns out that the man Blake shot was the son of the company owner who was to have given him a job—a man with the power to take out a contract on Blake.

Jarmusch spares few literary allusions, beginning with naming Depp's character after eighteenth-century poet and visionary William Blake. In *Dead Man*, Bill Blake's brief love interest's name is Thel, a direct reference to one of Blake's poetic works, "The Book of Thel." Calling Blake's Native American guide Nobody is an echo of the ploy Odysseus uses in Homer's *Odyssey* where, to escape the wrath of the murderous Cyclops, Odysseus tells him that he is called "Nobody." When later Odysseus puts out the Cyclops's one eye and the blinded monster cries out for help from his countrymen, he tells them "Nobody" has ruined his sight. Of course, his countrymen see no reason to take the Cyclops seriously after that. In Jarmusch's film, Depp's character has Nobody to guide him through the perils of being a hunted man.

Depp once again proved himself a gifted actor, deeply impressing his director. Jarmusch was particularly taken with Depp's ability to grow with his character and to maintain continuity of that character even when the filming of scenes may have been discontinuous. "What I love about Johnny for this character is that he has the ability to start off very innocently. This is a difficult role to play, to start off as a passive character in a genre that is based on active, aggressive central characters. What amazed me about Johnny was his ability to go through a lot of very subtle but big changes in his character, out of sequence but without ever telegraphing that character development. He was much more precise than I thought he would be. He was also very inventive."[3] Depp's inventiveness would take another interesting turn in June of 1995 when, after a movie project fizzled out, he signed on to be one of the artists who read or performed on the *United States of Poetry* program for PBS Television. Reaching back to his old love of the Beat poets, and especially of Jack Kerouac, Depp read from Kerouac's *Mexico City Blues*.[4]

In January 16, 1995, around a year after meeting her, Depp threw his girlfriend Kate Moss a surprise party for her 21st birthday. The party was at Depp's Viper Room, and Depp had arranged to have Moss's mother and father flown in from England, as well as a crowd of friends and family from throughout the country.[5] A week later, at the Golden Globe Awards ceremony, along with Arnold Schwarzenegger, Jim Carrey, and Terrence Stamp, Depp was a nominee for best actor in a comedy or musical (for *Ed Wood*) but lost to Hugh Grant. Depp's *Ed Wood* costar, Martin Landau, won for best supporting actor.[6] Depp had once more been beaten out for a Golden Globe, but he was very much the golden boy in show business.

*Empire* magazine named Johnny Depp one of the 100 sexiest stars in film history.[7] Not bad for a 32-year-old guy from Owensboro, Kentucky! What new movie project would Depp choose with which to dazzle his audiences? In what role would he cash in on his latest incarnation as one show business's sexiest stars? It was time for Johnny Depp to play... another accountant?

## IN THE *NICK OF TIME*... FOR A BIG PAYCHECK

As Gene Watson, accountant, in John Badham's *Nick of Time* (1995), Depp had accepted a role that many saw as purely commercial. One reviewer said of Depp's decision to act in the film, "You don't do a movie that crappy unless you think it's going to make a ton of coin."[8] Badham had made the wildly successful *Saturday Night Fever* (1977) starring a very young John Travolta and featuring hit songs from the Bee Gees. In *Nick of Time*, Badham had hopes of another young star generating another blockbuster hit. The script was hardly thrilling, and while Depp's character ends up tangled in an assassination plot against the governor of California, for many it did not seem like a role that Depp would have chosen as his next imaginative challenge. Yet, in an interview Depp did for *Playboy* magazine, when he was asked whether making *Nick of Time* was just selling out—"doing the Keanu thing"—he defended his choice: "I'm interested in story and character and doing things that haven't been done a zillion times. When I read *Nick of Time* I could see the guy mowing the grass, watering his lawn... and I liked the challenge of playing him. He's nothing like me... it gives me a chance to play a straight, normal, suit-and-tie guy."[9] Gene Watson, his character, is not really just a suit-and-tie guy as it turns out. He and his daughter are kidnapped by a couple who want to kill California's governor. One kidnapper is played by Christopher Walken, one of the stars with whom Depp was eager to share a script. In formulaic manner, Watson is given a gun and told to kill the governor or his daughter will be killed. The rest of the movie follows the pattern of a typical action thriller, and has its fun moments. But as one writer put it, Depp's Gene Watson is "colorless, flavorless," and merely a placeholder in a flawed plot.[10] The plot may have had its flaws, and *Nick of Time* may have been a more commercial endeavor than fans and critics would have predicted for Depp, but those in his inner circle knew otherwise. As his agent Tracey Jacobs said when asked about her client's turning down a role in the movie *Speed* (1994—starring Keanu Reeves and Sandra Bullock), "Let's make this really clear... he wants to be in a commercial movie. It just has to be the right timing and the right one, that's all!"[11] *Nick of Time* may not have been a gigantic box office hit, but it was a step in that direction. After wrapping up the filming, Depp and Kate headed off to France, to the Cannes Film Festival where *Dead Man* was in the competition for the coveted Palme d'Or. Although *Dead Man* did not win, Depp made the most of his stay in Cannes by teaming up with his director and friend Jim Jarmusch to appear in a movie spoof entitled *Cannes Man*. The two play themselves in the parody of the film industry.

From Cannes, France, Depp moved on to Ireland where he had been invited by Marlon Brando to be in the film *Divine Rapture*. The film was to be a comedy about miracles and the Catholic Church. But three weeks into shooting, the funding dried up, and the actors—including Debra Winger and one of Depp's *Dead Man* costars, John Hurt—were out of work. It was at that time, in June of 1995, that Depp got involved in the *United States of Poetry* program and, much to his delight, actually met poet Allen Ginsberg.

## "BABBLING LIKE AN IDIOT"

Ginsberg had been one of Depp's literary heroes back when he first discovered the Beat Generation writers. As Holly George-Warren explains it, the Beat Generation was named by Jack Kerouac, who "then divorced it." The "common thread running through the work was this: to say what hadn't been said in a language as unique as one's own thumbprint."[12] The great Beat writers included, in addition to Kerouac, William Burroughs, Neal Cassady, Charles Bukowski, Leroi Jones, Denise Levertov, Frank O'Hara, and of course Allen Ginsberg, to name just a few. Depp has said that Ginsberg's long poem, *Howl*, "left me babbling like an idiot, stunned that someone could regurgitate such honesty to paper."[13] In 1995, while rehearsing a bit of the Kerouac poem for the *United States of Poetry*, Depp spotted Ginsberg, who was also working on the project. The two were introduced, and Ginsberg recited a little of Kerouac's poem to show Depp how Kerouac himself might have read it. All Depp could think to say in response was, "Yeah, but I'm not reading it as him. I'm reading it as me." Immediately, Depp felt he had made a grave error in talking to the renowned poet in so contentious a manner. "I sucked down about half of my five-thousandth cigarette of the day in one monster-drag and filled the air around us with my poison." Then Depp remembered that Ginsberg had written a now-famous song entitled "Don't Smoke." "I looked at Ginsberg, he looked at me, and the director looked at us both as the crew looked at him, and it was quite a little moment." But Depp was redeemed an instant later when Ginsberg "smiled that mystic smile, and I felt as though God himself had forgiven me a dreadful sin."[14]

Ginsberg invited Depp back to his apartment where the two talked for hours. Ginsberg signed a few books for him including one for his brother, D. P. Depp, and then Depp went back to his hotel. "From that day forward, we stayed in touch with each other over the next few years, and even spent time together from time to time."[15] Sadly, three days before Ginsberg's death on April 5, 1997, he called Depp to tell him the end was near. Depp had hoped to get back to New York to say goodbye, but had to content himself with the memory of that last telephone conversation in which each said "I love you" to the other. One of the significant things about the story Depp relates about Ginsberg is the fact that it was published in a book about the Beats and the Beat Generation.[16] Johnny Depp—actor, musician, club owner, and now writer. The resume was growing.

By August of 1995, Depp and Kate had been together nearly a year and a half, and rumors had them heading for marriage—or splitting up! Still looking very much the loving couple, the two began to dabble in political issues, taking up the cause of protesting French testing of nuclear weapons in the South Pacific, and donating time and money to the War Child Project, an international organization that provides relief to children affected by war. In addition, Kate's new book was out, entitled, aptly enough, *Kate Moss Book*. It was a collection of photographs of the young supermodel, and its New York debut featured both Depp and Kate speaking out against the French. Ironically, France would become Depp's home country of choice a few years later.

At the end of that year, 1995, Depp and Kate vacationed in Aspen, Colorado. They were accompanied by her mother and brother. It was a trip that would prove enormously significant to Johnny Depp, as it was in Aspen that he first met the man whose book, *Fear and Loathing in Las Vegas*, had been as important to the young Depp as Kerouac's *On the Road*. While Depp, Kate, and her family were having a drink, into the bar strode the man who would, in effect, add voltage to Johnny Depp's star. The man was Hunter S. Thompson, one of Depp's boyhood idols. When Depp had been a teenager, his brother, D. P., had given him a copy of Thompson's *Fear and Loathing in Las Vegas* to read. The story of the two men, Raoul and Dr. Gonzo, drinking, drugging, and driving their way across the country and into the hallucinations of the American Dream left a lasting impression on Depp. "It was the most outrageous thing I'd ever read... those guys were heroes, man. I mean, they had to be, out there, living that."

Depp called the book "one of the greatest pieces of twentieth-century literature."[17]

## FEAR AND LOATHING

Hunter Stockton Thompson was born July 18, 1937, in Louisville, Kentucky, around 80 miles from Depp's birthplace of Owensboro. Thompson, who some have called the Godfather of Gonzo, was a writer, journalist, social critic, and national character whose outspokenness was matched only by his excesses with drugs, alcohol, cigarettes, and overall recklessness. A long-time member of the National Rifle Association (NRA), he was also a staunch advocate of civil liberties. Mostly, though, he was the man who pushed the limits of gonzo journalism—a style of reporting on things that entailed getting so involved in the subject matter that the writer became the main focus of the piece. His 1966 nonfiction book, *Hell's Angels*, chronicled the well-known bikers but mainly focused on Thompson's own experiences writing with the bikers. But perhaps Thompson's most famous work is *Fear and Loathing in Las Vegas: A Savage Journey to the Heart of the American Dream*. First published 1971, *Fear and Loathing* appeared in *Rolling Stone* magazine as a two-part piece. The two main characters are Raoul Duke and Dr. Gonzo, Duke's lawyer. The two are hard-drinking, drug-abusing men who head to Las Vegas to cover a motorcycle race. The trip becomes a weird vacation in which they get stoned, use LSD and hallucinate, and smash up a few cars. The story was part autobiographical and part fiction, and it was compelling enough to echo into the 1990s when it would be made into a movie starring Johnny Depp as Raoul Duke.

But before that film event, back at the Woody Creek Tavern in Colorado, Depp was treated to the arrival of Thompson. The two introduced themselves to one another and Depp discovered that Thompson had seen part of his movie, *Cry-Baby*. Thompson told him, "I never saw the end, of course...because I had a little acid."[18] The two hit it off, as Depp recalled. Thompson invited Depp and his entourage back to his compound where the two actually constructed bombs in Thompson's kitchen and then shot at them with some of Thompson's guns. Just a couple of years later, Depp would be shooting with Thompson again, this time on the set of Thompson's movie.

In 1996, new rumors began to circulate about the fading of the relationship between Depp and Kate, though the two continued to enjoy vacations and show-biz events together. They did not seem to pay much attention to the rumor mill. Depp had been named by *People* magazine as one of the 50 most beautiful people in the world.[19] A bit later that year, Depp won the London Critics' Circle Film Award's actor of the year for his work in *Ed Wood* and *Don Juan DeMarco*. More and more, he was receiving the kind of recognition that was putting him at the top of the star lists in Hollywood. In February 1996, TriStar Pictures director Mike Newell was able to get Depp to commit to the lead role in *Donnie Brasco*—another huge step up for Depp who would be costarring with Al Pacino, one of Hollywood's greatest actors. Donnie Brasco was the name taken by Joe Pistone, the FBI agent who infiltrated the Mafia in the 1960s and then later testified against scores of mobsters. To get ready for the role, Depp put on weight,[20] spent hours with Pistone to learn his story and his mannerisms, and did his customarily thorough job in becoming the part. Director Mike Newell said, "Johnny is, in part, a great impersonator. When he met Joe Pistone I could see him latch on to certain characteristics within seconds."[21] The movie provided Depp with an opportunity to further hone his craft, especially in working with Pacino. It also put Depp into contact with some interesting people. "I did meet some very heavy underworld figures through this project…and the thing is, I liked them very much." Depp's enjoying the company of a few ex-mobsters might not be that surprising. But he also enjoyed hanging out with "some very heavy upper echelon FBI guys who I could also identify with."[22] Equally intriguing about the film must have been the subtext of Pistone's gradual loss of identity over the course of the years he spent as a mobster. Depp's own roles and characterizations were finding ways of attaching themselves to him, and his portrayal of Pistone/Brasco was considered particularly convincing.

The movie was praised by critics, one writing that *Donnie Brasco* is "the best crime movie in a long while" and that Depp was excellent: "Surprise No. 1: Depp's tremendous talent is no longer surprising. With this film his career reaches critical mass, turning an assortment of varied, offbeat roles into the trajectory of a major star."[23] Depp *had* played a number of offbeat roles, it was true. That factor was most likely what prompted the phone call Depp received in early March of 1996, around a week into the shooting of *Donnie Brasco*. On the other end was Hunter S. Thompson, who told Depp that there was going to be a movie made from his novel *Fear and Loathing in Las Vegas* and asked, "What do you think about playing me?" Depp recalls saying "Absolutely,"[24] and the deal was, in effect, made.

Also in 1996, Depp had made plans to try his hand at directing. The story he wanted to do was called *The Brave*, based on the 1991 novel by Gregory McDonald. McDonald's was an extremely dark book about a destitute Native American man named Rafael and his wife and children.

Rafael is desperate to provide for his family but sees no hope to do so. He makes a bargain with a man named McCarthy who, it turns out, makes "snuff" movies in which the star is actually tortured to death. The bargain is that Rafael's family will receive $50,000 in exchange for Rafael starring in one of McCarthy's films. Rafael then has a week to reconcile himself to his fate and to say goodbye to his family before undergoing horrendous torture and death.[25] The film rights to McDonald's book were bought by a man named Aziz Ghazal, who hired Paul McCudden to write a screenplay that would be true to McDonald's story.[26] In a way, McCudden's script may have been too true to the original story; no producers stepped up to finance the film. In 1993, Ghazal committed suicide after murdering his wife and daughter, and the script fell through the cracks, through the hands of various potential producers, and eventually found its way to the interested gaze of Johnny Depp.

Depp thought that he could transform the script in collaboration with his brother, D. P. Depp.[27] The main change would be that Rafael would not die a horrible death at the hands of snuff-movie maker McCarthy; he would change his mind and redeem himself to his tormented family. But it did not quite work out that way once the shooting began. Marlon Brando played McCarthy, and the Depps rewrote his character to deemphasize the snuff-movie connection. Instead, Brando is a more mysteriously sadistic man who happens to get satisfaction from killing others. After weeks of discussion, argument, and experimentation, director Johnny Depp could not work out a suitable positive ending and fell back, more or less, on the ending from McDonald's book. For a first directorial effort, it was not so bad. He had brought together a worthy cast—Brando, his old *JumpStreet* buddy Frederic Forrest, Iggy Pop, and Clarence Williams III of *The Mod Squad*[28] fame, to name a few. While the storytelling abilities of the Depp brothers may have been flawed, the movie itself was an important step forward for Johnny Depp. As biographer Denis Meikle put it, *The Brave* "represents Depp's coming of age as an actor and as an artist. From here on in, he could walk tall with the best of them."[29]

It was time to get to work on the Thompson film, which was to be directed by Terry Gilliam—the brilliant animator of Monty Python fame. Making *Fear and Loathing* would, for Depp, entail some of the most in-depth character research he had ever done. After all, this was Hunter S. Thompson's life he would be portraying in the character of Raoul Duke who, according to Depp, was "ninety-seven percent Hunter." As Depp recounted to *Rolling Stone*, he told Hunter, "I need to spend time with you, and when you get sick of me being there, just tell me....I told him that I'd probably become a...pain in the ass, because I'd be asking him a lot of questions and taping the conversations and writing things down, and it'd be like I was a parole officer. But he never kicked me out, which was good."[30] Virtually everything about Depp's experience trailing Thompson was peculiar. Depp slept in a tiny basement room, surrounded by kegs of gunpowder; Depp and Thompson talked through much of those days, often drinking for hours at the bar; Depp tried on old clothes of Thompson's, some of which had not been washed in decades. Each time Depp visited Thompson he would spend up to two weeks, learning the man's mannerisms, nuances, and idiosyncrasies. Depp even shaved his head—or rather, he let Thompson shave his head for him to make him look even more like the eccentric writer.

## I . . . CANNOT BE YOU

Thompson was helpful, to a point. But as the date drew near to begin shooting the film, Depp and Thompson began to exchange a series of faxes that reflected Thompson's growing anxiety about the way in which he would end up portrayed and Depp's insistence that he would do his best to be true both to Thompson and to the part of Raoul as Thompson had written him. The exchange was as intimate as it was irritable. At one point, Depp wrote, "I am NOT and CANNOT be you. But I can come pretty close, and will. This is my work!!! If you remember back about a year or so ago, I asked you if you were sure that I should be the actor to play you in the film. Your reply was 'yes.' " Thompson reassured Depp, in his minimal way; he told Depp to "cheer up" and that it would be okay.[31] Depp's outburst is significant in that it constitutes his recognition that as an actor he can just about become someone else, and that his work entails laying claim to identities possessively and assertively. Interestingly enough, Depp is quite critical of the idea of *becoming* a movie role. "I despise those actors who say, 'I was in character,' and 'I became the character,' and all that stuff. . . . It's hideous."[32] But even for someone so critical of such total immersion in a character, Depp realized that playing Hunter S. Thompson was somehow different. "There was something that was stronger than me on this film. It was my experience of Hunter. Clearly I'd spent too much time with him, and it had taken over." When an interviewer asked Depp if people around him were concerned about his losing his identity over the role, he said, "Um, yeah. Yeah."[33]

Depp's portrayal of Raoul Duke as an out-of-control gonzo journalist prompted some to speculate that the role was an echo of Depp's life just as much as of Thompson's. Although few would argue that Depp came remotely close to Thompson's levels of drug use and other self-abuses, one

Johnny Depp biographer recognized Depp's almost too-close affinity for the part of Raoul. About Thompson, Depp told *Rolling Stone* magazine, "Man, he's a sickness. He's a disease that has penetrated my skin. I can't shake it."[34] In fact, Thompson got so far into Depp's skin that the actor convinced some that filming *Fear and Loathing* put him close to the edge of his own wreckage. As one biographer put it, in Depp's portrayal of Duke he was "continually threatening the integrity of the motion picture...balanced insecurely between the effortless performance and the open presentation of catastrophe."[35]

Depp was, in reality, in complete control of his acting in the film; the potential for catastrophe came at the hands of Hunter S. Thompson himself. After a day of shooting, Depp, Thompson, and a small group from the crew and the press met in one of the trailers. In the midst of chaotic conversation, Thompson announced, "I called the Viper Room about an hour ago and made a bomb threat." While it would not have been surprising had Thompson really done this, his announcement was a joke. According to *Rolling Stone* writer Chris Heath, who was with them at the time, "Depp's assistant had to grab the phone and tell the alarmed staff that they shouldn't evacuate."[36]

It had been an 11-week shoot, and it was difficult for a while for Depp to step away from his character, Raoul. Despite the raucousness of the shoot and the over-the-top relationship between Thompson and Depp, working on the movie had put a significant strain on Depp. According to one biographer, as a way of making the transition back to normal life, Depp took one of the film's props as a souvenir from the set and brought it home. It was "an eight-foot yellow gorilla with 'You Can Run But You Cannot Hide' emblazoned across its stomach." What was Depp planning to do with this gigantic souvenir? He put in right on his front lawn. Depp remembers thinking, "Aah, I've got a good idea...I'll rig him up for those bastard neighbors who've been complaining about the construction and the leaves in the garden....I had the construction crew on the film build his hand so he was flicking the bird.'"[37] This may seem a bit harsh, but the incident serves to demonstrate Depp's contempt for those who, in his view, judge him negatively, whether it is the press or neighbors. On the other hand, Depp very much wanted his work be recognized for the care and effort he put into it. In the case of *Fear and Loathing in Las Vegas*, Thompson had so thoroughly gotten to Depp that even after the filming was finished Depp worried he might not have done all he could with the role. In a post-shooting comment, Depp said, "I just hope he doesn't see the film and hate me. That's my biggest fear: that I'll do something that's close to him, that's proper, that's right, and he'll hate it...he deserves a good film, and I've tried to do that."[38] Thompson did not hate it; in fact, he and Depp had forged quite a friendship, complete with requisite exchanges of abuse (months after the shooting was over, Thompson affectionately referred to Depp as a "terrible little...hillbilly bastard"[39]).

It was time for Depp to take a deep, cigarette-smoke filled breath and do something else he did so well: play music. In the summer of 1997, he played slide guitar on a track for the band Oasis. The song, "Fade In-Out," on the album *Be Here Now,* could now boast having a Hollywood star among its musicians. Ironically, the reason Depp was even asked to play with the band was that one of the Gallagher brothers was too drunk to play for the studio recording that day! Depp, who had been visiting with the band members that day, grabbed a guitar and "nailed the part in one take."[40]

In 1997, *Empire* magazine ranked Johnny Depp 67th of the top 100 movie stars of all time.[41] This was an interesting achievement in that none of Depp's movies, at that time, had been real blockbusters, and although reviews of his performances were generally very good, he had not earned the kind of money that ordinarily determines who the really big stars are. Nevertheless, it was another feather in Depp's cap, and he had accomplished a good deal in 1997. Not only had he made *Donnie Brasco* and *Fear and Loathing,* he had made a cameo appearance as himself in the comedy *L.A. Without a Map* (1998). He had even lent his talents as a narrator for the video *Top Secret: Inside the World's Most Secret Agencies (National Security Agency, Scotland Yard, The Mossad),* released in 1998.[42] The next good deal should have been a major motion picture that could launch Depp further into the Hollywood stratosphere. It wasn't, quite.

## NEW YEAR, NEW MOVIE

As 1998 rolled around, it was time for Depp to get busy filming again. It was also time for the tabloids to get busy trying to figure out whether Depp and Kate Moss were still a couple. In January of 1998, Depp once again threw a surprise party for Kate, and took her to see the Rolling Stones at Madison Square Garden in Manhattan. A bit later that year, the two attended the Cannes Film Festival to see the screening of *Fear and Loathing in Las Vegas.* To those who were watching, it certainly looked like they were together and in love. A few days later, the press got its answer to the question about their relationship. On May 17, 1998, Depp told the *New York Daily News,* "Kate is somebody I care about deeply. We were together for four years, and she's a great, lovely, sweet, pure girl, really a great kid, and I care about her. I love her on a very deep, profound level. Distance is very difficult when you're trying to maintain a relationship, when you're thousands of miles apart for a lot of time. We still see each other, hang out and talk on the phone. We're close, but I'm not with anybody at all."[43] When asked why it seemed they had just attended the Film Festival as a loving couple, Depp responded, "That's because you can see we belong together. We like each other and love shines in us. We can't help it. But we were there as friends. Because of my stupid mistake. It's my own fault Kate left me. I can be a real pain in the butt and act really irritating. Especially when I'm working on a movie and it isn't going the way it is supposed to be. It gets on my nerves and I get annoying."[44]

Also a factor in the breakup was that Depp wanted children; Kate did not. "The time was obviously right for me and I started to talk about it with Kate. I thought she would react really enthusiastic, but she didn't. Kate immediately said that children weren't an option at the moment. That came as a shock to me. I was already getting happy about it and I never considered the fact that she might not be ready for it. I thought it was time. I was wrong...Kate couldn't give me what I wanted."[45] So, by mid-1998, Johnny Depp knew that he wanted a full-time lover, a family, kids—a somewhat more normal life. If he could not find it in the real world, perhaps he could in a film. A more romantic biography of the man would suggest that Depp's next film provided all of that. But while his next movie would provide a beautiful on-screen wife in Charlize Theron, and while his "wife" would become pregnant, this was hardly a storybook role into which Johnny Depp was about to step.

## SPACE MAN

Just about a month before the official breakup of Depp and Kate, Rand Ravich, who had written and was going to direct his story *The Astronaut's Wife* (1999), invited Depp to play the movie's lead, Commander Spencer Armacost. The movie has an interesting premise: During a NASA mission, Commander Armacost and his partner lose contact with the earth for two minutes when, during a space walk, they drift behind the ship. When he returns, he and his partner Alex Streck (played by Nick Cassavetes) are somehow different. Charlize Theron plays Jillian, Armacost's wife, and she senses something has changed in her husband—for one thing, he has become somewhat mechanical and almost insanely overprotective of their unborn twins (you'll need to see the movie to know what kind of "twins" they are!). One critic wrote that "Theron is the star of the movie, but the heart and soul of it relies on Depp, who just seems to be bored with the role."[46]

While the reviews of the film, and of Ravich's story and direction, were mostly negative—with complaints about Depp's phony-sounding Southern accent, and the movie's lack of an interesting plot—no one disputed that Depp managed to make his character look physically attractive. One reviewer wrote that *The Astronaut's Wife* is "a silly and inconsequential little thriller...despite the valiant attempts of its pretty players."[47] This was becoming Depp's trademark—quirky roles depicting alienated (or even alien) characters, all made at least somewhat appealing because of Depp's own unquestioned attractiveness. People were going to see Johnny Depp movies to see Depp. They were not, however, going to see him in the kind of droves that would come later. *The Astronaut's Wife* grossed only around a third of its $34 million budget.[48]

Wasting no time, as soon as he wrapped up filming on *The Astronaut's Wife*, Depp headed off to France. This would prove to be one of the most important trips of his life. It would give him a break from filming in the United States, it would allow him to take his mind off the end of his relationship with Kate Moss, and it would give him an opportunity to work with a director he admired—Roman Polanski. The film was entitled *The Ninth Gate*, and for Depp, the gate was about to open wide.

## NOTES

1. Jim Jarmusch, interview with Simon Hattenstone, *The Guardian*, November 13, 2004, http://film.guardian.co.uk/interview/interviewpages/0,6737,1348703,00.html (accessed June 6, 2007).

2. "Music Videos directed by Jim Jarmusch" at http://members.tripod.com/~jimjarmusch/videography.html (accessed May 6, 2007).

3. Gary Sussman, "*Dead Man Talking*," http://72.166.46.24/alt1/archive/movies/reviews/05–09–96/DEAD_BAR.html (accessed January 19, 2007).

4. *United States of Poetry*, DVD (Bay Books Video, 1995).

5. Johnstone, 70.

6. "The Envelope: the Ultimate Awards Site," LA Times, http://theenvelope.latimes.com/extras/lostmind/year/1994/1994gg.htm (accessed October 10, 2006).

7. Biography for Johnny Depp," IMDb.com, http://www.imdb.com/name/nm0000136/bio (accessed June 6, 2007).

8. Tara Ariano and Sarah D. Bunting, "Johnny Depp Does It Better Than Most," June 13, 2005, http://www.msnbc.msn.com/id/6434732 (accessed August 19, 2006).

9. Kevin Cook, interview with Johnny Depp. *Playboy*, January 1996, http://www.johnnydeppfan.com/interviews/playboy.htm (accessed April 29, 2007).

10. Pomerance, 33.

11. Quoted in Johnstone, 69.

12. Holly George-Warren, ed. *The Rolling Stone Book of the Beats*. (New York: Hyperion), 1999, ix.

13. Depp 1999, 411.

14. Depp 1999, 412.

15. Depp 1999, 413.

16. George-Warren, *The Rolling Stone Book of the Beats.*.

17. Chris Heath, "Johnny Depp's Savage Journey," *Rolling Stone*, June 11, 1998, http://www.johnnydeppfan.com/interviews/rs98.htm (accessed April 11, 2007).

18. Ibid.

19. *People*, 1996, http://www.imdb.com/name/nm0000136/bio (accessed May 5, 2007).

20. Meikle, 179.

21. Quoted in Johnstone, 80.

22. *Life Story*, 60.

23. Janet Maslin, "Donnie Brasco," *New York Times*, February 28, 1997, http://www.nytimes.com/library/film/donnie-film-review.html (accessed June 10, 2007).

24. Heath, "Johnny Depp's Savage Journey," June 11, 1998.

25. Gregory McDonald, *The Brave* (Fort Lee, NJ: Barricade Books, 1991).

26. Meikle, 189.

27. Meikle, 190.

28. *The Mod Squad* was a popular television show from 1968 to 1973; it had the same premise as *21 Jump Street*: young cops investigate crimes the older cops could not.

29. Meikle, 198.

30. Heath, "Johnny Depp's Savage Journey," June 11, 1998

31. Ibid.

32. Ibid.

33. Ibid.

34. Ibid.

35. Ibid.

36. Ibid.

37. Johnstone, 84.

38. Heath, "Johnny Depp's Savage Journey," June 11, 1998.

39. Ibid.

40. Johnstone, 84.

41. *Empire* 67, October 1997.

42. *Top Secret: Inside the World's Most Secret Agencies (National Security Agency, Scotland Yard, The Mossad)*, DVD (Goldhil Home Media, 1998). Johnstone, 84.

43. *New York Daily News*, May 17, 1998, http://www.johnnydeppfan.com/kate/sheet15.htm (accessed October 1, 2006).

44. Ibid.

45. http://www.johnnydeppfan.com/interviews/jeopie.htm (accessed June 6, 2007).

Ibid.

46. Matt Lawrence, 1999, FilmCritic.com, "review of *The Astronaut's Wife*," http://www.filmcritic.com/misc/emporium.nsf/reviews/The-Astronauts-Wife (accessed April 24, 2007).

47. David N. Butterworth, 1999, "review of *The Astronaut's Wife*,"http://reviews.imdb.com/Reviews/204/20423 (accessed January 4, 2007).

48. Johnstone, 84.

Johnny Depp, pictured here on November 21, 1995, is known for his remarkable portrayal of eccentric and quirky characters in his films. Credit: AP Images/Damian Dovarganes.

Johnny Depp and Vanessa Paradis at the Hand and Footprint Ceremony held at The Grauman's Chinese Theatre in September 2005. Credit: AP Images/Luis Martinez.

Johnny Depp, pictured here in 2006 is know for his offbeat, anti-establishment, anti-Hollywood approach to his own stardom. Credit: AP Images/Matt Sayles.

Johnny Depp signing autographs for fans at the 2006 Disney-land premiere of Pirates of the Caribbean: Dead Man's Chest. Credit: AP Images/Chris Pizzello.

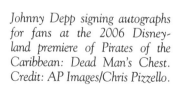

*Johnny Depp at the May, 2007 premiere of Pirates of the Caribbean: At World's End in Disneyland. Credit: AP Images/Matt Sayles.*

# Chapter 7

# "SLOOP JOHN B":
# FINDING PARADIS(E)

By 1998, both the unnatural and the supernatural had become subtexts to Johnny Depp's career. He had appeared in *Nightmare on Elm Street* and *Freddy's Dead: The Final Nightmare*; he had played a robot-boy with scissors for hands and the role of Ed Wood, director of (bad) science fiction films; he had been snuffed by a sociopath in *The Brave*; his character Don Juan DeMarco may or may not have been a reincarnation of a centuries-old fictional character; and he had played an astronaut who becomes an alien. Depp was establishing himself as a regular resident of worlds not quite like ours. It was only fitting, then, that his next film project be one in which his character would be forced to confront the pure evil of hell. It was equally fitting that his foray into the netherworld would also bring him that much closer to a kind of paradise—at least twice, in fact.

## A MOVIE, A GIRL, A PLACE, A BABY

A lot of people claim that a particular experience completely changed their lives—and Johnny Depp is certainly no exception. In fact, each time he made a new movie, started (or ended) a relationship, played guitar with another cool band, or spent a few weeks with a highly eccentric and drug-soaked journalist, chances were good that he found the experience to be life changing. But nothing had so thoroughly altered his life as his arrival in France to begin filming Roman Polanski's *The Ninth Gate*. In important ways, making this particular movie was hardly a blip on the radar of changes Depp was to undergo.

Depp's character, Dean Corso, is a 40-something rare book dealer. After having played so many parts of people younger than him, Depp now got to tack on a half-dozen years. Corso is hired by Boris Balkan, a wealthy publisher, who has found a copy of an ancient book called *The Nine Gates of the Kingdom of Shadows* that allegedly describes the process by which to summon Satan himself. Balkan wants Corso to locate the two extant copies of the book supposedly so that they can determine whether Balkan's copy is genuine. The Devil, in this case, comes in the form of a woman—Polanski's real-life wife, Emmanuelle Seigner—who is able to fly and do other odd things. A writer for the *New York Post* suggested that *The Ninth Gate* is "the worst occult film to star big-name actors in many years, and a startlingly inept and unsatisfying piece of storytelling."[1] But if the movie was not a great piece of storytelling, the story beneath it was. One of the people who had auditioned for the part of the Devil (listed only as "The Girl" in the credits) was a 25-year-old actress by the name of Vanessa Paradis. She did not get the part, but she did not come away from the experience empty-handed.

Vanessa Chantal Paradis was born on December 22, 1972. By the time she was 15 years old, Vanessa had recorded the song, "Joe le Taxi," that vaulted her to the top ten on the British charts. In 1988, she recorded her first album, *M & J*, which made it all the way to 13th on the French charts. Two years later, her album *Variations Sur Le Même T'aime* rose to number 6.[2] Between the two albums, Vanessa appeared in her first film, entitled *Noce Blanche* (1989). Perhaps the movie was a sign of things to come. In it, Paradis plays a teenage girl both wise and jaded beyond her years who falls in love with her older philosophy teacher. Her performance was good enough for her to win France's version of the Oscar, the César, in 1990. Two years later, her boyfriend at the time, musician Lenny Kravitz, produced her third music album, titled, simply, *Vanessa Paradis* (1992). Already Vanessa had appeared in print advertisements for Chanel fragrances and was a sought-after model. She was just 20 years old and already a rapidly rising star. Vanessa made three more movies and was working on another in 1998 when she stepped (with a newly mended broken leg) right through Johnny Depp's *Ninth Gate*.

The short version is: they met, they started seeing each other, fell in love, and soon after, Vanessa was pregnant and Johnny was pleased. For those who might like to retrace the steps of that inaugural meeting, Depp was having dinner with his director, Roman Polanski, at Hotel Costes K at 81 Avenue Kleber in central Paris.[3] According to Depp, he was smitten from the start: "I pretty much fell in love with Vanessa the moment I set eyes on her." No longer adrift, by mid-1998, he had found his anchors. "I came over here to make a movie, met a girl, got a place, had a baby."[4]

The place he and Vanessa purchased was in the south of France, one of several homes the two would eventually own. About France as his new home, the chain-smoking Depp said, "In France when you go somewhere they say right away: if you want to smoke, do as you please. That's what I call hospitality."[5] Hospitable France proved to be the right place for Depp and Vanessa to start a family. As Depp finished filming *The Ninth Gate*, he and Vanessa were spending more and more time together; when she became pregnant, he was ecstatic. He was 35 years old and had finally met someone with whom he could have the family he had been wanting. Vanessa was 26 and was, evidently, comfortable not only with the eccentric man with whom she was about to have a baby, but with life as the object of increased media scrutiny. In fact, she was quite accustomed to it herself.

Now with a baby on the way and a few films in the works between them, Depp and Vanessa had some decisions to make about what to do next and where to go. The two arranged to have Vanessa move back to her family home where she would be comfortable and looked after. By November 1998, Depp had yet another reason to be, as he put it, "consciously very happy."[6] He was scheduled to fly off to England to discuss his part in a movie being made by his old directorial friend, Tim Burton. "It's just amazing for me, going back to work with Tim," Depp remarked. "It's like returning home after a war."[7] Evidently, Depp was referring to his experience working with Polanski, with whom he had often had conflicts while filming *The Ninth Gate*. At around the same time, unfortunately, Kate Moss was going through a rough time, checking herself into rehab in London. She had lost her million-pound-per-year contract with Calvin Klein a month or two before, and she was obviously buckling under the strains. Depp, on the other hand, was soaring.

## MAN OF LEGEND

Tim Burton was making *Sleepy Hollow* (1999), based on Washington Irving's 1819 story, "The Legend of Sleepy Hollow." It was a tale already familiar—at least in bits and pieces—to many adults and children. It is an intriguing story with all the best elements of mystery, humor, romance, and a touch of tragedy, and Burton recognized in it the makings of a compelling film. The plot of Irving's story is that of a young, gawky, and nervous young man named Ichabod Crane, who comes to Sleepy Hollow to be their schoolteacher. Before long, Ichabod finds himself attracted to the beautiful Katarina van Tassel, and to her family's wealth.

Katarina, however, is the object of fancy for a large number of young men, especially the large, powerful, and aggressive Brom Van Brunt, who is irritated over the Ichabod's courtship of Katarina. In an act of jealousy tinged with his customary mischief, Brom plays a terrible trick on Ichabod, disguising himself as the Headless Horseman of Sleepy Hollow (using a pumpkin as his severed head) and frightening Ichabod nearly to death. Ichabod flees Sleepy Hollow, never knowing the cruel trick by which he has been victimized.

Depp said of Irving's story, "I loved it as a kid,"[8] suggesting that Depp's taste in reading had extended farther than he had previously let on. While other young male stars were taking on roles that reinforced their masculine public personae, Depp would be taking on another role in which he would play the odd-looking outsider whose inner weaknesses threaten to overwhelm him. Johnny Depp had played a number of roles where he had to disguise his age and his good looks, but he had never before played a character who, as he is described in the original text, is so completely contradictory to the actor's physical type. As Washington Irving described him, Ichabod Crane "was tall, but exceedingly lank, with narrow shoulders, long arms and legs, hands that dangled a mile out of his sleeves, feet that might have served for shovels, and his whole frame most loosely hung together. His head was small, and flat at top, with huge ears, large green glassy eyes, and a long snipe nose, so that it looked like a weather-cock perched upon his spindle neck to tell which way the wind blew."[9] It would be up to Burton and Depp to figure out how to reshape the story in order for Depp to become Ichabod Crane.

To transform Irving's story into a sharp screenplay, Burton employed playwright Tom Stoppard (uncredited in the film) to refine the script and add more humor. Burton then added a killer cast, including Christina Ricci, Christopher Walken, Miranda Richardson, and Sir Michael Gambon. When filming was over, Depp commented that "working with Tim Burton on *Sleepy Hollow* was like an exorcism. It was a cleansing of my *Ninth Gate* experience." But not all of Depp's demons had been cleansed.

In January, 1999, during a break in the filming of *Sleepy Hollow*, Depp and Vanessa had gone out to dinner to celebrate her pregnancy. They had now been together for just six months, and their relationship had progressed quickly. They went to a French café in the heart of London and were bombarded by photographers and tabloid journalists. Never happy to face the paparazzi, and after drinking a bottle of expensive wine, Depp was even less in the mood for the flashbulb assault. He ended up belting a photographer with a wooden stick and was arrested for disturbing the peace. Several hours in a jail cell sufficed as punishment. The event was evidence that the darker, edgier Depp was never far below the calmer surface he generally showed.

Five months later, Depp's life would change as he took on the most dramatic, and rewarding, role of his life; he became a father when Vanessa gave birth on May 27, 1999 to Lily-Rose Melody. For Depp it was a "monumental revelation: the most pure, less egoistic moment of my life and this is the understatement of the century." Lily-Rose's birth also caused Depp "one moment of panic, because I thought we would have a son, and I looked at her and thought: Oh God, there is something missing!"[10] Not only was there nothing that was missing, Depp discovered that the birth of his daughter meant a new beginning for him as well. "All my past became negligible, everything that was necessary to lead to Lily."[11] Depp was ecstatic. Now there would be a new kind of challenge for the Depp/Paradis family: how to keep working while also raising a child. Both Depp and Vanessa were in constant demand not only for performances but for speaking engagements, endorsements, and more. They had to come up with some kind of plan for how to handle the Lily-Rose effect!

## "I ONLY NEED TO WEAR A BRA AND A DRESS..."

The plan was relatively simple: "Vanessa and I agreed never to work simultaneously. We don't want other people to take care of Lily. So small parts that allow me not to be away for long are welcome."[12] One of those small parts came in an offer from artist Julian Schnabel. Known more for very large paintings than for film work, Schnabel had, nevertheless, made a feature film entitled *Basquiat* (1996) based on the life of graffiti artist Jean-Michel Basquiat. Now Schnabel wanted to make a movie about Cuban dissident and writer Reinaldo Arenas. Arenas was a poet who happened to be gay and who led a flamboyant lifestyle. In the Cuba of 1959, when Castro took over the Cuban government, gays were among those who were denounced by the new regime as corrupt. In the cultural purge that followed, many were imprisoned—or worse. Arenas himself was eventually jailed for years before he had an opportunity to flee to Miami in the hope of finding freedom to write and live as he wished. Instead, he found more intolerance in Miami's large Cuban community, and after 10 years of struggle, Arenas committed suicide in a New York City apartment.

This was the story that Schnabel wanted to tell in a film entitled *Before Night Falls* (2000). According to Depp, Schnabel called him "and asked if I wanted to play a small part as a Transvestite. I thought: easy enough, I only need to wear a bra and dress, nice that he asked me."[13] It was not the first time Depp had played a transvestite. In *Ed Wood*, he had learned to walk in heels, wear a bra and stockings, and to walk the walk. In *Before Night Falls*, Depp took his talent for playing transvestites to a new height, making a cameo appearance as Bon-Bon, the heavily made-up, blond wig–wearing transvestite who smuggles Arenas's manuscripts out of the prison. Not content with one cameo, Depp also makes an appearance as Lieutenant Victor, an official of the Cuban Communist military who forces Arenas to denounce his homosexuality and his writings.[14]

For a man who was looking to trim his film commitments, Johnny Depp had about as busy a year in 1999 as one could have. He starred in three movies—*Sleepy Hollow*, *The Astronaut's Wife*, and *The Ninth Gate*; his daughter was born; he played his old hero, Jack Kerouac, in a documentary entitled *The Source* (1999), about the Beat writers; he appeared as himself in several episodes of various television programs; and he received a great deal of professional recognition in the form of nominations and awards. In 1999 alone, Depp was nominated for a Golden Satellite Award for best actor in a comedy or musical (*Sleepy Hollow*); was nominated for an award from the Academy of Science Fiction, Fantasy & Horror Films (*Sleepy Hollow*); won the Blockbuster Entertainment Award for favorite actor in a horror movie (*Sleepy Hollow*); and won the prestigious French César for his body of work.

He was hardly finished and hardly slowing down. In September 1999, he took on another small role in a film directed by Sally Potter, entitled *The Man Who Cried* (2000). Not wanting to spend time away from Vanessa and Lily-Rose, Depp had them accompany him, which worked out well since he would be filming in France and England. Indeed, his work on the film would take only about three weeks. Still, it was a part tailor-made for Depp. Whereas Christina Ricci had been a supporting actor to Depp's lead in *SleepyHollow*, in *The Man Who Cried*, Depp would play the small supporting role of Cesar the Gypsy, and Ricci would be the star. Ricci's character, Suzie, is a young Jewish woman whose father leaves their Russian village shortly before World War II to try to establish a new life in America. He plans to send for her as soon as he is settled. But Suzie, whose name is originally Fegele, loses contact with her father and sets out to try to find him.

Along the way, she travels to England and then France just as the war is about to begin. Suzie meets a handsome young Gypsy named Cesar—played by Depp—to whom she is powerfully attracted. Before long, she has lost her virginity to Cesar. She cannot remain in Paris, however, as the

German army storms into France, so she once again resumes her quest to find her father. It was a role familiar to Johnny Depp—an outcast, a lover, a man whose facial expressions say more than his few lines in the script do. As one biographer points out, "The fact that [Depp] consciously had opted to accept more cameo roles in order to reduce his workload since the birth of Lily-Rose meant also that the types of roles which would be offered him were going to play to his looks."[15] *The Man Who Cried* was essentially a flop, receiving poor reviews, including one in which the reviewer said the film ought to have been entitled "The Audience Who Yawned."[16]

## TIME TO SWEETEN THINGS UP

As the year 2000 approached, Depp and Paradis were spending time at three homes: their apartment in Montmartre, Paris, his house in the Hollywood Hills, and their newest address—an old farmhouse in the south of France. Life in the French countryside was rapidly becoming a paradise for Depp and Vanessa. "I love America—I love going back, seeing my family and friends—but it's wonderful to get back to France and be living in a tiny village with nothing around. There is still the possibility to live a simple life."[17] While life may have felt simple for the Depp/Paradis family, that simplicity was supported by two very lucrative careers. Accounts differ with regard to salaries, but one report has Depp earning two million dollars for his three weeks of work on *The Man Who Cried*.[18] Oddly enough, Depp's career was still in a kind of limbo. Over a 10 year period, he had acted in 17 feature films (18 if you count *Freddy'sDead*) and only a few were real hits.

His delight in the home life he and Vanessa were making was perhaps taking the edge off of the need to succeed, but for the public to keep up its interest in Johnny Depp, they were going to have to see him in a movie that would make more of a splash. *Sleepy Hollow* was, for that reason, a timely movie for Depp. This third collaboration between Depp and Tim Burton was a major success, earning over 200 million dollars worldwide.[19] The day before the world premiere of *Sleepy Hollow*, November 16, 1999, Johnny Depp received his own star on the Hollywood Walk of Fame.[20]

Depp's star was rising, and with a beautiful life partner and a lovely daughter, a steady stream of film offers, several gorgeous homes, and an ever-increasing list of awards to his credit, his next role seemed a fitting extension of the way his life was going. One of the directors for whom he had retained a great deal of respect was Lasse Hallström, who had directed Depp in *What's Eating Gilbert Grape*. What surprised Depp was that Hallström thought highly of him as well. According to Depp, they had "had a good experience on Gilbert Grape but it was also difficult. I was surprised that he'd want to go through something with me again, thinking that I was some kind of moody, brooding, horrible shithead."[21] Obviously, Hallström thought nothing of the kind.

In Hallström's newest project, *Chocolat* (2000), actress Juliette Binoche plays Vianne Rocher, the proprietor of a quasi-magical chocolate shop. Vianne and her young daughter move to a mannered little French village and open a chocolate shop during the holiday of Lent. The mayor of the town would like to shut them down, but Vianne's chocolates and charm seem to have won the town over. Before long, a boat full of drifters hits town and Vianne falls for one of these drifters, an eccentric, guitar-playing, handsome, and charismatic Gypsy named Roux, played by Johnny Depp. It really is not a big part in the movie—Roux does not appear at all for the first hour or so. But the role gives Depp a chance to ply his charms on another leading lady, and another occasion to create a notable hairstyle—this time a kind of ponytail/braid that makes him seem at once exotic and stylish.

And as long as his hair was long, why not put it to use in another film? This time, however, Depp would not be playing a romantic lead or a particularly admirable figure. From the aphrodisiac of Vianne Rocher's chocolates to the addictions and dangers of cocaine, Depp took the plunge into another memorable character performance.

## COMING TO BLOW

For his next job, Depp chose a role that, if anything, highlighted and reinforced one aspect of his public image that he might have liked his audiences to forget: that of a drug-using, hard-drinking, out-of-control man. He had moved away from drug use before the birth of Lily-Rose, and had limited his drinking, he said, to the occasional cocktail or glass (or bottle) of wine. True, he was as heavy a smoker as ever, but to a great extent he had cleaned up his act—at least in his personal life. But he was about to dirty that act up again in his next movie. In it, he would play George Jung, the notorious drug smuggler whose story had been told by Bruce Porter in the book entitled *Blow: How a Small-Town Boy Made $100 Million with the Medellin Cocaine Cartel and Lost It All* (1993).

Director Ted Demme hired Johnny Depp with the idea that Depp, more than most actors, could not only become the character but also maintain the kind of visual fascination that Hollywood's top stars evoked in audiences. In other words, Demme wanted George Jung with Johnny Depp's visual appeal. As Demme put it, "I wanted an actor to give me George

Jung. I didn't want a movie star to come in and star in 'Blow.' I really wanted the guy to be George. Johnny has done that on every film. You put Edward Scissorhands, Ed Wood, Donnie Brasco, and George in the same room, and they don't look a like [sic] at all. I needed someone who was also sexy. Someone who would walk into a room and everyone would be like 'wow, who is that guy.' "[22]

In a way it is ironic that Depp would be cast as Jung; George Jung's "career" had been a steady trajectory downward into the world of drug smuggling and dealing. He had made a fortune then lost it all, lost his family, and finally lost his freedom. Depp's prospects looked to be quite opposite Jung's, and yet in his usual manner, he approached the part with the idea of getting as deep into his character's head as possible. He spent a couple of days with Jung in prison, talking with him and observing him. While there was not much admirable about the man, Depp explained that Jung "was doing what he knew best. What he got from his upbringing. He became exactly what he didn't want to be, a greedy person who doesn't think of anything other than money, just like his mother. I figured that my goal would be to take what seemed to be nothing but a party boy and turn him into a real man that you can relate to."[23]

What audiences did not see was the Johnny Depp offscreen who had purchased a fart machine and was breaking up the cast members with fart sounds at strategic moments in shooting. Costar Penelope Cruz, in particular, found Depp's practical jokes to be hilarious. She said, "Johnny is the funniest man. I don't think people know this but he is always the joker....You know, I am screaming, pulling at my hair [in a scene from *Blow*]. All of a sudden I hear 'pfggggggggg' and I think 'Incredible, just ignore it.' But it comes again and I start smiling. Then everybody laughs."[24] Depp's pranks may have helped to keep things loose on the set, but he worked at his performance with usual intensity. According to one biographer, Depp's "towering performance" as George Jung "is pure craftsmanship."[25] Sadly, director Ted Demme's career did not benefit much from what was, by most accounts, a very successful film about the dangers of the cocaine trade. Demme died of a heart attack while playing basketball in 2002. An autopsy showed that there had been cocaine in his blood.[26]

## PIT STOP IN HELL

It seems that every few years, no matter what other roles he has taken on, Johnny Depp comes back to playing a detective—first as a teen detective in *21 Jump Street*, then as an undercover detective in *Donnie Brasco*, and more recently for the 2001 film *From Hell*, directed by the Hughes brothers, Allen and Albert. The time was the late nineteenth century, and the place was London. Depp was now Detective Chief Inspector Frederick George Abberline.[27] Originally the part was going to go to Sean Connery. Then, it was to be offered to Daniel Day-Lewis or Jude Law. When none of these actors could commit to the project, the Hughes brothers enlisted Depp, who was happy to take the part. "I must confess that I've always been fascinated by Jack The Ripper. When I was young I was attracted to everything that was dark and I discovered this figure when I was seven or eight years old. Since then I practically read every book about this subject."[28]

Abberline, both detective and psychic, is trying to solve the case of Jack the Ripper, who has been kidnapping and murdering prostitutes in the Whitechapel area of London. To make things more interesting—and perhaps more fitting for a Depp role—the screenwriters made Abberline into an opium user, a radical departure from the real facts of Abberline's life. In fact, Albert and Allen Hughes ended up departing so much from the facts of the Ripper case that *From Hell* became a mostly fictionalized story of Abberline's involvement in it. Depp did not seem bothered by the historical inaccuracies. Instead, he looked at the character that had been created in the screenplay. "This is an inspector who follows the case helping himself with methods which aren't exactly conventional, such as the visions based on opium and absinth; he is a bloodhound who chooses the side of the subproletariat and the prostitutes, against the establishment; he is an original and human character who takes big risks to carry on his investigation." Besides, he would add, "the Hughes brothers were passionate about this, I couldn't say no to them."[29] Reviews were mixed; while Depp was praised for his performance—including his excellent English cockney accent—it was hardly the tour de force on which to hang a career. It was, in a sense, a speed bump along the way for Depp and he was heading for another.

Toward the end of 2000, Depp found himself being served with a lawsuit by Anthony Fox over control of the Viper Room. Fox contended that Depp and Sal Jenco had made deals behind his back and was seeking damages. In a 2003 decision, Los Angeles Superior Court Judge Allen Goodman wrote that "The facts establish persistent and pervasive fraud and mismanagement and abuse of authority...Depp...abdicated his duties of loyalty and fidelity to the corporation and to plaintiff-shareholder and failed to exercise any business judgment with respect to the affairs of Safe."[30] However, Anthony Fox had been missing since December 2001 and as of March 2003, his whereabouts were still unknown.

What was also missing was the final push to make Terry Gilliam's long-awaited *The Man Who Killed Don Quixote*, which had been in and out of the works for many years. Through a series of retracted deals by potential producers in Germany and France, Gilliam once again found that project he had hoped to have shot in 1999 was jinxed. Although Johnny Depp had told Gilliam that he would be happy to star in the film, Gilliam could not get the necessary commitments from producers. Depp began to feel "jerked around," perhaps especially because the film would have given him an opportunity to star opposite Vanessa Paradis.[31] Depp's role would have been to play Toby Grosini, a contemporary advertising genius who gets mysteriously whisked back into the seventeenth century. He is mistaken by Don Quixote for his faithful companion, Sancho Panza.

Toby is a rough character, and the part had been written for Depp. Director Terry Gilliam explained, "I wanted to take the entire range of Johnny and who he is and what he's capable of, and play with it. He tends to get these parts where he's lovely or innocent or whatever, and I thought, let's stretch him and let him really play on a broad canvas. He's much more interesting than the world knows. There's a sting to Johnny's tail that most people haven't seen, and I thought we should incorporate some of that."[32] Unfortunately for Gilliam, and for Johnny Depp, the film never got off the ground. Instead, the various cast members, director, producers, and crew members appear in a documentary, made in 2002, entitled *Lost in La Mancha*, in which Gilliam and others, including Depp, speak about the project and its being doomed to failure. From Gilliam's account, it would seem that *The Man Who Killed Don Quixote* could have been a shining moment for Johnny Depp's acting career. Instead, Depp would have to look toward his next role, his next opportunity to show the world that he was more interesting than anyone knew.

## INTERESTING ISN'T ALWAYS GOOD

As 2001 drew to a close, someone else from Depp's life was showing the world that she was more interesting than people thought—but not in a good way. On December 12, 2001, Depp's ex-girlfriend, Winona Ryder, was arrested for "grand theft and possessing pharmaceutical drugs without a prescription" while shopping in Beverly Hills.[33] Winona was convicted of grand theft—a felony—and vandalism. She was sentenced to three years probation and 480 hours of community service.[34] Although not at all involved in Winona's troubles at this point, and despite the string of movies and even a bit of directing he did for two of Vanessa Paradis's music videos, the incident served to mark a less-than-satisfying start of the new millennium for Johnny Depp.

After appearing in *Before Night Falls*, he became a self-professed expert on the paintings of Jean-Michel Basquiat, about whom he wrote, "Basquiat is not for everyone. Much like pork is not for everyone. You either get it, or you don't"[35]—the obvious implication being that Depp got it. After making *From Hell*, Depp professed a deep background in Ripper literature—"I must have 25 books on the case"—and a theory on the truth about the Ripper's identity: "There's a line of thought that it was an American quack doctor who was in London at the time....That makes sense to me—an American serial killer."[36]

When he had done research for his *The Man Who Cried* role by meeting with and speaking to some Gypsies, he became wise in the ways of Gypsy life. On James Lipton's program, *Inside the Actors Studio*, Depp responded to a question from an audience member about what he had learned from spending time with Gypsies. "Life. Yeah, great lessons in life. These guys ...really know the definition of living, you know, and I don't mean that in terms of a constant festival or a constant party, I mean...I mean these guys live every single moment."[37] It's difficult to tell what, precisely, Depp really had learned from his experience. Johnny Depp's strength had always been his looks, and later, his ability to play great characters. Perhaps he was playing a new public character—that of a somewhat professorial actor-intellectual. But it was time to get back to doing what he did best: creating memorable characters in movies.

In keeping with his desire to work in as brief intervals as possible so as to be available to his daughter, Lily-Rose, and his girlfriend, Vanessa, Depp accepted a role in a film being made by a young director, Robert Rodriguez, entitled *Once Upon a Time in Mexico* (2003). To shoot all of his scenes as insane CIA agent Sands, Depp would only have to be on set for eight days. The movie proved to be so much fun for him that he was not quite ready to leave the shoot after the eighth day. He begged Rodriguez for more to do. According to Rodriguez, Depp had "never shot a full movie in eight days and at the end of that he was like, 'Is there anything else I can do, man?' He said, 'Who's playing the priest?' and I said I hadn't cast it yet. He said, 'How about I do a Marlon Brando voice and dress up as someone else? Can I do the priest before I leave?' So there's a confessional scene which wasn't supposed to feature Johnny Depp."[38]

Not everyone enjoyed Depp's work in the movie as much as he himself did. One reviewer wrote, "*Once Upon a Time in Mexico*, a movie that goes so wrong so abruptly it's as if a meteor were heading for the set and everyone had to evacuate." That same writer, however, added that "if there's a star of the film, it's Johnny Depp."[39] One of Depp's biographers writes, "Depp is everything to the piece. He turns a brain-dead B-movie into an acceptable A-feature by his presence alone."[40] Depp's signature was, by this point in his career, that he could make something out of virtually nothing in almost any film in which he appeared.

Depp returned to France and to Vanessa and Lily-Rose after filming *Once Upon a Time in Mexico,* and by September of 2001, Vanessa was pregnant again. Suddenly things were looking up for him—for his career and his family. But just as he could now turn his eyes toward bigger and brighter things, the world found its eyes riveted to televised newscasts of the catastrophe in New York City. On September 11, 2001, terrorists attacked and destroyed the twin towers of the World Trade Center, effectively murdering thousands. In a bizarre exchange, as reported by his good friend Hunter S. Thompson in his regular column, Depp phoned up Thompson on the Sunday after the attack.

According to Thompson, Johnny Depp called him from France to find out what Thompson knew about Osama bin Laden. When Thompson replied that he knew "Nothing at all" about bin Laden, Depp replied, "I'm terrified of him.... All of France is terrified." When Thompson pointed out that everyone was terrified and going a bit crazy, Depp said, "Never mind that.... Who won the Jets-Colts game?" Thompson informed Depp that the game had been canceled and that the stock market had been closed for six days. Depp's response was, "Ye gods.... No stock market, no football—this is Serious."[41]

For Depp and his family, his decision to live in France may have provided him with a small sense of security. However, he had a commitment to fly to the United States in early October to help promote *From Hell,* so within less than a month of September 11th, Depp was back aboard a plane. It was, by his account, odd to be talking about movies in the wake of tragedy; he was eager "to get back to my family to be with my girls, and then from there, I don't know. I can't say that I'm very comfortable putting my two-and-a-half-year-old daughter and my girl [Vanessa Paradis] on a plane." But Depp's discomfort did not mean he would discourage people from going to see his new movie. "We've gotta keep moving forward, and movies are escapism, and if people want to go and get out of reality for a couple of hours, why not?"[42]

## I WANT TO DO KIDDIE MOVIES NOW

Depp had his own little escape from movies themselves for a while; for the first few months of 2002, he spent most of his time with family.

Vanessa was expecting the baby in early spring, and on April 9, 2002, she gave birth to a son, Jack, whose name would soon become a new tattoo on Johnny Depp's right forearm. The Depp/Paradis family was now symmetrical—two males, two females, and as his 39th birthday approached, Depp experienced yet another rebirth—that of an increasingly responsible and doting dad, with an appreciative sense of humor about the whole enterprise. When asked by David Letterman what it was like to now have two children, Depp replied, "I guess once they hit one years old, it's sort of like running around with a miniature drunk. A tiny drunk.... You always gotta hold on to them, they bump into things, they laugh, they cry, they urinate, they vomit.... It's great, it's really great."[43]

Often much more effusive than that, Depp is rarely reluctant to gush about his kids. Director and friend Terry Gilliam joked, "[Depp] talks about his children all the time...it's boring beyond belief! If he shows me one more picture of his kid, I'll kill him."[44] Depp had become so much the family man, he had to come up with a new outlook on the direction he wanted his career to take. With the age of 40 well within his sights, Johnny Depp decided to step back into childhood.

"I want to do kiddie movies now," he told the *Daily Telegraph Magazine* in August 2002. "I'm fed up with adult movies—most of them stink. At a certain point with movies it becomes all about mathematics: this has to lead up to this, this has to lead up to that—you're always bound by some kind of formula. But since having kids and watching lots of animated cartoons and all those great old Disney films, I think they're better, they're much better."[45] Between 2003 and 2004, Depp would make two hit movies for kids of all ages: *Finding Neverland* (2004) and the first of his blockbuster pirate films, *Pirates of the Caribbean: The Curse of the Black Pearl* (2003). No matter what other film work Depp would do in his career, films like these, and subsequent kiddie projects, would mark him forever as one of the great child-fantasy actors.

In *Finding Neverland*, Depp's portrayal of Sir James Matthew Barrie, creator of Peter Pan, drew praise from reviewers. One wrote that Depp "throws himself so totally into Barrie's giddy sense of innocent glee, it's hardly noticeable that there is little substance to the movie."[46] It was as though all of Depp's youthfulness and enthusiasm for play managed to come through in this story of Peter Pan's "father." Indeed, like an overgrown kid, he could not resist bringing out his notorious fart machine, this time distracting costar Kate Winslet and causing gales of laughter among the cast.[47] Another reviewer, remarking on Depp's ability to convey so much emotion and intensity, wrote, "Depp delivers an extraordinary performance, one marked again by meticulous attention to detail."[48]

But there was, as usual, a potentially dark side to the character Depp had chosen to bring to life. As Depp himself noted, "there was always some speculation about Barrie that maybe there was some kind of pae-dophilia going on, which I actually don't think there was....What I do believe is he was an incredibly dark figure, really depressed...morose."[49] Fueling the speculations about Barrie's relationship to the theme of boys who do not grow up were other Hollywood events that were grabbing headlines. In November of 2003, pop icon Michael Jackson was arrested on charges that he had molested young boys at his Neverland Ranch in Santa Barbara, California. Jackson, a Peter Pan fan, denied all charges, but the very name of the Neverland Ranch could not help but be linked to Barrie's story. By the time *Finding Neverland* was released in October 2004, fans across the globe had to find ways to separate the fantasy world portrayed in the film from the fantasy world actually lived by Michael Jackson. Depp, however, was not about to slow down for whatever contro-versies might arise. He had a growing family and there was work to do.

Based on a ride at the Disney theme parks, *Pirates of the Caribbean* would be the movie that would put Depp's career into the stratosphere. All of Depp's pirate movies are discussed at length in another chapter of this biography, but suffice to say here that Depp managed to transform the character of Captain Jack Sparrow into one of the most imaginative crosses between a cartoon character, a comedian, a swashbuckler, and a jolly madman. With a phenomenal cast including Geoffrey Rush, Keira Knightley, and Orlando Bloom among others, *Pirates* was nominated for and won dozens of awards throughout the world, and Depp was widely recognized as the creator of a character so memorable that he sparked the making of sequel after sequel. In typical Depp style, however, he played down his success with self-deprecating remarks to the press. "I think I'm getting all this attention right now because people feel sorry for me. I'm an underdog. Other actors look at me and think, 'That poor bastard is still hacking away at it.' "[50] Despite his own reticence, Depp had fulfilled his mission to make kiddie movies that his own kids would be happy to watch. But he was not finished making more grown-up movies, as well.

## OPENING NEW WINDOWS

2004 was a busy year for Depp. *Finding Neverland* was meeting with great success, and *Pirates* was wowing audiences everywhere. But 2004 also saw the release of a much different kind of movie, entitled *The Secret Window*, written by Stephen King and David Koepp. In it, Depp plays a writer, Mort Rainey, who is accused of plagiarizing the work of another man who seeks revenge. Rainey's work is actually original, but he cannot seem to dissuade his stalker, John Shooter, played by John Turturro in another collaboration with Depp. The movie has a surprise ending that casts Depp in a new light as a monster of sorts.

A number of critics compared the film to *The Shining* (1980), also written by Stephen King along with Stanley Kubrick. This was a particularly interesting comparison in that one of the classic lines from that film had been "Heeeeere's Johnny!"—uttered by Jack Nicholson's Jack Torrance as he wreaked havoc on his family. Now, in *The Secret Window*, while the character's name is Mort, there is little doubt that audiences came to see how *this* Johnny was going to morph into a man with a sinister secret. While critical reviews of the movie were often lukewarm, once again Depp's performance drew raves. As one writer put it, "Depp may be the only actor around today who's able to turn washing and drying his hands into a dramatic clue about the character he's playing."[51]

Depp would wash and dry his hands a number of times more in the next year, first with a somewhat less memorable portrayal of John Wilmot, the Earl of Rochester, in Laurence Dunmore's *The Libertine* (2004)—a film that also received little praise. He did, however, receive recognition from the Motion Picture Academy; he was nominated for an Oscar for his work in *Pirates of the Caribbean*. He also won the Screen Actors Guild award for *Pirates*, and in keeping with his image as one of show business's most beautiful people, in 2004 VH1 ranked Johnny Depp as number five among the 100 "hottest hotties" in the world. On his way to a remarkable 2005, Depp paused long enough to appear briefly in a 2004 French film entitled *Ils se marièrent et eurent beaucoup d'enfants* (They Married and Had Lots of Children) for director Yvan Attal, who also had a starring role. But for a man who had, to date, around 30 films, whatever he was going to do next would have to be something challenging to the actor, who told *Playboy* magazine in a typical understatement, "I consider myself a guy with a good job, an interesting job."[52]

## NOTES

1. Jonathan Foreman, "Polanski's Latest is a Loser Right Out of the Gate," *New York Post*, March 10, 2000, http://pqarchiver.nypost.com/nypost/access/68851400.html?dids=68851400:68851400&FMT=ABS&FMTS=ABS:FT&date=Mar+10%2C+2000&author=Jonathan+Foreman&pub=New+York+Post&edition=&startpage=57&desc=POLANSKI%27S+LATEST+IS+A+LOSER+RIGHT+OUT+OF+THE+GATE%27(accessed August 15, 2007).

2. Celebrity Link, Vanessa Paradis, http://www.celebrity-link.com/c1/showcelebrity_categoryid-115.html.

3. Denis Meikle, *Johnny Depp: A Kind of Illusion*. Rev. ed. (Surrey, England: Reynolds & Hearn) 2007, 232.

4. Jan Jannsen, "Johnny Depp: Pan Handler," *Ms.London*, September 27, 2004, 10.

5. Ab Van Ieperen, "Johnny Depp: I never wanted to be a star," *Vrij Nederland*, May 19, 2001 (The Netherlands), http://www.johnnydeppfan.com/interviews/vrij.htm (accessed August 15, 2007).

6. Quoted in Meikle, 240.

7. Quoted in Meikle, 241.

8. Mark Salisbury, "Into the Woods: On the Set of Burton's *Sleepy Hollow*," *The Guardian*, December 17, 1999, http://www.johnnydeppfan.com/interviews/guardian1299.htm (accessed August 15, 2007).

9. Washington Irving, *The Legend of Sleepy Hollow*. (Rockville, MD: Wildside Press), 2004, 8.

10. Ab Van Ieperen. "Johnny Depp: I Never Wanted to be a Star May 19, 2001.

11. Ibid.

12. Ibid.

13. Ibid.

14. IMDb, Full cast and crew for Before Night Falls, http://www.imdb.com/title/tt0247196/fullcredits#cast (accessed June 1, 2007).

15. Meikle, 264.

16. Marc Savlov, review of *The Man Who Cried*, *Austin Chronicle*, June 8, 2001, http://www.austinchronicle.com/gyrobase/Calendar/Film?Film=oid%3a141715 (accessed June 11, 2007).

17. Gregory Katz, "An American in Paris," *USA Today*, July 6, 2003, http://www.usaweekend.com/03_issues/030706/030706johnny_depp.html (accessed November 11, 2006).

18. Meikle, 261 (It should be noted that another biographer, Nick Johnstone, reports that Depp acted in both *The Man Who Cried* and *Before Night Falls* for no compensation at all. See Nick Johnstone. *Johnny Depp: the Illustrated Biography*. (London: Carlton Books), 2006., 97).

19. Meikle, 267.

20. IMDb, "Awards for Johnny Depp," http://www.imdb.com/name/nm0000136/awards (accessed June 11, 2007).

21. Martha Frankel, "A Man Apart," *Movieline*, March 2001, http://www.johnnydeppfan.com/interviews/movieline.html (accessed May 14, 2007).

22. Steve Behnke, "Ted Demme: Great Movie, Great Person," April 5, 2001 http://www.countingdown.com/features/?feature_id=15763 (accessed June 13, 2007).

23. Ersie Danou, "Johnny Depp: Closer to the Light," *Cinema Magazine*, June 2001 (Greece), http://www.johnnydeppfan.com/interviews/cinema601.htm (accessed June 12, 2007).

24. IMDb Movie/TV News, http://www.imdb.com/news/wenn/2000-06-21 (accessed August 15, 2007).

25. Meikle, 275.

26. IMDb, "News for Ted Demme," http://www.imdb.com/name/nm0001130/news (accessed May 31, 2007).

27. IMDb, *From Hell*, http://www.imdb.com/title/tt0120681/ (accessed April 4, 2007).

28. No Author, "Johnny's Paradise," *Grazia*, November 20, 2001, http://www.johnnydeppfan.com/interviews/garzia.htm (accessed June 6, 2007).

29. Ibid.

30. Amanda Bronstad, "Viper Room's Twisted Tale Takes New Turn: Johnny Depp, Anthony Fox Nightclub Lawsuit," *Los Angeles Business Journal*, March 3, 2003, http://findarticles.com/p/articles/mi_m5072/is_11_25/ai_100733612/pg_1 (accessed June 5, 2007).

31. *Lost in La Mancha* (2002), DVD, directed by Keith Fulton and Louis Pepe (Eastcroft Productions, 2002).

32. Jessamy Calkin, "One that Got Away," *Daily Telegraph Magazine*, August 3, 2002, http://www.johnnydeppfan.com/interviews/telegraphmag.htm (accessed February 2, 2007).

33. "Lawyer: Ryder's Arrest a 'Misunderstanding'," CNN.com, December 13, 2001, http://archives.cnn.com/2001/SHOWBIZ/News/12/13/ryder.arrest/ (accessed June 2, 2007).

34. Matt Bean, "Winona Ryder Gets Probation for Shoplifting," *CourtTVNews*, December 6, 2002, http://www.courttv.com/archive/trials/ryder/sentence.html (accessed June 2, 2007).

35. Johnny Depp, "Basquiat Paintings-for Enrico-under the Influence of Pork." 2003, http://www.johnnydeppfan.com/interviews/basquiatforward.htm (accessed May 14, 2007).

36. Thomas Quinn, "Ripper Star is Reborn as Mr Deppendable," *The Mirror*, February 8–14, 2002, http://www.johnnydeppfan.com/interviews/mirror.htm (accessed January 6, 2007).

37. *Inside the Actors Studio*, Bravo, September 8, 2002, transcript by Heather, http://www.johnnydeppfan.com/interviews/ias.htm (accessed August 15, 2007).

38. IMDb Movie/TV News, "Two Johnny Depps for the Price of One," September 15, 2003, http://www.imdb.com/news/wenn/2003-09-15 (accessed December 20, 2006).

39. John Anderson, "Once Upon a Time in Mexico," *Newsday.com*, September 12, 2003, http://www.newsday.com/entertainment/movies/ny-etmovto pr3450322sep12,0,7431053.story (accessed March 13, 2007).

40. Meikle, 307.

41. Hunter S. Thompson, "When War Drums Roll," Page 2, *ESPN.com*, September 2001, http://espn.go.com/page2/s/thompson/010918.html (accessed June 11, 2007).

42. IMDb Movie/TV News, "Depp Boards Plane to Promote Movie," October 9, 2001, http://www.imdb.com/news/wenn/2001-10-09 (accessed June 5, 2007).

43. Johnny Depp, interview with David Letterman, June 18, 2003, http://www. johnnydeppfan.com/interviews/lettermantranscript03.htm (accessed November 2, 2006).

44. Jessamy Calkin, "One That Got Away," August 3, 2002.

45. Ibid.

46. Phil Villarreal, "Gleeful Depp in Tip Top Form," *Arizona Daily Star*, November 24, 2004, http://www.azstarnet.com/sn/ent_index/49417.php (accessed August 11, 2006).

47. "Depp's Fart Machine Interrupts Winslet," *Female First*, 2004, http://www. femalefirst.co.uk/celebrity/10892004.htm (accessed March 20, 2007).

48. Betty Jo Tucker, "The Play's the Thing," ReelTalk Movie Reviews, http:// www.reeltalkreviews.com/browse/viewitem.asp?type=review&id=1060 (accessed May 30, 2007).

49. Johnny Depp, interview with the *Daily Record*, July 11, 2003, http://www. discoverkate.com/movies/neverland/press-03_0711_daily-record-depp-int.htm (accessed May 16, 2007).

50. "Confessions of Depp," *Sydney Morning Herald*, March 17, 2004, http:// www.smh.com.au/articles/2004/03/17/1079199254355.html (accessed October 17, 2006).

51. Betty Jo Tucker, "Writer's Shock," ReelTalk Movie Reviews, http://www. reeltalkreviews.com/browse/viewitem.asp?type=review&id=782(accessed May 30, 2007).

52. Bernard Weinraub, "Playboy Interview: Johnny Depp," *Playboy*, May 2004, http://www.johnnydeppfan.com/interviews/playboy2004.htm (accessed April 4, 2007).

# Chapter 8

# "JOHNNY B. GOODE": LOVE, DEATH, CHOCOLATE, AND PIRACY

If you were a kid or had young children in 2005, then chances were good that even if you had somehow managed not to have heard of or seen Johnny Depp previously, you were going to. In 2005, Depp collaborated with his old buddy Tim Burton on not one but two movies: *Corpse Bride* and the strange and wonderful *Charlie and the Chocolate Factory*. In *Corpse Bride*, we meet an animated version of Johnny Depp, who lends his voice to the unfortunate Victor Van Dort. Victor, whose family has arranged for him to marry Victoria Everglot (voiced by Emily Watson), is too shy to get his wedding vows straight and runs into the woods to practice them over and over. At one point he places the ring on a twig that is really the hand of the voluptuous-but-dead "corpse bride" (voiced by Helena Bonham Carter) who claims, now, to be lawfully wedded to Victor. Despite its macabre-sounding title, *Corpse Bride* is, as Roger Ebert put it, "a sweet and visually lovely tale of love lost."[1]

If *Corpse Bride* is a lovely tale, it is also one of Burton's gothic visions of the world in which the underworld contains as much beauty, in its way, as does the land of the living. In keeping with his predilection toward gothic tales, Burton's *Charlie and the Chocolate Factory* emerged out of the book by that title, written by Roald Dahl in 1964. Dahl had been known for his peculiar approach to children's stories, and this was no exception. Originally made in 1971 as *Willy Wonka and the Chocolate Factory*, starring comedian Gene Wilder, Depp's challenge—and one he relished—was to remake the character of Willy Wonka in his own way. As he put it, "it's time to take it somewhere else."[2]

## SOMEWHERE ELSE

Dahl's story is about a boy named Charlie Bucket who lives in poverty with his parents and grandparents near a huge chocolate factory owned and operated by Willy Wonka. Charlie finds one of five Golden Tickets that grant recipients a tour of the factory. The other four kids are greedy and are punished by Willy in gruesome fashion. Only Charlie survives, in large part because he does not much care about chocolate but cares deeply about his family. He ends up inheriting the entire factory. It is a cautionary tale about the dangers of greed and the inevitable punishment of those who value the wrong things in life.

So, where did Depp—who had been allergic to chocolate as a child[3]—take this role? How did he deviate from the portrayal given Willy Wonka by Gene Wilder? While some critics argued that Depp and Burton had actually improved upon Wilder's portrayal, saying things like "this inventive, delightful and visually rich fantasy is more faithful to Dahl's source material,"[4] others said more or less the opposite: "The new Burton and Johnny Depp collaboration might be more faithful to Roald Dahl's classic children's book. It's got a bigger budget and more a fearsome hype machine hooking in audiences. But at the same time, the new version is about as charismatic as a pet rock minus one googley eye."[5]

Moreover, Depp's performance—with his androgynously styled hair and paler-than-a-ghost makeup—was criticized by some as being an example of forced weirdness. One writer said that Depp's portrayal of Willy Wonka was "mechanically stylized" and felt "strained and excessively conceptual...the performance feels like shtick, a tired riff on one uncomplicated idea. We don't necessarily have to like Willy Wonka, but should just looking at him give us a headache?"[6] This kind of criticism did, indeed, suggest that Depp had reprised Wilder's Wonka by taking it somewhere else, just not necessarily a good place. It was the fifth collaboration between Depp and Burton, and although the results may not have thrilled critics, the two of them were not at all unhappy with the results.

Not willing to just come out and give himself credit for a job he had done, Depp said about his Willy Wonka, "I have no idea what I did.... And I have no idea of it's anywhere near where it needs to be. I can only go by what I feel, and I feel good."[7] Even if critics did not love *Charlie,* Depp had plenty of reasons to feel good. At age 40, he had accomplished a great deal of film and television work, he had been in a committed relationship for a half-dozen years, and now had two children, ages five and two. His career had survived his speaking unpatriotically in 2003 when he declared that "America is dumb, it's like a dumb puppy that has big teeth that can bite and hurt you, aggressive."[8] And he had the adoration of Vanessa Paradis who, when asked what she finds attractive about Depp, replied, "Everything. Even his faults."[9]

Vanessa Paradis's career had also progressed. When she made her album *Bliss* in 2000, she dedicated it to Depp and their daughter.[10] In early 2005, she appeared in the French film *Mon Ange,* in which she plays a love-lorn prostitute named Colette. She also starred in the science-fiction tale, *Atomik Circus – Le Retour de James Bataille* (2004) and had a small part in Roger Paradiso's *Tony 'n' Tina's Wedding* (2004). She also provided the voice for a character in *The Magic Roundabout* (2005).

Yes, both Johnny Depp and Vanessa Paradis could feel very good about their lives, but in restless Depp fashion, he would not wait long to return to his role as Captain Jack Sparrow; he would be making a grand return not once but twice in 2006 and 2007. His *Pirates of the Caribbean* movies would make millions, and his star would continue to rise, making him the prime candidate for a number of projects to come. The enormous success of his Jack Sparrow ventures prompted David Wild of *Rolling Stone* to ask Depp if he found the intensity of the response to the *Pirates* movies surprising. *Not* surprisingly, Depp's answer was a mixture of self-deprecation and disingenuousness: "It surprised me, because I'm used to about eighteen people seeing my movies."[11] Indeed, even if he had said 18 million, he would have underestimated his audiences by a wide, wide margin. Audiences were flocking to see Jack Sparrow, and virtually any other role Depp cared to create.

It's time to ask, not why, but how; how did and does Depp select and then create such memorable, off-center, and...Depp-like roles?

## NOTES

1. Roger Ebert, "Tim Burton's Corpse Bride," September 23, 2005, http://rogerebert.suntimes.com/apps/pbcs.dll/article?AID=/20050922/REVIEWS/50921002/1023 (accessed June 1, 2007).

2. Johnny Depp, interview with Chris Nashawaty, *Entertainment Weekly,* September 19, 2003, http://www.johnnydeppfan.com/interviews/ew2003.htm (accessed June 1, 2007).

3. Johnny Depp, interview with *Swiss TV Magazine,* August 2005, http://www.johnnydeppfan.com/interviews/teleswiss.htm (accessed April 11, 2007)

4. Jeff Vice, "Charlie and the Chocolate Factory," *Deseret News,* July 15, 2005, http://deseretnews.com/movies/view/1,1257,405000625,00.html (accessed June 16, 2007).

5. Mike Ward, "Chocolate Diss: Johnny Depp Tries and Tries To Be Weird, but Ultimately Comes Up Annoying," July 15, 2005, http://www.richmond.com/

ae/output.aspx?Article_ID=3771588&Vertical_ID=127&tier=1&position=6 (accessed June 1, 2007).

   6. Stephanie Zacharek, "Charlie and the Chocolate Factory," Salon.com, http://dir.salon.com/story/ent/movies/review/2005/07/15/charlie/index.html (accessed May 6, 2007).

   7. Erik Hedegaard, "Johnny Darko," *Rolling Stone*, February 10, 2005, http://www.johnnydeppfan.com/interviews/rollingstone205.htm (accessed June 4, 2007).

   8. "Johnny Depp: U.S. is Like a Stupid Puppy," *CNN.com*, September 3, 2003, http://www.cnn.com/2003/SHOWBIZ/Movies/09/03/depp.us.reax.reut/ (accessed July 7, 2006).

   9. Michael Peyrard, "Vanessa's Paradise," *Elle*, August 2001, http://www.johnnydeppfan.com/interviews/elle082001.htm (accessed May 8, 2007).

   10. Ibid.

   11. David Wild, "Blood Brothers," *Rolling Stone*, May 31, 2007, 54, http://www.rollingstone.com/news/coverstory/johnny_depp__keith_richards_ipirates_of_the_caribbeanis_blood_brothers (accessed August 15, 2007).

# Chapter 9

# "JOHNNY ANGEL":
# THE CHARACTER ACTOR

In an interview with Charlie Rose in November 1999, Johnny Depp stated that he really would like to be known as, and work as, a character actor. Depp cites Lon Chaney as his model and hero, "the greatest character actor of all time."[1] Chaney, who acted in early silent films, lived from 1883 to 1930 and was called The Man of a Thousand Faces for his remarkable ability to create distinctive characters with makeup and prosthetics. He is most noted for his role as the Phantom of the Opera in 1925 and the Hunchback of Notre Dame in 1923 but created about 150 other roles as well.

A character actor is generally someone who does not have the qualities to be a leading man, the romantic interest, or hero of a story. It is someone whose face or body or voice or style somehow disqualifies him for the lead role. But Johnny Depp is not disqualified for any of these reasons. His face is often described as beautiful, his body perfect, and his manner elegant or gentle. His voice is a leading man's voice, deep and clear. As one critic described the whole package, "his performances are most often off-kilter, angled and light, full of soul, tenderness, toughness, sincerity and grace, expressed through the liquid cadences of his voice and his diction, his beautiful man-boy face, the unerring and particular use of limbs to amplify and enhance."[2] Another stated, in awe, that he is "possessed of a handsomeness that is almost otherworldly: big, burning eyes; soft, elegantly mussed hair; strong yet delicate hands. The hollows of his cheekbones have hollows."[3]

So why does he want to be a character actor if his appearance suggests he could easily have it the other way? Part of the answer lies in what Depp thinks of acting as a job, as a career, and as an artistic form. What is

Johnny Depp's take on acting? Does he believe the Marlon Brando quote he has used that dismisses acting as a childish and basically dumb activity? In an interview in *Vogue* magazine in 1994, Depp quoted Brando as saying that "acting is a strange job for a grown man."[4] Brando was considered one of the great actors of his time and during the 1950s he set the definition of acting with his intense dramatic roles. He was usually described as the actor who defined his times as well as his profession yet he became, in his last years, someone who chose bizarre and ridiculous roles that made him look like he had forgotten how to act (most notably *The Island of Dr. Moreau* in 1996).

Depp and Brando appeared in two movies together, *Don Juan DeMarco* in 1995 and *The Brave,* which Depp also directed, in 1997. The 2004 movie *The Libertine* starring Depp was dedicated to Brando's memory. Brando and Depp discussed acting together, as Depp explained: "Once, he said to me, 'How many movies do you do a year?' I said, 'Last year, I think I did three.' And he said, 'Don't do too many.' I said, 'Why is that?' He said, 'Because we only have so many faces in our pockets.'"[5]

## MAKING FACES

Depp seems to defy this rule, having taken on many faces, like his other hero Lon Chaney. Johnny Depp has played a singing teen rebel, one of Freddy Krueger's victims, several different kinds of cops and federal agents, two accountants, a drug dealer, a cross-dressing movie director, an astronaut, a soldier, a guy with scissors for hands, a candy-making recluse, and most famously, Jack Sparrow, eccentric pirate. He has usually deliberately and thoughtfully selected these roles, often without regard for their box office potential. He explains: "I look at the story and the character and say, 'Can I add any ingredients to make a nice soup? In some sense there is a monofilament running through the guys I've played. They are outsiders. They're people society says aren't normal, and I think you have to stand up for people like that.'"[6]

On the other hand, Depp has also described his job as "stepping in front of a camera, making a few faces, doing some goofy stuff" and getting paid for it.[7] When asked in 2004 if he was happy being an actor Depp replied, "Yeah. I'm a lot happier now than I used to be. 'Cause for a lot of years I was really freaked out. Maybe I took it all too seriously, you know? I was freaked out about being turned into a product. That really used to bug me. Now, more and more, I enjoy the process. Creating a character, working that character into a scene, into the movie. I mean, the last couple of things have been just a ball."[8]

## MAKING SENSE WITH THE MOVIES

When we look at actors in a movie, what is it that we expect to find out? First we should understand why we have movies, what they are for, what they do for us, and why we watch them, sometimes over and over again. There is only one thing that all scholars of the cinema agree on and that is that movies are stories. Beyond that, they want to claim that movies either reflect life or create life or express our cultural neuroses or the private psychosis of the director, actor, or producer. But these extra explanations are not necessary. Movies are stories no matter what their style or content and we know what stories are for. Stories are for making sense of the world.

We frame our lives as stories, and things we observe are put in a narrative mode when we think about them ourselves or share them with others. Instead of looking at the world as a place of rationality where people make decisions based on evidence and logic, a narrative view of the world thinks of people as storytellers and value is judged on the quality of the story and its ability to explain things. How people come to adopt certain stories to explain and guide their behavior is the most important thing to understand.

This is the approach taken by Depp's characters, and perhaps Depp himself, but certainly by his mentor for many of his most memorable characters, Tim Burton. Burton, in a non-Depp movie called *Big Fish* (2003), presents a fabulous storyteller whose tall tales are valuable not because of their connection to the truth but because they create community and give people a reason to act and believe. The stories, told by a dying man one last time to his cynical son, are supposed to be judged on their capacity to evoke emotions, memories, and connections. Instead the son is a pragmatist and wants nothing to do with the stories if they cannot be proven true.

All Tim Burton movies, but especially those with Johnny Depp, are movies that value good stories and the characters that relay them to us. Is Depp especially important in Burton's storytelling because, as many commentators have noted, Depp seems to be Burton's on-screen stand-in, his double, his alter ego? Burton says that is not how it works. He chooses Johnny Depp for his movies not because he represents Tim Burton in each movie but because Depp likes to work the same way he does, being open to new ideas, seeing characters in a different way, and making characters that defy easy categorization. It is this dislike of rigid categories that both Depp and Burton talk about and that the characters they create together come to represent on the screen.

## WHAT ACTORS DO

Actors are carrying out the stories and scenarios that are the essence of a movie. Through the actors we see the possible stances that can be taken in a situation, the different points of view that people can hold, the varying ways passion and reason and irrationality clash, and how elements of narrative, of storytelling, require us to react and think. That is a lot of work for an actor to do, and it is a different description than the one that describes actors as simply vehicles for a prewritten story that would get played out no matter how they acted. The actor is a translator or interpreter, bringing to a role not only the script but also everything else in his own world that might affect that translation. As Depp says of the animated character he voiced in *Corpse Bride* (2005), "He's a little bit an outsider, bumbling, deeply insecure, nervous—a lot like me in life. It's like Victor is represented in the same way as Edward Scissorhands, of not feeling comfortable in life. That universal feeling we all drag around with us for the rest of our days, of being inept, unable to be understood."[9]

Depp describes his approach to a role as being a combination of all the classic acting styles: part comes from outside influences, part comes from flashes of insight and images that pop into his head: "I think one of the greatest gifts that we, as human beings, have is our instinct . . . that initial feeling you get about something, I think that's a great gift and sometimes we overlook it. Generally, when I'm reading the screenplay, I begin to get flashes, flashes of things, images," he has said.[10] He also observes people and extracts bits and pieces of what he sees: "One of the primary responsibilities and luxuries of an actor is to the art of observation, being able to watch people and watch their behaviour. Now that is fascinating, because people are really nuts . . . . Over the years, I've really enjoyed just stealing little bits from people, incorporating them into characters."[11]

His most interesting and unique characters can be seen as a collage of these influences and, when we can trace them, they provide vivid examples of the process of making compelling stories and the characters that carry them. A few examples of the characters Depp has produced, a couple of them in collaboration with Tim Burton, demonstrate just what he has contributed to the stories of the cinema.

## EDWARD SCISSORHANDS

When he first read about the character Edward Scissorhands, Depp said, "Oh, I read the screenplay and I was devastated, I mean, I was just devastated, um…it was one of the most beautiful things…themes, that I've ever read, not just screenplay. And I knew Edward when I read that, I just knew it, and it was such a universal feeling…that feeling, you know, of not feeling quite like you fit in." In addition, Depp said, because he believes that a character "has to be built on that foundation of truth, so it has to come from a place of honesty, from a place of truth within you," that since "there's quite a lot of Edward in me," that Edward ended up with "a lot of me in him."[12] This description is somewhat vague, however, and it is instead the specific references that Depp used for Edward Scissorhands that are more fascinating.

It is with Edward that Depp has been most specific about how his inspirations work, how the flashes of images end up being incorporated into a character. He said, "the two things that came to me…the two initial images were a baby, you know, a brand new little baby was one, and a dog that I had…when I was growing up, and the unconditional love of that dog and the way that that dog…even when he'd done something wrong and you'd reprimanded him, he would cower away. You use these images as your foundation," he explained, and then "essentially, you throw it all away"[13] and let things develop as the character and story unfold. Interestingly, Depp now uses the same idea of relying on a foundation in his off-screen life too, referring to his kids as the source of his new stability, his new foundation.

Another obvious influence was Depp's fascination with silent-movie stars that could express emotion and ideas with just their eyes, their body language, and their expressions. He especially cited Buster Keaton, who was known for his expressive face and sad eyes as well as his comic timing. That sadness is a part of Edward's character and Depp often blends feelings and thoughts with his own: "I realized that Edward was all alone, and inside of all of us is this lonely little kid," Depp has said. "Edward is a total outsider. I really know how that feels. And so, then, eventually, I found him. And Edward—he just clicked."[14] Ending his relationship with Edward was thus harder than leaving other characters: "He's a character that I deeply understood. Still now, I miss Edward. I remember the last time in makeup, I really had the feeling that I was leaving somebody. Somebody who was very close to me."[15]

## WILLIE WONKA

The insistence by many reviewers and fans that Willie Wonka was based on Michael Jackson is a story Johnny Depp wants to put to rest and he denies looking to Jackson for inspiration. The Michael Jackson connection comes from the fact that Jackson was under suspicion of molesting young boys at the time the movie was being made. Jackson also has an odd, mask-like face like Willie Wonka, and both share a shyness about interacting with the public.

Depp defines other influences on his development of Willie Wonka: "I was thinking more of Howard Hughes, or Brian Wilson when he installed a sandbox in his house."[16] Howard Hughes was the eccentric, germ phobic billionaire aviator and movie producer (1905–1976) who became a recluse towards the end of his life. Brian Wilson was a member of the 1960s California surfer band, The Beach Boys. Wilson once had a nine-by-nine-foot sandbox built in his house to hold his piano so he could feel like he was composing music while on the beach. It was used for an odd music project that also included musicians playing vegetables, an orchestra wearing toy firefighter's helmets, and sound-recordings in an empty swimming pool.

It's possible that musician/artist Marilyn Manson (of the band by the same name), a friend of Depp's, was also an inspiration, as was Pee-Wee Herman; the look of Depp's hairdo was said to come from *Vanity Fair* editor Anna Wintour or any number of other famous women with bobbed hair.[17] At any rate, Depp says he and Burton have "this kind of mutual understanding of things, and a mutual fascination with people, human beings, weirdness, character flaws, human tics and all of that stuff,"[18] and this shows up in the characters they create together.

An even more direct influence that both Depp and Burton cite comes from the hosts of children's television programs and game shows. Depp explained, "There was this guy called Captain Kangaroo. Even then it was strange, but if you go back now and watch it, it's really out there. He had his pal Mr. Green Jeans and Bunny Rabbit. So it was memories of watching those guys as a child."[19] "Even then," Depp explained, "how odd it was, the way they spoke—this bizarre musical rhythm cadence to their speech pattern" and the fact that they had "that perpetual grimace/grin on their face. I kept thinking—they're certainly not like that at home. You feel like they go on stage, put a mask on, and do their thing—and take it off. It's almost like a clown."[20]

## ICHABOD CRANE

Although Edward Scissorhands has often been noted as Depp's most intriguing character, Ichabod Crane in *Sleepy Hollow* is an equally complex and captivating creation, one put together from multiple sources. As a foundation, Ichabod had "a façade of bravado, but in fact would be on the verge of tears, like, if an insect comes near him." He was so on edge, so fragile that in a sense "you'd feel his butt cheeks clench," Depp continued. This feminine element was surprising and if somewhat stereotyped at least it resulted in a character who was hard to predict. Depp added, "I just liked that the hero of the story, whom one would expect to be romantic—I liked the idea that he's more than half a woman."[21]

Ichabod Crane as a grown-up Nancy Drew was another of Depp's contributions to character development. His movements and bearing were very feminine and not at all expected. Ichabod's meticulous approach to his work came, said Depp, from actress Angela Lansbury,[22] who played the amateur sleuth Jessica Fletcher in the television series *Murder, She Wrote* from 1984 to 1996. But Depp actually traces her influence to the movie *Death on the Nile* (1978), which he had seen as a child. She was "this force, she was this presence,"[23] he tried to explain. From Lansbury's character he drew an "energy and righteousness." From another cinema detective, Sherlock Holmes as portrayed by British actor Basil Rathbone, Depp drew the kind of drive a focused, even obsessed detective needs.[24]

Tim Burton explains that a characteristic he saw in Depp served him well in creating Ichabod Crane. "We really wanted to evoke the spirit of the old Hammer horror films, Vincent Price movies, Roger Corman's work," Burton says. Price had a role in *Edward Scissorhands*, and was the inspiration for Burton's early animation short, *Vincent* (1982). Burton continued, "The heroes in those films are always kind of separate, ambiguous, absorbed in their work. They're there, but you don't know much about them. And Johnny is perfect for that; he radiates like a silent-movie actor. He hardly has to say anything. It's something you can't manufacture."[25] From some of the most famous horror movie actors he borrowed the "horror-movie posturing of Bela Lugosi, Boris Karloff, Peter Cushing and Christopher Lee."[26] Both Depp and Burton were "obsessed with horror movies, monster movies and found great sanctuary in those dark places."[27]

Another possible source of inspiration for Ichabod Crane is the character Withnail, an unemployed actor from *Withnail & I*, a 1987 British movie that follows two men on an eventful trip to the countryside. Withnail is played by Richard E. Grant, who also has a voice part in Tim Burton's *Corpse Bride* (2005). Finally, Depp credits actor and friend Roddy McDowall with providing Ichabod Crane with an "ethereal quality."[28] McDowall (1928–1998) was best known as a child actor and then for his work as a chimp in the *Planet of the Apes* movies as well *The Poseidon Adventure*

(1972), *Cleopatra* (1963), and dozens of other movies, TV movies, plays, and TV series. McDowall was, says Depp, "a great actor. Very original actor. He was a fascinating actor to watch," and so his persona and many others contributed to Ichabod Crane's composite nature: "So those are the ingredients and you just sort of mash then all together and see what you come up with. And it's always dangerous when you try that stuff."[29]

## ED WOOD

There was not a lot of footage of Ed Wood to help Tim Burton and Johnny Depp construct a biographical reflection of the cross-dressing director. So in another clever collage, Johnny Depp drew inspiration from some really disparate sources that on the surface have nothing to do with this oddball hack director from Hollywood. Repeated in endless interviews is the following trilogy of inspirations for Ed Wood's construction. The "blind optimism" of Ronald Reagan, president of the United States from 1981 to 1989, was the first ingredient. Reagan was known for being one step removed from reality, making policies and decisions based on the movies, and often mixing up whether an idea or a quote came from reality or from a film.

Next came the enthusiasm of the Tin Man from *The Wizard of Oz* (1939). The Tin Man was the one who needed a heart so that he could feel things and have genuine emotions but it turned out that he had lots of heart already, he just needed confidence in his feelings. The third ingredient is a more obscure one: the radio host Casey Kasem who for years has been presenting American Top 40 radio shows, which count down the top popular music hits in a category or time period. Kasem is also a noted voice actor for cartoons and commercials and is the inspiration for Ed Wood's funny voice.

In describing the experience of creating this oddest of characters Depp has said, "Even if you're playing a sort of heightened character and living inside of a heightened reality, you can apply your own truths to the character. But it certainly is more fun. I'll tell you what's more fun. It's just being able to try something that maybe hasn't been beaten to death. To try and do something a little bit different—What's the risk? The risk is you fall flat on your face or make an ass of yourself or you get fired.[30] To another reporter he added, "With characters like this Ichabod Crane, or with Raoul Duke from "Fear and Loathing" or with Edward Scissorhands, you know it's only going to happen one time, this opportunity to do this. So you just take your best shot. Somebody hands you the ball and you run as fast as you can."[31]

## JACK SPARROW

Getting fired was apparently on Johnny Depp's mind when he created Jack Sparrow. It should be noted that Depp often likes to describe his characterizations as so odd, so innovative, that the studio executives often get nervous or he thinks they are getting nervous. This seems to be a way of explaining the off-center quality of his work, something that challenges the status quo of Hollywood. Whether he really was in danger of being fired from any of his films is questionable. But in the case of the first manifestation of Jack Sparrow, everyone associated with the project now likes to tell the story of nervous Disney executives making frantic phones calls and sending e-mails asking what the hell was going on. After all, if you did not make Disney at least a little nervous, maybe your work was not all that off the mainstream.

So, the stories go something like this, as Depp describes: "There were a couple of high-end Disney executives who were fine with what I was doing. But there were a couple who were very worried. You know, like, 'He's ruining the movie! Why is he acting like that? What's he doing with his hand? Is the character a complete homosexual?' There was a lot of that going on for a solid month and a half. And I understood their worries, but I felt so in tune with this character and so confident that what I was doing was right that I had to say, 'Look, I understand your fear. But you've hired me to do a job. You know what I've done before, so you know it's going to be something along these lines. So please trust me. And if you can't trust me then you probably should replace me.'"[32]

As the *Calgary Sun* described it, "It is well known that, during production on the original *Pirates*, Disney executives—including the now deposed Michael Eisner—were freaked out because of how eccentric Depp chose to play Jack Sparrow. He teetered on land, like a man who spent his life balanced on the rolling deck of a ship. He drank, swore, whored, lied and played the coward if it suited his purposes.... Eisner thought he was nuts. Depp kept his job only because producer Jerry Bruckheimer, a man with real power in Hollywood, protected him, supporting the eccentric performance choices"[33]

Depp had decided soon after getting the role the type of pirate he wanted to create. "I knew pretty early on. I mean, right away, actually, when I read the script. Because the whole challenge initially, even before the script came, was to come up with a pirate that hadn't been done before, to come up with a pirate character who's fun, interesting, a lot going on in his past, but that hadn't been done before, who could be dangerous, but at the same time funny."[34]

Part of the foundation for this character was, ironically, to make that foundation shaky. Making Jack's sexuality ambiguous was one method: "With Jack, it was more that I liked the idea of being ambiguous, of taking this character and making everything a little bit...questionable. Because women were thought to be bad luck on ships. And these pirates would go out for years at a time. So, you know, there is a possibility that one thing might lead to another."[35]

The screenwriters of the *Pirates* movies, Terry Rossio and Ted Elliot, had another idea that really set Jack off from traditional pirates. Recognizing the mythological potential of the character, they decided to make Jack a type of trickster figure rather than a hero. As they explain, "We created this kind of trickster, fast-talking type of character...using a lot of language to kind of confuse people and keep them off guard."[36] Johnny Depp picked up this idea and used it to explain Jack, saying in interviews that he was a kind of trickster.

The varied and colorful descriptions of this delicious pirate that made their way into news reports, movie reviews and everyday conversations are a tribute to just how innovative and creative this character was conceived to be. Jack Sparrow, everyone seemed to agree, was colorful, splashy, swishy, and swashbuckling. He was definitely "channeling Keith Richards."[37] Hollywood has seen mascara-painted pirates before, but never one so sexually ambiguous, with an effeminate walk and lispy, slurred speech yet with a very masculine, roguish appeal. He was a "tweaked out pirate,"[38] both a drag queen and smelly scoundrel who brandished a mean sword and a keen mind.

The screenwriters describe Jack this way: "The point of the first film, I'm surprised no one has brought it up, is that we each set our own limitation. Jack states his moral stance, beyond what anyone thinks, beyond the guidelines of society, there is simply what a man can do, what a man can't do. Also, the Jack character is much like Bugs Bunny, when things go bad, Bugs' strategy is to just hang on, until fate and chance come around to work in his favor....Jack will take actions to create chaos, not knowing how they will pay off or if they will pay off, but knowing that something will emerge that he may turn to his advantage....Jack counts on chance coming into play down the line, for good or ill."[39]

It became widely known that Depp fashioned Captain Sparrow on two cultural icons: Rolling Stones guitarist Keith Richards and the animated character Pepé Le Pew. Reporters around the world took off with the Keith Richards angle, especially promoting the idea spread by both Depp and Richards that rock musicians and pirates were the same thing. It meant, among other things, that with Jack Sparrow Depp had achieved his dream of becoming a rock star. His connection to Richards, he explained, went back to the 1990s and for a musician like Depp, Richards was one of rock music's gods.

The Pepé Le Pew connection was generally relegated to a small reference, but it does, in fact, tell a lot more about Jack. Pepé Le Pew is a skunk in the Warner Brothers Looney Tunes cartoon series and was created by famed cartoonist Chuck Jones. Pepé spoke broken French and smelled like a skunk so when he tried to be amorous, all his targets of affection were repelled. Depp explained, "Pepé Le Pew, he's a skunk who believed he was a ladies' man, who believed it wholeheartedly. And I kind of had that feeling about Jack, that no matter what the actual reality was, he would only see his reality. He would only believe his reality, his version of the story—a guy whose two main objectives are, number one, getting his ship back, which really represents his freedom, because he can move forward towards the horizon, and number two, to propagate the myth. He's a guy who understood that the legend is infinitely more important than the truth."[40] Cartoon characters were interesting to Depp's character formation because they "are not bound by the same laws as regular human-being actors. So I thought that would be a fun way to approach a movie character, to push the boundaries."[41]

Director Gore Verbinski sums up Depp's performance this way: "Somebody asked me the other day how this character is different from others Johnny has played. He's always played against type—that's been his thing, the way he's escaped being typecast as a good-looking leading man. He's always Bud Cort, never Clint Eastwood. There's always an internalization, where he's standing back and watching things. But with Jack Sparrow, he's a guy who's a braggart, who makes the big speech, who can go with the grain. And so you get this virtuoso performance."[42] Verbinski also commented, "I think this is the closest thing to who Johnny really is. It's the easiest thing for him."[43]

## OTHER CHARACTERS

When Johnny Depp is depicting a real-life character, however, the approach is quite different. For Joe Pistone in *Donnie Brasco* and Hunter Thompson in *Fear and Loathing in Las Vegas*, Depp chose to imitate them, studying their speech patterns and mannerisms. This is an odd choice since his other approach with fictional characters is so creative and so much more of a collage, pulling bits and pieces from different places and putting them together to form a unique characterization.

For common, everyday characters, he seems to have less of an established process. For example, for antique book dealer Dean Corso in *The Ninth Gate*, or accountant Gene Watson in *Nick of Time* or astronaut Spencer Armacost in *The Astronaut's Wife*, there seems to be what one reviewer described (looking at *Nick of Time*), as "a modern Everyman, colorless and average, and he plays the part in such a minor key that he practically disappears."[44]

## NOTES

1. *Charlie Rose Show*, "Johnny Depp Discusses 'Sleepy Hollow,'" aired November 15, 1999, show #2552, transcript at http://www.johnnydeppfan.com/interviews/charlierose2.htm (accessed August 15, 2007).

2. Erik Hedegaard, "Johnny Depp: He's Found Neverland with The Woman He Loves and Their Kids, but 'Rage Is Still Never Far Away'," *Rolling Stone*, no. 967 (February 10, 2005), http://www.rollingstone.com/news/coverstory/johnny_depp_found_neverland (accessed August 15, 2007).

3. Johanna Schneller, "Where's Johnny?" *Premiere*, December 1999, http://interview.johnnydepp-zone2.com/1999_12Premiere.html (accessed August 15, 2007).

4. James Ryan, "Depp Gets Deeper," *Vogue*, September 1994, http://www.johnnydeppfan.com/interviews/vogue.htm (accessed August 15, 2007).

5. Mark Binelli, "The Last Buccaneer," *Rolling Stone*, July 13, 2006, http://www.rollingstone.com/news/story/10714717/the_last_buccaneer (accessed August 15, 2007).

6. Kevin Cook, interview with Johnny Depp, *Playboy*, January 1996, http://www.johnnydeppfan.com/interviews/playboy.htm (accessed August 15, 2007).

7. "Jonathan Ross Presents Johnny Depp," VH1, http://www.youtube.com/watch?v=M4xExtp45E4&mode (accessed August 15, 2007).

8. John H. Richardson, "The Unprocessed Johnny Depp," *Esquire* 141, no. 5 (May 2004).

9. Hanh Nguyen, "'Corpse Bride's' Johnny Depp Is a Man of Character," *Greenville News*, September 26, 2005, http://www.timburtoncollective.com/articles/cb5.html (accessed August 15, 2007).

10. *Inside the Actors Studio*, "Johnny Depp," Bravo, season 8, episode 812, original air date September 8, 2002, http://www.bravotv.com/Inside_the_Actors_Studio/guest/Johnny_Depp; transcript also at: http://www.johnnydeppfan.com/interviews/ias.htm (accessed August 15, 2007).

11. Paul Fischer, "Interview: Johnny Depp," Moviehole.net, September 15, 2005, http://www.moviehole.net/news/6258.html (accessed August 15, 2007).

12. *Inside the Actors Studio*, "Johnny Depp," Bravo, season 8, episode 812.

13. Ibid.

14. Glen Collins, "Johnny Depp Contemplates Life As, and After, 'Scissorhands'," *New York Times*, January 10, 1991.

15. Christophe d'Yvoire, "Johnny Depp by Johnny Depp," *Studio Magazine*, February 2000, http://www.johnnydeppfan.com/interviews/studio00b.htm (accessed August 15, 2007).

16. Binelli, "The Last Buccaneer," July 13, 2006.

17. "Charlie and the Vagina Monologue Factory," Culture blog, SFGate.com, http://www.sfgate.com/cgi-bin/blogs/sfgate/detail?blogid=3&entry_id=250 (accessed August 15, 2007).

18. Alicia Quarles, "Playing Willie Wonka His Way," *Milwaukee Journal Sentinel*, July 12, 2005, http://www.jsonline.com/story/index.aspx?id=340240 (accessed August 15, 2007).

19. Anwar Brett, "Charlie and the Chocolate Factory," BBC, http://www.bbc.co.uk/films/2005/07/25/johnny_depp_chocolate_factory_interview.shtml (accessed August 15, 2007).

20. Stephen Snart, "Johnny Depp," TheCinemaSource.com, http://www.thecinemasource.com/v3/spotlight.php?id=321&wordcount=500 (accessed August 15, 2007).

21. Schneller, "Where's Johnny?" December 1999.,

22. *Inside the Actors Studio*, "Johnny Depp," Bravo, season 8, episode 812.

23. Jeffrey M. Anderson, "Snoopy Dances," Combustiblecelluloid.com, November 12, 1999, http://www.combustiblecelluloid.com/intdepp.shtml (accessed August 15, 2007).

24. Michael Sragow, "Depp Delves into the Stories behind His Characters," *Baltimore Sun*, July 14, 2006.

25. Schneller, "Where's Johnny?" December 1999.

26. Sragow, "Depp Delves into the Stories behind His Characters," July 14, 2006.

27. Anderson, "Snoopy Dances," November 12, 1999.

28. Sragow, "Depp Delves into the Stories behind His Characters," July 14, 2006.

29. Anderson, "Snoopy Dances," November 12, 1999.

30. Pat Grady, "Johnny Handsome: From Jump Street to Sleepy Hollow, Johnny Depp Has Proven He's More Than a Pretty Face," *Reel.com*, http://www.reel.com/reel.asp?node=features/interviews/depp (accessed August 15, 2007).

31. Rob Blackwelder, "Deppth Perception," SPLICEDwire, November 12, 1999, http://www.splicedonline.com/features/depp.html (accessed August 15, 2007).

32. Chris Nashawaty, "Johnny Depp," *Entertainment Weekly* 1, no. 729 (September 19, 2003), 28–34.

33. Bruce Kirkland, "A Pirate's Life for Depp," *Calgary Sun*, July 2, 2006, http://www.calgarysun.com/cgi-bin/publish.cgi?p=144830&x=articles&s=showbiz (accessed August 15, 2007).

34. Cindy White, "It's a Pirate's Life for Johnny Depp and Disney's Other Seaworthy Stars," SciFi.com, http://www.scifi.com/sfw/issue325/interview.html (accessed August 15, 2007).

35. Binelli, "The Last Buccaneer," July 13, 2006.

36. Aaron Wallace, "UltimateDisney.com's Interview with Ted Elliot & Terry Rossio," UltimateDisney.com, http://www.ultimatedisney.com/pirates-tedandterry-interview.html (accessed August 15, 2007).

37. Binelli, "The Last Buccaneer," July 13, 2006.

38. Scott Warren, "Pirates of the Caribbean," Premiere.com, July 9, 2003, http://www.premiere.com/moviereviews/1091/pirates-of-the-caribbean.html (accessed August 15, 2007).

39. Terry Rossio, "Walking the Plank-2005," wordplayer.com, http://www.wordplayer.com/archives/rossio07.Plank.Walk.html (accessed August 15, 2007).

40. White, "It's a Pirate's Life for Johnny Depp and Disney's Other Seaworthy Stars,"

41. Associated Press, "Johnny Depp Finds Himself, and Success, as Captain Jack Sparrow," abc12.com, http://abclocal.go.com/wjrt/story?section=entertainment&id=4319945 (accessed August 15, 2007).

42. Binelli, "The Last Buccaneer," July 13, 2006,

43. Bruce Kirkland, "A Pirate's Life for Depp," *Calgary Sun*, July 2, 2006, http://www.calgarysun.com/cgi-bin/publish.cgi?p=144830&x=articles&s=showbiz (accessed August 15, 2007).

44. Edward Guthmann, "Depp's 'Nick of Time' Misses the Mark," *San Francisco Chronicle*, D-12, http://www.sfgate.com/cgi-bin/article.cgi?f=/c/a/1996/05/24/DD21923.DTL (accessed August 15, 2007).

# Chapter 10

# "JOHNNY'S REEL": AT THE MOVIES

Until his first *Pirates of the Caribbean* movie came out, millions of people worldwide knew who Johnny Depp was but probably had not seen him in a movie. The celebrity that they may have heard about who dated famous women, had an incident at his nightclub, and starred in some TV show now had a face for a wider audience. For Depp, having more than a handful of people see his hard work was a new thing. As he explained in an interview, "The interesting thing is, like, for the most part, I've kind of been able to glide through this weird little thing they call a career in terms of the business world and in terms of the industry in many movies that were considered absolute failures, flops. So I've kind of made a career of...failing."[1]

So despite the appreciation of film aficionados and critics, his film choices marked him, at least in the business sense, as a failure. Even after the first *Pirates* movie, Depp released several more films that had mixed reviews and some that were downright bombs. But Depp claims that this was always part of his plan, to make the movies he wanted to, when he wanted to, and in the way he wanted.

That, of course, caused problems with the kind of roles that he as an actor had until recently been offered. The story on Depp seemed to be that by choosing art and specialty films instead of commercially successful ones, he was not the automatic choice for many studio heads. As a result, *Sleepy Hollow* producer Scott Rudin had to work hard to convince his studio to hire Depp, just as Tim Burton has had to, and even powerhouse Jerry Bruckheimer had to for the first *Pirates* movie.

The change in Depp's status from box office poison to box office gold can be tracked through his movie career. "I think he's probably the premier actor of his day," says Miramax head Harvey Weinstein, who adds, "I think he's been frozen out for years. I think he was looked at as too risky for a lot of the top stuff. A lot of people are going to be kissing his butt now. But what they don't understand about Johnny is that he can smell BS 10 miles away. The same guys who a year ago were saying 'Him? Are you kidding? He's box office poison' now [think] he's the hottest thing in the universe."[2]

Here, then, are Johnny Depp's films: failures and triumphs, flops and fantastic successes, along with some insights on what he and others thought about these contributions to the history of the cinema or merely to our entertainment schedule. Taglines are listed because they tell how the movie was marketed, how the story of the movie can be put into a few carefully chosen words. Directors are listed because Depp has purposefully sought out some of the most famous and talented directors and is an actor who relies on their vision and guidance. His collaborations with Tim Burton are his most well-documented attempts at making movies in conjunction with a kindred spirit.

## MOVIES 1984–2007

Title: *A Nightmare on Elm Street*
Release Date: 1984
Role: Glen Lantz, a teen in Springwood, Ohio
Director: Wes Craven (*Last House on the Left*, 1972; and *The Hills Have Eyes*, 1977)

### TAGLINES:
She is the only one who can stop it . . . if she fails, no one survives.
If Nancy Doesn't Wake Up Screaming She Won't Wake Up At All . . .
Sleep Kills

### STORY:
When the *Nightmare on Elm Street* movies began (there are now seven with a prequel in the works), they were an imaginative and gory entry into the teen slasher genre. The backstory was that Freddy Krueger had been a child murderer who was burned to death by angry townspeople

after the court failed to convict him. He returns to Elm Street to haunt the dreams of the teenage children of his killers. When he cuts them apart with his razor-fingers, it is not only a dream, but rather a dreamed murder from which the dreamer can never again awaken. Essentially everyone dies, except for one girl, Nancy, who lives to recall the horrors of Freddy Krueger over and over. *Nightmare* and its creepy star, Freddy Krueger (Robert Englund), moved beyond most slasher films and became cultural icons.

The presence of Johnny Depp in this first *Nightmare* movie (before that he was a teen TV heartthrob) was not a significant event in film history but it does mark his screen debut. Depp plays Glen, Nancy's boyfriend, and he is adorable as a teen jock with big hair and an intense look. The teens are staying at Nancy's friend Tina's house because her mom went to Las Vegas with a boyfriend, a typical slasher movie example of negligent parents leaving their kids alone to get into trouble. While 15-year-old Tina and her boyfriend Rod are having sex in an adjoining room, Depp is on the couch because his girlfriend, Nancy, is unwilling to do it in her friend's house. "Reality sucks," he gripes when he is awakened by his friends' groaning.

But reality is nothing compared to what a Freddy Krueger–infested dream world has in store for these teens. It turns out that all the teens are having the same nightmare about Freddy Krueger. When Tina falls asleep, Krueger enters Tina's dream world and kills her. Depp is warned by Nancy not to go to sleep but he does and gets sucked into his bed and a gusher of blood fills his room. Nancy finally confronts Freddy and demands her friends back and sure enough Glen, Tina, and Rod drive up in a red convertible, but it has a striped top like Freddy's sweater. In the sequels, Freddy gets into the dreams of other teens in the town and seemingly endless slaughter ensues as is the custom in teen slasher movies following the tradition of John Carpenter's *Halloween* (1978) and the *Friday the 13th* series beginning in 1980. While Depp's activities in this movie are generally dismissed as insignificant for his career, it was his first exposure to Hollywood moviemaking, and he himself would later play another famous character with blades for hands.

Title: *Private Resort*
Release Date: 1985
Role: Jack, a teen at a tropical resort
Director: George Bowers (*The Hearse*, 1980; and *Body and Soul*, 1981)

## TAGLINES:

Spend a weekend with no reservations!

They're looking for hot times. And they came to the right place ...

## STORY:

In his second movie, Depp and new actor Rob Morrow starred in an obscure teen farce as teenagers who are on the prowl for beautiful rich girls at a wealthy Miami resort. Like many of the other dumb teen comedies churned out at the same time, including *Private Lessons* (1981) and *Private School* (1983) by the same producer, this one features lots of flesh and innuendo about guys acting out their sexual fantasies, mostly in the company of women with big breasts and wearing bikinis. It is partially this inane image of Depp that is spoofed in his 1990 John Water's comedy musical, *Cry-Baby*. Depp described the movie as a "teen kind of exploitation ... basic filthiness."[3] Not having acting aspirations at that point, he did not care.

Title: *Platoon*

Release Date: 1986

Role: Private Gator Lerner

Director: Oliver Stone (*Salvador*, 1986; *Born on the Fourth of July*, 1989; *JFK*, 1991; and numerous other films as writer, director, or producer)

## TAGLINES:

The first real casualty of war is innocence.

The first real movie about the war in Vietnam is *Platoon*.

## STORY:

Johnny Depp had a small role in the star-studded cast of *Platoon*, an early feature film by one of America's most prolific and controversial directors, Oliver Stone, who won the Oscar for best director. Alongside Tom Berenger, Willem Dafoe, Charlie Sheen, and Forest Whitaker, Depp is a member of a platoon of soldiers in Vietnam who bond as a group of men in battle and eventually have to test their loyalties when they get involved in an attack on civilians in a village, evoking the 1968 My Lai massacre. Stone was a Vietnam veteran from the same era and conveys a sense of war as a messy, chaotic, and ridiculous affair: nearly every review of the film called it "gritty." The movie was considered authentic because of Stone's experiences in Vietnam. Depp receives high billing in the credits, right after the stars and the main supporting characters. He is not mentioned in most of the reviews but neither are the other supporting actors.

Depp's character, Private Lerner, is a translator and fits in well with the boozing and pot-smoking members of the platoon. When the group goes into a village in search of the enemy, Lerner speaks Vietnamese to the villagers and translates that they are forced to let the Viet Cong use the village. Despite his efforts to tell the villagers' story, the more aggressive members of the platoon want to slaughter the villagers, and one woman is shot. The village is burned and Lerner helps carry the children out. Later the platoon is ambushed and Lerner is shot, although he gets rescued by a platoon member and is taken away with the other wounded and dead in a helicopter.

Stone says he told Depp that he could tell "from a mile away that he was going to be a star" and that with his good looks he was going far in Hollywood. But more than that, he was an "original character" and had "a quality."[4] Depp joined the cast for the grueling shoot in the jungles of the Philippines that lasted several months. Depp said he had never been out of the country before and it was a dramatic introduction to international politics; while they were there the Philippines burst into revolution when dictator Ferdinand Marcos was deposed by the People Power revolution.

Title: *Cry-Baby*
Release Date: 1990
Role: Wade "Cry-Baby" Walker, a teen who can only cry one tear
Director: John Waters (*Pink Flamingos*, 1972; and *Polyester*, 1981)

## TAGLINES:
Too young to be square.... Too tough to be shocked.... Too late to be saved.
Good girls want him bad. Bad girls want him worse.
He's a doll. He's a dreamboat. He's a delinquent.

## STORY:
John Water's *Cry-Baby* is a delightful and affectionate spoof of Johnny Depp's own situation as a teen idol after *21 Jump Street*. Depp's character is a musician teen from a gang who falls in love with a beautiful girl who is one of the town "squares." The tone of the film is both bizarre yet kind, and neither the boring squares nor the oddball members of the Drapes gang are ridiculed.

By the time the movie came out, Depp had finished his *21 Jump Street* role and had plans to move onto the big screen full time. Director John Waters, known for his bizarre and campy movies, picked Depp for the role of a singing juvenile delinquent after seeing him in the same teen magazines that Depp claimed to hate. Waters is quoted as saying, "He certainly has those handsome, smoldering good looks, but Johnny is gonna go way beyond being a teen idol. I think he's going to mature incredibly well, like Robert Mitchum. He could play a sophisticate or a suit, that whole look, or a redneck—all types."[5] Waters is also quoted as imagining Depp as, "the best looking gas-station attendant who ever lived" or as a "sexy mass murderer," a bit shady and tattered in his ragged clothes.[6]

In another interview for a teen magazine, Depp describes his take on the movie: *Cry-Baby* was marketed as the ultimate juvenile-delinquent musical comedy but it had more than that. It presented an idea that was to appear in numerous Depp films: people are not always what they appear to be and they should be given a chance to show who they are. For Depp it also had a Romeo and Juliet theme, which also recurred in many of his films, even if this one had a John Waters twist to it. Depp told Waters in an interview they did together that, "That was one of the great things about *Cry-Baby*—it gave me a chance not only to make fun of the whole situation, but to do something really different. To be able to work with someone like you, who's an outlaw in filmmaking and has always done his own thing."[7]

For Depp, *Cry-Baby* was the chance to begin doing the kinds of movies he wanted to do After "21 Jump Street", he did not receive many offers he found interesting. When John Waters contacted him with the idea for a movie that ridiculed his own teen idol image, Depp saw his chance for a new beginning. It was from this movie that I swore to myself to do just what I wanted to do."[8]

The cast of *Cry-Baby* was something of a freak show, typical for a John Waters movie. It featured Ricki Lake (who acted in *Hairspray* and later became a talk show host), Iggy Pop (a punk rocker known for his wild stage antics), Traci Lords (famous star of adult movies and a nude *Penthouse* pictorial), Polly Bergen (a panelist for several years on the game show *To Tell The Truth*), actress Kim McGuire (whose odd looks earned her character the nickname Hatchet-face), and perhaps most remarkably the heiress Patty Hearst (she had been kidnapped by the Symbionese Liberation Army in 1974 and then joined them, carrying a machine gun, in a bank robbery that landed her in jail).

*Cry-Baby* is scheduled to be a stage musical in the 2007 season in both New York and La Jolla, California.

Title: *Edward Scissorhands*
Release Date: 1990
Role: Edward Scissorhands, a boy with scissors for hands
Director: Tim Burton (*Pee-Wee's Big Adventure*, 1985; *Beetle Juice*, 1988; and *Batman*, 1989)

## TAGLINES:

Innocence is what he knows. Beauty is what she sees.
His story will touch you, even though he can't
> Edward lived alone where he could hurt no one and no one could hurt him. Until the day the Avon Lady came calling...

## STORY:

It was with this role in his first Tim Burton movie that Johnny Depp established himself as an actor who often (but not always) created characters that are astounding in their uniqueness and breathtaking in their intensity and focus. Depp's Edward Scissorhands is a cobbled-together boy created by a scientist (Vincent Price) who dies before he can finish his creation. As a result, Edward has to live alone in his hilltop castle with scissors for hands. It is not until a local suburbanite selling Avon products comes to his door and then invites him home that he has contact with the supposedly normal world. But in classic Tim Burton fashion, suburbia is as bizarre as Edward's world, with its uniform houses all painted icky pastels and housing humdrum people and oblivious Avon ladies.

Edward's introduction into this world disrupts everyday routines and expectations, and like all Burton films it explores notions of machines vs. humans, the wisdom of adults vs. children, the fluidity of time, and being an outsider in a closed society. But the themes are never heavy-handed because Burton has Edward, acted innocently and earnestly by Depp, find a way to adjust and even gain acceptance. With heavy makeup, serious scarring, a tight body suit, and sharp instruments for hands, you would think Depp could do little with the role, but his expressive eyes, gentle voice, and delicate actions make Edward a genuinely precious character. Critics raved about Depp's performance, saying that he was perfectly cast and his performance was tender and moving.

Burton describes the film as being about the difference between how people see you and how that is different from what you feel inside, very much like Depp's role in *Cry-Baby* and an idea often related by Johnny Depp about himself over the years. Depp often described the experience as being one where he immediately identified with the outsider, Edward Scissorhands. That Depp felt so comfortable in a role that, as it happens, required quite a bit of physical discomfort to play, was an early sign of the relationship he and director Tim Burton would build over the years. In a number of ways, it would be a collaboration that would allow both artists to refine their crafts in profound ways.

The most bizarre and yet relevant scenes are those when Edward cuts topiary in the neighborhood and eventually moves on to cutting the hair of women and dogs. All topiary, like Edward, are an odd attempt to make a natural thing unnatural, to equate the inanimate with the animate, to reverse the order of nature and culture. It is another idea that Burton and Depp explore in all their movies together.

Burton's films always skimmed the mainstream. In 1985, he made *Pee-Wee's Big Adventure*; a few years later, he made *Beetlejuice* (1988), which featured Winona Ryder, among others. In 1989, Burton's movie *Batman* was an unexpected hit with both fans and critics. So by the time he made *Edward Scissorhands* in 1990, Burton already had a strong fan base who eagerly awaited his next cinematic fantasy.

It was this wild imagination in Burton that helped to cement his relationship with Depp. Of their collaboration, Burton remarked, "We do have a certain shorthand; a connection that we don't have with other people. We like the same obscure things;" Depp concurred that "at times, it's as if our brains are connected by some invisible hot wire that can shoot sparks at any second."[9] Those sparks have led to five collaborations plus another that is soon to be released. After *Edward Scissorhands*, Depp and Burton made *Ed Wood* (1994), *Sleepy Hollow* (1999), *Charlie and the Chocolate Factory* (2005), and the animated *Corpse Bride* (2005). Their sixth collaboration, *Sweeney Todd*, due to be released, once again casts Depp in the role of a dark, tormented, and violent man who somehow evokes our sympathy as much as our fear.

*Edward Scissorhands* was turned into a musical and was performed in a nationwide tour in late 2006 and early 2007 after it premiered in London and Japan.

Title: *Freddy's Dead: The Final Nightmare*
Release Date: 1991
Role: A teenager who appears on a TV show
Director: Wes Craven (*The Hills Have Eyes*, 1977; and *A Nightmare on Elm Street*, 1984)

## TAGLINES:

You Think You Know About Dreams.... You Know Nothing!
They saved the best for last.
Evil has finally met its match.
Take Him Home in a Box!

## STORY:

Freddy's back again, and so is Johnny Depp, who sort of died in the first movie but reappears here as a character on a TV show with the inexplicable name of Oprah Noodlemantra.

Title: *Arizona Dream*
Release Date: 1993
Role: Axel Blackmar, a young man exploring his dreams
Director: Emir Kusturica (*Time of the Gypsies*, 1988)

## TAGLINES:

A rebellious young man. With his own vision of the future. And
  his own fantasy of love.

## STORY:

This is a movie that includes everything from flying fish to a romp with Faye Dunaway, all presented with a touch of the fantastic. But before the scene of sex with and aging and botoxed Faye Dunaway, the movie presents us with Dunaway shooting a shotgun at comedian Jerry Lewis who minces away like he was in one of his Dean Martin pictures; then Depp imitating a rooster while wearing a white petticoat over his shoulders; then a woman playing an accordion to her turtles; then a game of Russian roulette. The idea behind this style of filmmaking is taken from surrealism, where the juxtaposition of odd elements is what creates a narrative. Any movie that ends, like this one does, with Jerry Lewis and Johnny Depp as philosophical Eskimos fishing for flounder, cannot be taken in normal narrative terms.

Serbian director Emir Kusturica is interested in cinema as art and found in Johnny Depp a good vehicle for his messages. Kusturica is also a musician and appreciated that in his lead actor. "That is more important than how good an actor he is. Acting, who cares? Everyone could be an actor." He continued, "He has a certain self-destructive side which I like very much.... He's one of the great young actors, in that he has a rich mythological eruptive internal life. In America I stopped seeing people with secrets. They just become part of the CNN global system. He has *secrets*, and secrets are the main sign of human existence. It's beautiful to have a guy who was not eaten by TV civilization, who is still human in its shadow."[10]

Title: *Benny & Joon*
Release Date: 1993
Role: Sam, an odd young man with a silent-movie persona
Director: Jeremiah S. Chechnik (*National Lampoon's Christmas Vacation*, 1989)

## TAGLINES:
A romance on the brink of reality.

## STORY:
Johnny Depp plays Sam, a seemingly simple-minded fellow who ends up living with the mentally fragile Joon and her brother Benny because his cousin won a poker game in which Sam's living situation was put in the pot. Sam, it turns out, makes a good companion for Joon and the two eventually fall in love, much to the horror of Benny, who wants to put his volatile, mentally ill sister in an institution. Sam is interesting as another of Depp's damaged, non-conformist, and very much alive characters. Sam uses scenes, slapstick routines, and facial expressions from Buster Keaton, Charlie Chaplin, and Harold Lloyd movies to entertain Benny and Joon but also to bridge the gap between her withdrawal from reality and Sam's reinterpretation of it. Keaton and Chaplin, stars in both the silent and sound film eras during the teens to the sixties, also acted, directed, and wrote great early comedies; Lloyd acted and produced during the same period. All were known for their command of physical comedy and they provide both Sam and Johnny Depp with role models for their acting styles.

Depp's performance as Sam recalled for many his turn as Edward Scissorhands in the way he acted mostly with gestures and without saying more than a word or two, but some saw this as Edward Scissorhands without the scissors. *Rolling Stone* had this more jaded view and said of Depp's performance, "Our condolences to Johnny Depp—he's trapped in this pot of curdled whimsy as Sam, a free-spirited dyslexic with a Buster Keaton fixation."[11] One interviewer saw a connection to the real Johnny Depp and told him that. He recalls, "The Johnny Depp in this film, with his pauses and gazes and untamable flights of imagination, is the closest I've seen on-screen to the Johnny Depp I've met. When I tell him this, he is silent, and I can't tell whether he feels that it's his personality or his acting ability that has been insulted."[12]

Title: *What's Eating Gilbert Grape*
Release Date: 1993
Role: Gilbert Grape, a grocery store clerk in a small town
Director: Lasse Hallström (*My Life as a Dog,* 1985; and *The Cider House Rules,* 1999)

## TAGLINES:
Arnie knows a secret. His big brother Gilbert is the greatest person on the planet.
Life is a terrible thing to sleep through.
Living in Endora is like dancing to no music.

## STORY:
Gilbert Grape is a young man with no future: he lives in a present occupied by a boring job in groceries, an affair with a desperate local married woman, a retarded brother (Arnie, played by Leonardo DiCaprio), and a morbidly obese mother. Gilbert takes care of them all and, along with his sister, tries to make a normal life for them. But small changes disrupt the routine of the family, not in one large dramatic crash but in slow and simple ways. A large chain grocery opens up nearby, a burger chain opens in town, Arnie gets into more trouble every time he climbs a water tower and finally gets arrested, and a girl that Gilbert is attracted to gets stranded in town for a few days. Around these small shifts in the status quo, tremendous changes take place and eventually Gilbert has to decide what his family's future will look like. The story is simple without being simplistic and always shows Gilbert as someone who is serious about his responsibilities while longing for something more.

The role of Gilbert, like that of Sam, Cry-Baby, and Edward, moved Depp away from playing pretty boys and into the realm of angst-ridden young men who are nevertheless sensitive and kind, the kind of person Depp has often described himself as. In an interview after the film opened, Depp remarked, "[Director] Lasse thinks that I like to hide behind weird characters so that I'm not exposed, and that Gilbert is the most real thing I've played; closer to reality and closer to me."[13]

Title: *Ed Wood*

Release Date: 1994

Role: Ed Wood, a cross-dressing director of really bad movies in the 1950s and 1960s

Director: Tim Burton (*Edward Scissorhands*, 1990; and *Batman Returns*, 1992)

## TAGLINES:

Movies were his passion. Women were his inspiration. Angora sweaters were his weakness.

When it came to making bad movies, Ed Wood was the best.

## STORY:

Edward D. Wood Jr. is considered one of the worst directors Hollywood has ever seen. In an age of YouTube videos, where everyone tries their hand at directing moving pictures, it may be hard to imagine a time when a passion for directing could only be satisfied by making films in the Hollywood style—in studios with sets and the proper cameras and even an old star or two. What Ed Wood seemed to lack was even a basic sense of how to get a story onto film in a way that other people, his audience, could comprehend. As a result, Ed Wood films used cheesy sets, visual clichés, some of the worst acting ever recorded on film, and wacky storylines.

A documentary about him, featuring the actors and crew who worked with him, included contradictory descriptions of him as a "sweet man," "self-destructive," "a con-artist," "a user and a loser," "completely undaunted," "child-like in his enthusiasm," and "the most sincere and honest person that I have ever met."[14] He might have been completely forgotten if not for the fact that his 1959 film, *Plan 9 from Outer Space*, has been widely considered the worst movie ever made, topping lists like those of The Golden Turkey Award; it also was horror film actor Bela Lugosi's last film.

*Ed Wood*, starring Johnny Depp in a luscious angora sweater and bra, covers some of the production of *Plan 9*, Wood's relationship with Lugosi, and Wood's cross-dressing activities. Depp's Wood is a delightful optimist, a real lover of movies who has a nearly perpetual smile and a quizzical eyebrow raised to the endless criticism he encounters. Burton shot the film in black and white and this gives it a vintage look like Wood's own films. Depp is perfect as the enthusiastic director. Part of the charm of the movie is that Ed Wood never seemed to notice how incompetent he was and this is what makes Depp's depiction of him so much more touching.

In a scene after Wood has been turned down by a major studio, he sadly states, "All I want to do is tell stories, the things that I find interesting." It could be Depp speaking about his own work. In describing why he took this role Depp says, "He was totally pure. It really all came from an absolutely right place. That was why Ed Wood was so important to Tim [Burton, the director] and I. It was really like a love letter to him. We appreciate this guy, you know?"[15]

Title: *Don Juan DeMarco*
Release Date: 1995
Role: Don Juan DeMarco, a man who thinks he is the great fictional lover, Don Juan
Director: Jeremy Leven (*Alex and Emma*, 2003, writer and producer; and *The Notebook*, 2004, writer)

## TAGLINES:

The story of the man who thought he was the greatest lover in the world…and the people who tried to cure him of it!
The Best Part of Love is Losing All Sense of Reality.
If you can't get laid after seeing this film, you can't get laid.

## STORY:

Although this is not a Tim Burton film, it is another example of a movie that makes a statement about the power of storytelling. Like Sam in *Benny & Joon* or even Jack Sparrow, Depp's character here lives in his own reality and he has to face a world that does not want him to act it out. Depp plays a young man who thinks he is the legendary lover Don Juan, a womanizer whose tales date back to the seventeenth century. When he attempts suicide, he has to convince a psychiatrist (played by Marlon Brando at Depp's request) that he really is the legendary lover and should be released from a psychiatric hospital. The psychiatrist listens to his story, and has his own life changed in the process.

The film garnered interest because it was a chance for Brando to return to the screen and show again that he could act, but the general impression was that he made little effort in the film. Depp, on the other hand, was seen as a quality actor in this slight film. Roger Ebert explained that Depp "has an openness to fantasy that makes his strange characters—also including Edward Scissorhands and Ed Wood—touching and convincing. Actors often talk about how they'd like to work with Brando. This kid could teach him some things."[16] Some reviewers, however, thought the two made a remarkable combo and that the movie succeeded because both were strong actors.

About this character Depp has suggested that Don Juan is a man who truly believes in himself. At the same time, Depp has been careful to draw distinctions between this movie role and himself because, despite his reputation as a lover of beautiful women in real life, he has never had the audacity to call himself the world's greatest lover. Nevertheless, it is another role in which Depp plays an outsider, a person different from the normal, who tries to show others an alternative way to live. Depp has shown that he likes the idea of addressing issues like, what is reality, what is madness, and what is normal.

The story also plays with the concept of whose reality should rule, whose reality should set the rules. While it is not a great revelation that people have different realities and that this causes conflicts, Depp's character does help us question what happens when conformity is demanded of all people in a community.

Title: *Dead Man*
Release Date: 1995
Role: William Blake, an accountant from Cleveland
Director: Jim Jarmusch (*Ghost Dog: The Way of the Samurai*, 1999; and *Broken Flowers*, 2005)

## TAGLINES:
No one can survive becoming a legend.

## STORY:
Directed by independent film superhero Jim Jarmusch, costarring heavyweights Robert Mitchum, Gabriel Byrne, Billy Bob Thornton, and John Hurt, and shot in gorgeous black and white, this is a self-absorbed, very hip, and rabidly surreal tale of a man's journey west for a job in an end-of-the-line town called Machine. Blake does not get the job he came for and ends up shooting a man and becoming a fugitive. That actually is too mundane a description for a film that revels in bizarre-looking characters and scenarios that do not in any way create a narrative.

"What name were you given at birth, stupid white man?" asks a Native American in *Dead Man*. When Johnny Depp's character replies, "I'm

William Blake," the Indian replies, "Is this a lie or a white man's trick?" When Blake insists that is his name, the man replies, "Then you are a dead man." The Native American, named Nobody, befriends the wounded Blake and is upset because he is unfamiliar with the poetry of the original William Blake. He helps the Depp version of Blake discover his destiny. Nobody quotes a Blake poem, saying, "Some are born to sweet delight. Some are born to endless night," and you can be sure if it is a Johnny Depp film, his character is destined for the latter.

Blake's destiny, it turns out, is part "collecting white man's metal" (getting shot) and part appreciating Native American views of reality. For some critics the only value to the film was that it encouraged people to go and read Blake's poetry. *Variety* decried its lack of narrative, slow pace, and mystical-poetic elements."Perhaps most important for Depp is that he gets to play another odd character, one that connects to Native Americans. Some aspects of this film seem to pop up in Depp's own directorial debut, *The Brave*, which was released in 1997.

Jarmusch said about Depp's performance, "What I love about Johnny for this character is that he has the ability to start off very innocently. This is a difficult role to play, to start off as a passive character in a genre that is based on active, aggressive central characters. What amazed me about Johnny was his ability to go through a lot of very subtle but big changes in his character, out of sequence but without ever telegraphing that character development."[17]

Title: *Nick of Time*
Release Date: 1995
Role: Gene Watson, an accountant and father
Director: John Badham (*Saturday Night Fever*, 1977; *War Games*, 1983; and *Short Circuit*, 1986)

## TAGLINES:
Within 90 minutes, someone is going to die . . . . And the clock is ticking.
Ninety minutes. Six bullets. No choice.
Nick of Time: Real Terror in Real Time

## STORY:
Johnny Depp as an accountant (again) with short hair, glasses, a dull suit, and a little kid? Remember that in the mid 1990s, Depp was also making *Ed Wood* and *Donnie Brasco*, both rather bold characters. You

have to wonder what would attract Depp to this story of a man whose child is kidnapped and in order to get her back has to assassinate the governor of California.

Since it turns out that people on the governor's staff, including her husband, are in on the plot, Gene has trouble finding someone to help him get out of his mess. Both the plot and Depp's handling of his character resulted in reviews that were dismissive of his efforts. The best most reviewer's could say was that Depp proved he could play an ordinary guy, though not with much relish. Depp does not seem like an action hero throughout the story and he resorts to asking a shoeshine man to help him; the shoeshine guy is the real hero, eventually foiling the kidnappers and getting Gene's daughter back.

What reviewers could not know at the time was that the gimmick that director John Badham used to give the movie a unique pacing—having it play out in real time—would a few years later, in 2002, become the reason that the television program *24* seemed so fresh and challenging. But unlike *24*, *Nick of Time* inserts so many stylistic images (often of ticking clocks) that they neutralize the tension even as they remind you how much time you have already spent on this story. Depp plays desperate and befuddled well but leaves no lasting impression as a man caught in an unsolvable puzzle and under an impossible deadline.

Title: *Donnie Brasco*
Release Date: 1997
Role: Donnie Brasco/Joe Pistone, an undercover agent posing as a mobster.
Director: Mike Newell (*Enchanted April*, 1992; and *Four Weddings and a Funeral*, 1994)

**TAGLINES:**
Donnie Brasco. Based On A True Story.
In 1978, the US government waged a war against organized crime.
One man was left behind the lines.

**STORY:**
Johnny Depp describes his preparation for this role as a series of discussions with the real Donnie Brasco, an undercover FBI agent who really did infiltrate the mob and eventually bring about a series of mob arrests and convictions. Depp spent time with Joe Pistone, the real Donnie Brasco, in order to learn his every mannerism. "He's got an interesting rhythm to his

speech. I did my best to get that."[18] The real Pistone confirmed that Depp captured his mannerisms and way of walking and talking.

Relying on the real character instead of using his trademark character development techniques may be why this Depp portrayal seems so indifferent. Depp as Brasco, a slimy mob wannabe that gets vouched for by Al Pacino's "Lefty," is hard to distinguish from Depp as Joe, the supposedly honorable FBI agent. If the strain of carrying two identities and two loyalties is at the heart of the movie, it should be clearer that there is, at least initially, a difference between the two men. *Donnie Brasco* was a darling of critics if not audiences and domestic receipts barely covered the cost of making the film with its two stars.

Title: *The Brave*
Release Date: 1997
Role: Raphael, a Native American
Director: Johnny Depp

## TAGLINES:
-none-

## STORY:
Depp directed, starred in, and wrote the screenplay for this movie, which debuted at the Cannes Film Festival in 1997 but was never released in the United States. Depp plays a Native American named Raphael who is down on his luck and money. He meets a businessman played by Marlon Brando who offers him $50,000 for his life (descriptions of the movie say it is for Raphael to appear in a snuff film but that is not revealed in the movie). At Cannes it was nominated for the highest award, a Golden Palm. Nevertheless, it is a film considered generally lacking in all the qualities that make a compelling movie, from the storyline to the timing and the visuals. The story is slow and lacks drama, and the camerawork, dialogue, and directing contribute little to the story.

So why would Depp make such a film as his directing debut? Certainly playing a Native American must have something to do with the appeal of this story. In discussing the film, Depp expressed his commitment to using movies to explore social issues that are important to him. "It's a project in which I totally involved myself, in a very personal and even intimate way. It was the chance for me to talk about things that I really cared in my heart of hearts: this deplorable condition in which the American Indian really lives, and broadly speaking, all people who have dark skin: black people, Mexicans, Indians. I tried to do something honest, not to imitate any existing model, certainly not to try to get entertainment from it."[19]

Depp has repeatedly referenced his Native American heritage in interviews although he is ambiguous about the details. Depp got a tattoo to honor his Native American grandfather and says also that his great-grandmother was Cherokee. The problem with claiming his Cherokee heritage is that it is not just a matter of thinking or knowing that you have Cherokee blood. The Cherokee, like most native tribes, have specific criteria for membership. For the Cherokee, it involves meeting strict requirements: being able to provide documents that you are the ancestor of someone who was enrolled in the Cherokee Nation between 1899–1906 and resided in Indian Territory (Oklahoma).[20]

Whether or not he meets the tribal criteria, there is nothing in this film to suggest knowledge of Native American life or an affinity for it. Having Cherokee blood is no guarantee that you understand Cherokee or any native culture. In fact the Cherokee struggle with who is Cherokee, and who gets to decide that is part of that question. Marlon Brando is also often cited as a supporter of Native American rights because, in protest about the historic treatment of Native Americans, he sent a woman named Sacheen Littlefeather to the Academy Awards in 1973 to refuse his *Godfather* Oscar. Littlefeather's native credentials were eventually questioned (although she has since promoted her Native heritage) and Brando's actions generally ridiculed.

Title: *Fear and Loathing in Las Vegas*
Release Date: 1998
Role: Raoul Duke, a famous writer based on Hunter Thompson
Director: Terry Gilliam (*Brazil*, 1985; and *The Fisher King*, 1991)

## TAGLINES:
Give us your brain for two hours and you will never be the same again...
If there was a trip to be taken, they were there.
Four Days, Three nights, Two Convertibles, One City
Buy the ticket, take the ride.

## STORY:
Based on the real-life writer Hunter Thompson, this absurdist film by Terry Gilliam succeeds in bringing to the screen Thompson's book about a

drug-filled trip to Las Vegas during the Vietnam War era. It does this with a wild portrayal by Depp and a series of hallucinogenic scenes staged by Gilliam. The result is another bizarre character in Depp's repertoire. For Gilliam it was less a druggy movie and more one that showed what drugs were used for: as a ticket to an adventure, as a way of seeing the world differently.

Johnny Depp says he read Hunter Thompson's book when he was 17 and it was one of his favorite books, and while you might expect that Thompson was a madman he really was a southern gentleman. Preparing for the role, Depp moved into Thompson's Colorado home to study his subject and instead, says Gilliam, "stole his soul."[21] Depp says he spent about four months with him in Colorado, studying his habits and voice and accompanying him on his book tour. As Depp described it, "Hunter is indelible! He is like a disease you've got. He slips under your skin, takes root into your blood and your pores. Hunter impregnates you. He haunts you. His rhythm, the way he speaks, his language, are very interesting. And it's hard to get rid of it after mixing with him for a time."[22]

Thompson and Depp became friends and Thompson described the actor in glowing terms: "Johnny has an outlaw personality. He identifies with the outlaw image in what he reads, the movies he makes. He's not faking it." Gilliam added his admiration for Depp's work: "Johnny's particular path in life is to constantly nudge people awake," Gilliam says. "The films he chooses force you to reconsider what you think of the world."[23]

Some critics felt the combination of Thompson, Depp, and Gilliam did not work so well even though the film seemed to respect its source. Roger Ebert described the film as "a horrible mess of a movie, without shape, trajectory or purpose—a one joke movie, if it had one joke." He found the movie devoid of plot, relying almost entirely on scenes of greater and greater euphoria and hallucination in its two principal characters.[24]

While some critics found Depp's portrayal hammy or ridiculous, others were impressed by the way Depp captured the essence of Thompson's persona and experiences. Anyone who didn't know that Depp could act, anyone who thought he was just a pretty face, could find in this role the proof that Depp was an actor worth noticing.

Title: *The Ninth Gate*
Release Date: 1999
Role: Dean Corso, a dealer in antique books
Director: Roman Polanski (*Rosemary's Baby*, 1968; and *Chinatown*, 1974)

**TAGLINES:**

Leave the unknown alone.

The only thing more terrifying than searching for the Devil…is finding him.

**STORY:**

Johnny Depp went to France to make a film with the infamous director Roman Polanski who was exiled there since 1978 because he had sex with a 13-year-old girl in the United States. Depp ended up with a turkey of a film, but met the woman who was to become his love and the mother of his children. Whether another dumb film is a fair price to pay for a transition to a new and satisfying life is what critics should have been asking Depp ever since.

Depp wanted to work with Polanski and was not attracted by the story of *The Ninth Gate* or the quality of the writing: "I think Polanski is one of the few filmmakers who nearly did a perfect film, a couple of them. Chinatown is almost perfect. It may be perfect. And I was really excited about the prospect of going to work with him. The screenplay was sort of like, all right, you know. Maybe when we get in there, we can float around a little bit and find some stuff and change it. But he doesn't want to do that so much."[25]

The story, co-written by Polanski, is somewhat convoluted: Depp's Corso, a well-known but slightly disreputable book dealer, is hired to find and authenticate copies of an old book supposedly written by the devil himself. The purpose of having all the known copies of the book is to open the gates to another world, presumably the one occupied by Satan. Corso is endlessly pursued and attacked by others who also want the books. He is also protected by a woman who appears to have some kind of supernatural powers and who may or may not be the devil in disguise.

Carrie Rickey of the *Philadelphia Inquirer* was taken aback by this ill-conceived film: "Leaping Lucifer! Is it possible that Polanski, the legendary director of Repulsion, Rosemary's Baby and Chinatown, concocted this bloodless, soulless and airless affair?"[26] Other reviewers concurred that the film never made its point very well or that what looked like an ideal coupling of Polanski and Depp never panned out and that Depp appeared almost bored with the story. Salon.com claims the whole movie is purposely "deadpan" with the actors in on the joke and Depp's performance sleek and mischevious.[27]

Title: *The Astronaut's Wife*
Release Date: 1999

Role: Commander Spencer Armacost, an astronaut
Director: Rand Ravich (*The Maker,* 1997, writer and coproducer)

## TAGLINES:
How well do you know the one you love?
Imagine the face of terror is the one you love.
Witness the birth of pure evil.

## STORY:
It is somewhat surprising that Depp would take a role with a first time feature director after all his experiences with the industry's top talent and his claim after *Don Juan DeMarco* that he would never work with a freshman director again. The choice proved disastrous, as the film never attracted an audience. Even more surprising is that the film is really a vehicle for the lovely Charlize Theron, who plays his wife and is given extensive close-ups and long scenes. Depp's role does not fit in with the type of characters he had been playing to that point.

Depp plays an astronaut who together with his crewmate is exposed to something dangerous while on a mission in space. When they return the crewmate dies and his wife shockingly commits suicide. Theron and Depp move to New York and begin a new life that is complicated by the fact that she, like her friend who just died, is pregnant by what appears to be some alien force. The movie plods through a story that has Depp barely acting since an alien force also occupies him. Depp's performance was considered unremarkable and predictable and like his character in *The Ninth Gate;* he was never allowed to give it his characteristic flair.

Reviewers found the film derivative especially in its resemblance to *Rosemary's Baby* (1968). A viewer commenting on the film at IMDb.com defined the problem with the film clearly: "What do you get when you mix six parts "I Married a Monster From Outer Space" with four parts "Rosemary's Baby," "The Omen" and "Village of the Damned," shake it and stir it, then add "Invasion of the Body Snatchers" and the "Alien" movies as chasers? You end up with "The Astronaut's Wife," a film cobbled together from so many disparate and familiar sources that the audience is always ten giant steps ahead of both the plot and the characters."[28]

Title: *Sleepy Hollow*
Release Date: 1999
Role: Ichabod Crane, a New York City prosecutor
Director: Tim Burton (*Edward Scissorhands,* 1990 and *Ed Wood,*
   1994)

**TAGLINES:**
Watch your head!
Who will it come for next?!
Heads Will Roll.

**STORY:**
Tim Burton and Johnny Depp joined forces again to bring to life the classic early-American short story written in 1820 by Washington Irving. "The Legend of Sleepy Hollow," as Irving wrote it, had a Connecticut school teacher, Ichabod Crane, driven out of a small New York town, apparently by the apparition of a headless horseman but more likely by his romantic rival. Burton's Ichabod Crane is not a teacher but a New York detective with the job of investigating the decapitations of citizens in the small Dutch town in 1799. Written this way, *Sleepy Hollow* seems more contemporary, like another version of CSI with a touch of homage to old horror films and maybe *Kolchak: The Night Stalker*, a television series (1974–75) about hunting supernatural creatures.

Many critics found Burton's take on the story spellbinding and Depp's Ichabod Crane a fascinating and unexpected character. Depp makes Ichabod a delicate and fragile man, a proponent of scientific methods, and a man attached to the security provided by his instruments of investigation and his precise style of forensic science. Ichabod does not believe in the supernatural and his whole system of beliefs is challenged in Sleepy Hollow. Making Ichabod Crane so vulnerable and swooning while spouting scientific certainty was an important inspiration that makes the character so multifaceted.

Depp's Ichabod Crane is a forerunner of Jack Sparrow: "Anyone surprised at Depp's outre buccaneer Jack Sparrow in his Pirates of the Caribbean movies probably never saw his astonishingly fey Ichabod....As a progressive 1799 policeman exiled from New York and ordered to test his theories of deduction on a series of horrific beheadings, Depp combined intellect and swooning effeminacy to dazzling effect. He molded himself into a male ingenue who mixed the aura of a tortured poet with the unisex glamour of late Carnaby Street."[29]

There was some consideration, at first, for Depp to play the part of Ichabod complete with a prosthetic nose and ears, to more closely match Irving's description of the character. But Burton did not want to dress his star up in this way. Instead, Burton directed Depp to create Ichabod's look by emphasizing his prissiness. Depp's ability to use gesture and nuance to create unusual physical types was consistent with Burton's view of him as being very much like a chameleon, able to change with the requirements of the role.

Burton's vision for the movie gave Depp another role in which to show that the two of them shared a way of storytelling that is an unprecedented combination mixing "old-style horror melodrama with borderline camp; it mixes gruesome decapitations (an R-rated raft of them) with drawing-room drollery; it mixes trippy dreamscapes with quaint village settings."[30]

Title: *The Man Who Cried*
Release Date: 2000
Role: Cesar, a Gypsy horse rider
Director: Sally Potter (*Orlando*, 1992; and *The Tango Lesson*, 1997)

## TAGLINES:
-none-

## STORY:
Johnny Depp finally gets to be a Romani in this story of a Jewish girl who leaves Russia to find her father but ends up in Paris as the Nazis are about to invade. Critics found it odd and unmoving.

Elvis Mitchell had fun with Depp playing a Gypsy again: "Johnny Depp, who apparently had a Gipsy King layover in this picture while on his way to 'Chocolat'.... does his hot-eyed misterioso number, and while he is quite good, he should be served with papers that enjoin him from ever playing a Gypsy again. When Cesar courts Suzie, he makes speeches that belong in an opera. 'They're all my children, and these older people here are all my parents,' he intones ominously when Suzie follows him to the Gypsy camp."[31]

In fact there is nothing about the character of Cesar, a horseback rider in a stage show, that requires Depp's unique abilities. What may explain his taking this role is his interest in Gypsy music and culture. The people who play Cesar's family in the movie are members of Romanian music group Taraf de Haidouks. About meeting them on the movie set Depp said, "For me they are a model in the way they approach life. Despite all that they went through—I'm talking about racism against gypsies which went on for centuries and still exits today—these guys can play a music which expresses the most intense joy. They have this gift to make you feel alive. They are among the most extraordinary people I ever met."[32]

Title: *Before Night Falls*
Release Date: 2000

Role: Lieutenant Victor and Bon-Bon, a transvestite
Director: Julian Schnabel (*Basquiat*, 1996)

## TAGLINES:
-none-

## STORY:
Based on the memoir of Cuban writer Reinaldo Arenas (1943–1990), this low-budget film looks at the life of Arenas as he joins the Cuban revolution, writes openly about being gay in post-revolutionary Cuba, gets imprisoned, and eventually commits suicide while suffering from AIDS. It is written and directed by artist Julian Schnabel and has Johnny Depp in two small roles: as a transvestite, Bon-Bon, in prison with Arenas, and as a prison guard.

Very little commentary was made at the time about Depp's roles except to note Depp's odd dual appearances. *Variety* found some delight in Depp's short scenes: "In the film's most amusing sequence, Johnny Depp makes one of two brief but memorable appearances as Bon Bon, a gutter-glamorous transvestite with a talent for rectal smuggling, who shifts several chapters of Reinaldo's book out of the prison at a time."[33]

Title: *Chocolat*
Release Date: 2000
Role: Roux, an itinerant musician
Director: Lasse Hallström (*What's Eating Gilbert Grape*, 1993; and
    *The Cider House Rules*, 1999)

## TAGLINES:
One Taste Is All It Takes.
One taste is not enough.
What do you see?
… and the world is still indulging!

## STORY:
Johnny Depp is not the star of this delicious story of a woman who causes a stir in a small French town when she opens a chocolate shop just as Lent begins. Her tempting confections and her advice on love and life stir up trouble with the locals. Vianne (Juliette Binoche in an

Oscar-nominated performance) provides the town with a glimpse of an alternative life, one where the willingness to open up to sensuousness, represented by fine chocolate, will be rewarded. The film was nominated for a Best Picture Oscar but the reviews tended to use sugary metaphors to put this adult fable in its place, calling it gooey, too sweet yet very tasty.

Johnny Depp is an itinerant musician traveling on the river. He presents an opportunity for Vianne to put her lessons on love into practice, and her carnal relationship with Roux is just another reason for the townspeople to hate her. Salon.com's Charles Taylor felt that Depp exuded a "laid-back sexiness" that illustrated his acting skill: "Depp can fool you into thinking he's not doing anything, but if you've got liquid eyes that take in a woman the way he takes in Binoche, that's enough."[34]

For Depp, this role as a gypsy-like Irish traveler and the one as a Romani Gypsy in *The Man Who Cried*, also released in 2000, associated him with Gypsy characteristics, including the style of clothes he wears. Depp has supported Gypsy music and performance. On the website for a documentary about Gypsy life that he appears in, he is quoted as saying, "It would be great if by experiencing the Romani people and their music, people can learn more about them and understand that—what you've believed about these people has been a lie your entire life."[35] Gossip magazines even claim Depp is going to have a Gypsy wedding.

Title: *Blow*
Release Date: 2001
Role: George Jung, a drug dealer
Director: Ted Demme (*Life*, 1999; and *Monument Ave.*, 1998)

## TAGLINES:
Based on a True Story.

## STORY:
Adding to his history of playing disreputable characters, Johnny Depp stars in this movie about real-life drug dealer and smuggler George Jung. Jung became a major U.S. cocaine dealer in the 1980s and Depp plays the lowlife Jung simply as someone who makes bad business deals and has parents who can be blamed for his problems.

In this "deeply mediocre dope opera...hopefully ambitious yet hopelessly lightweight,"[36] Jung's life is glorified even if he does finally end up in prison. Depp's acting is certainly adequate for the role but does not suggest any sense of the tragic consequences of Jung's actions. In fact, the *New York Times* thought it worth mentioning that "Johnny Depp has the kind of face that justifies the existence of cinema," and "he makes even dull films watchable,"[37] which is presumably a reference to this film.

> Title: *From Hell*
> Release Date: 2001
> Role: Inspector Frederick Abberline, a drug-addicted detective with Scotland Yard
> Director: The Hughes Brothers (*Dead Presidents*, 1995; and *Menace II Society*, 1993)

## TAGLINES:
Evil has a new address…
Only the legend will survive

## STORY:
In several interviews, Depp has confessed an interest in the story of Jack the Ripper, a notorious murderer of prostitutes in late-nineteenth-century London. In this movie he gets to help solve the case by playing an opium-addicted detective who has visions about the killer while in his drug haze. In keeping with Depp's other interest in questioning what is reality and who has the right to define it, this movie is based on a theory about Jack the Ripper that was popular in the 1970s and was the basis for the graphic novel *From Hell* by Alan Moore, whose visual style influenced this movie. Depp is "a rogue detective who does not buy into the illusions of the age."[38]

Depp's role is noted as being similar to the one he had in *Sleepy Hollow* but even more interesting; "Mr. Depp is probably prettier than the hookers he is questioning, and that his need to play against his looks is so strong that it translates into a separate undercurrent of ferocity."[39] After falling in love with one of the prostitutes, and then realizing he must silence himself because he knows her location once she escapes London, he goes back to the pipe and opiates himself to death.

The movie did not make money but it does have its fans. As one commented on IMDb, "Don't let the detractors put you off. It's hardly surprising a generation weened on MTV—folk with the attention span of a gnat and the emotional depth of a paper cup—didn't like it. They've got their Screams and their Scary Movies, and they're welcome to them. This is super stuff."[40]

Title: *Pirates of the Caribbean: The Curse of the Black Pearl*
Release Date: 2003
Role: Jack Sparrow, a pirate
Director: Gore Verbinski (*The Mexican*, 2001; and *The Ring*, 2002)

## TAGLINES:

Prepare to be blown out of the water.
Over 3000 Islands of Paradise—For Some it's A Blessing—For
    Others...It's A Curse.

## STORY:

We might like to think that very successful movies like this one are
all neatly calculated and precisely planned and predetermined to have
box office appeal. But the stories circulated about the creation and production of this first *Pirates* movie suggests that intuition, fate, luck, and
a dash of "sea turtles"are really the ingredients of such stories. Jack Sparrow explains how he got off a deserted island in the middle of the ocean
by saying he rode off on sea turtles. It became a phrase used again as
shorthand to say the story of how something happened is better than
the reality.

Screenwriters Ted Elliot and Terry Rossio reveal in their website that
the movie almost did not get made. They explain, "As Michael Eisner
tells the story, he was fully prepared to tell Gore [Verbinski, director] and
Jerry Bruckheimer he wasn't going to make the film, but then Gore took
Eisner on a tour of the development art, and Eisner thought, what the
heck, there's a movie I'd like to see, and let it continue."[41] This was even
before Johnny Depp was associated with the project.

In discussing how he came to the project Johnny Depp has said, "I was
sitting in a meeting with Dick Cook over at Disney, a kind of a general
meeting, and he said, 'What kind of stuff are you looking to do?' I said,
'I don't know. I'd kind of like to do some kiddie stuff. Something a bit
more accessible for mine, you know.' He said, 'We're thinking of doing
this thing, Pirates of the Caribbean,' and I just said, 'I'm in.'" Apparently Depp apparently surprised both himself and his agent with his quick
response. When the interviewer responded, "That's the last thing I would
have expected you to do, a movie based on a theme park," Depp replied,
"I can't explain it, you know. I just had a feeling. I don't know why. And
there was every chance in the world for it to be something horribly embarrassing. I just had a good feeling, and then all the elements came together
and it worked fine."[42] Depp attributes the urge to do a Disney film to his

daughter's interest in Disney films: "My daughter, she was about three then, and I'd watched every single animated Disney hoo-ha that existed. I'd gotten quite close to these movies and enjoyed the fact that these cartoon characters were without limits."[43]

He explained to *Rolling Stone*, "I don't know why I said yes. I didn't think, 'I must do a commercial movie.' I've never been the guy who can predict...'This one will take a giant dump,'" Though, Depp believed, Disney was thinking, 'This is going to be a huge flop.' "Later, when they were telling me I had to approve my image on cereal boxes, I still never felt compromised. It wasn't like selling out to me. It was like I had infiltrated the enemy camp and stuck my flag in, and now it's taken root and you're on the ride, so let's see where it goes."[44]

*Pirates* is not just a blockbuster movie and the beginning of an over-three-billion-dollar franchise, but it is a story that we have taken into our everyday lives. It has spread pirate lore, gear, gaming, and language like no other tale of the high seas and it revived the career of a creative actor who needed this role to show his ability to a wider audience. One of the most noted aspects of the film is Johnny Depp's creation of Jack Sparrow. Jerry Bruckheimer, producer of the series, describes Depp's contribution as essential to the movie's success: "He makes this movie more offbeat. He wanted to play Jack Sparrow as half-baked, out at sea too long, drinking too much, but very smart underneath it all. And he's very visual; he created the look of the character."[45]

Perhaps the most widespread aspect of the Jack Sparrow lore was that Disney's head honchos were terrified when they saw Depp's reinterpretation of the classic figure of the pirate. In all the DVD extras, documentaries, books, websites, and media coverage of the origin story of *Pirates of the Caribbean*, all the major players feel it is necessary to prove that they were defying the Disney aesthetic and Disney's hold on the pirate image. They proved this by saying that the corporation was initially horrified at Depp's swishy, somewhat fey, and always seemingly drunk pirate. As Depp describes it, "The executives did panic. I mean, bless 'em, they did panic on the first one. And probably to some degree for good reason."[46]

*Pirates of the Caribbean: The Curse of the Black Pearl* is in many ways a reverse of the traditional pirate story. The thing that may have broken the curse of pirate movies is that instead of searching for treasure, the cursed pirates have to put back all the pieces of Aztec gold they stole in order to break the curse. Reviews for this first *Pirate* film were mixed. "It could have been worse, but that's no excuse. *Pirates of the Caribbean: The Curse of the Black Peal* is a $125 million Jerry Bruckheimer epic that drags on for an unconscionable 143 minutes and buries its treasures—mainly Johnny Depp in eye shadow and dreads as Captain Jack Sparrow—in briny cliches."[47] Another review observed that the film "seems blinded by its own dazzle."[48]

There was definite hesitation to admire a film based on a ride: "Despite its derivation from a Disney theme-park ride, this is one of the more engaging of the summer blockbusters."[49] The movie was blamed for daring to use a story that had carny origins: "'Pirates of the Caribbean' is an amusement park ride at Disneyland, and now it's a movie based on the ride. Is this a sign of the apocalypse? No, but it does suggest a dearth of inspiration and portends a movie made up entirely of surfaces, filled with air—a shell game with all shells and no pea."[50] The *Portland Tribune* liked it, however, saying it was "a flat-out delightful, hilarious joy ride featuring scoundrels, bounders and edge-of-your-seat thrills....It's an honest-to-God pirate movie, boys and girls, and a really good one at that."[51]

Title: *Once Upon a Time in Mexico*
Release Date: 2003
Role: Sands, a renegade CIA agent
Director: Robert Rodriguez (*Desperado*, 1995; and *Spy Kids* 1–3, 2001–2003)

## TAGLINES:
The Time Has Come.
Legends play by their own rules.

## STORY:
Director Robert Rodriguez directed this third part of his trilogy, an homage to the spaghetti westerns of Sergio Leone. His legendary outlaw, El Mariachi, is pursued by a renegade and corrupt CIA agent, played by Johnny Depp, who recruits him for a job: to prevent the assassination of the president of Mexico. Depp wanted to work with director and writer Rodriguez and take on a role he thought was different: "Here was a chance to play a guy who's a little against the grain of what you'd expect to see in a CIA agent. He wasn't someone who was clichéd or who I felt I had seen before...Sands is a man who has no regard for human life. I've never played someone like that before—who's not a good guy in any way."[52]

Coming out right after *Pirates*, this version of Depp may have been surprising for fans of Jack Sparrow but at least one critic had no trouble with the transition: "Johnny Depp is on a roll. First he swashbuckles off with *Pirates of the Caribbean*. Now he steals every scene he's in as Sands, a rogue CIA agent who doesn't let a small thing like getting his eyes gouged out stop him from a gunfight. He slips on a pair of shades to hide the blood dripping from his peepers and hires a kid to tell him where to aim. You don't want to miss Depp in this movie—he knocks it out of the park."[53]

Title: *Secret Window*
Release Date: 2004
Role: Mort Rainey, an author of successful novels
Director: David Koepp (*Stir of Echoes*, 1999, writer/director; and
    *Panic Room*, 2002, writer/producer)

## TAGLINES:
Some windows should never be opened.

## STORY:
This tale of supposed suspense and maybe even horror from Stephen King found Johnny Depp playing a writer holed up in a cabin by a lake because his wife cheated on him and he can no longer write. It is typical Stephen King territory: "the film lurches tiredly through the author's favorite masochistic-narcissistic fantasy, subjecting a woebegone writer to a gauntlet of abuse."[54] Mort is accused by a creepy farmer from Kentucky of stealing his ideas for a book and Mort is unable to get rid of him. The farmer, played by John Turturro, never looks quite real, and that hints at the source of his claim against Mort.

Depp says that this story about a solitary writer who is stalked by an odd man hit close to home: "It's almost like having my own worst private nightmares come true. I'm paranoid about being watched, and so playing someone who's basically being stalked was a very weird experience."[55] Yet this is not really a stalker film: the twist of the story is that the stalker is not really a farmer from Kentucky but Mort's alter ego, an alternative personality, maybe even his unconscious manifested. It is Mort himself, not a stranger, who frightens Mort, makes him see crazy things, and eventually murders several people. Did Depp miss the point of the story or was he just being coy about the twist?

The movie does little with Depp's abilities as an actor and one reviewer felt that Depp presented a "deliciously baroque take on the writing life" but really was being gracious to yet another film that did not deserve his effort: "another daunting mission accomplished with wit and ingenuity."[56] For another reviewer, "That doesn't mean that it isn't fun to watch Depp, only that it's not fun enough considering his gifts."[57]

Title: *Ils se marièrent et eurent beaucoup d'enfants (And They Lived Happily Ever After)*
    Release Date: 2004
    Role: L'inconnu
    Director: Yvan Attal

## TAGLINES:
-none-

## STORY:
Roger Ebert's comment about Depp's cameo appearance in this French movie perhaps expresses the value of this movie in understanding Depp's career. Depp appears in a silly elevator scene where he makes love to a woman he has just encountered: "Scenes like this cause me to become unreasonably restless. Does Gabrielle know this man is Johnny Depp? Does the movie? Does Depp? Is the movie so cool everybody knows he's *Johnny Depp* but just doesn't say so? Is his appearance intended as an endorsement? Or is he not supposed to be *Johnny Depp*, in which case why was he cast?"[58] We could assume he was cast because he is Johnny Depp and because Johnny Depp represents temptation perhaps better than anyone can.

Title: *Finding Neverland*
    Release Date: 2004
    Role: James M. Barrie, author of *Peter Pan*
    Director: Marc Forster (*Monster Ball*, 2001)

## TAGLINES:
Unlock your imagination.
How far can your imagination take you?
Where will your imagination take you?

## STORY:
Johnny Depp received an Academy Award nomination (one of seven for the film) for best actor in this story about James Matthew Barrie (1860–1937), the man who wrote the play, *Peter Pan, or The Boy Who Wouldn't Grow Up* in 1904. The concept of a boy who never wants to grow up was drawn from Barrie's relationship with the sons of a woman he befriended in early-twentieth-century London and has become a way of explaining the behavior of men who act childish or do not take responsibilities seriously. Both musician Michael Jackson and director Steven Spielberg have

identified with Peter Pan, and Jackson's ranch (where he was accused of molesting children), in Santa Barbara, California, is named Neverland.

Barrie himself has been nearly accused of pedophilia in his dealings with the boys, not in his own time but recently, as scholars have looked at his writings as having, from a contemporary point of view, too much interest in the lives of children. Reviews suggested that this Johnny Depp version of Barrie's life would redeem him from the nasty rumors.

This is another story in which an adherence to accepted reality is banished in favor of the imagination. On its official website, *Finding Neverland* is described as showing "the wonder of the imagination, the nostalgia for childhood innocence and the longing to believe in something more enchanted than everyday life."[59] One review celebrated it for taking you "back to a time in which people—children, in particular—still created whole worlds in their heads, inventing characters and situations as far away as their flights of fancy would take them."[60]

Depp's performance may have impressed the Academy but not all reviewers: "Johnny Depp neither soars nor crashes, but moseys forward with vague purpose and actorly restraint."[61] On the other hand, he impressed others with his portrayal of a man who understands and appreciated children, something that happened to Depp late in life: "Despite his identification with youth, Depp's Barrie is no antic man-child. Nor is he a mugging creep, which is a huge relief, considering the precedent. Depp never stoops to juvenile behavior, never turns himself into the butt of the joke. Instead, he portrays that rare adult who can relate to kids without pandering or condescending."[62]

Title: *The Libertine*
Release Date: 2004
Role: John Wilmot, Earl of Rochester, poet
Director: Laurence Dunmore (no previous credits)

## TAGLINES:
He didn't resist temptation. He pursued it.

## STORY:
What a shock this must have been for audiences expecting the kid-friendly version of Johnny Depp that they met in *Pirates*. In this release, Depp plays John Wilmot, a poet in the court of King Charles II of England who had inherited the title Earl of Rochester. He was known for his witty poetry as well as his perpetual drunkenness and lascivious sexual exploits.

Depp plays Rochester in this movie as "a cross between Casanova and Richard III" and looks like "a debauched rock-star musketeer" in what this critic thinks is probably "the most sexless film about a seducer ever made."[63] When Rochester tells us in his opening monologue that we will not like him because of his odious deeds, we hope he is wrong. The *New York Times* reminds us that the use of Depp in this film is supposed to make Wilmot's life more acceptable: "Mr. Depp's beauty and talent do not lend themselves to our displeasure, and neither does his stardom, which is partly why he was cast."[64]

Depp's connection to the character he plays was explored in one interview. Depp told the author about his own drinking in his early life, "At the time, it was more self-medicating. It never had anything to do with fun for me." The author remembered that, in discussing *The Libertine* on the DVD, Depp used the same words "to describe the alcoholism of the debauched antihero he plays in that wretched movie: it's 'self-medication,' not 'fun.' As an insight into a certain kind of addiction, it isn't earth-shattering, but as a sign of an actor's ability to expose an intimate part of his personal history in even the most far-out characterization, it's tremendously moving."[65]

Title: *Charlie and the Chocolate Factory*
Release Date: 2005
Role: Willie Wonka, an eccentric candy maker
Director: Tim Burton (*Planet of the Apes*, 2001; and *Big Fish*, 2003)

## TAGLINES:
Oompa-Loompas are crazy for Coco-Beans.
The Factory Opens July 2005.
Willy Wonka: Is semi-sweet and nuts.

## STORY:
*Charlie and the Chocolate Factory* brings together three men who have strong visions of how we should view and engage with the world: Roald Dahl, whose perverse children's story was the basis for the movie, Tim Burton whose films always toy with the border between reality and the unreal, and Johnny Depp himself in whom Burton found the ideal representative for his strange imagination. With Jack Sparrow already out there as a contribution to the world's wacky screen characters, it is interesting that so many people enjoyed another bizarre and very different Depp creation: Willie Wonka, a truly weird candy maker who

clearly revels in the torture of bad children and their indulgent parents. Depp commented, "I enjoy playing someone with slightly twisted social skills,"[66] as if Willie Wonka's only problem was not knowing how to treat his guests.

In this story of a boy who wins the chance to visit Willie Wonka's chocolate factory and maybe better his poor family's lot in life, children are seen as obnoxious and spoiled creatures. It is interesting, then, that Depp's children visited him on the set of this movie. As he describes it, "They came to visit me on the set and they walked into my trailer and there I was decked out with the top hat and Prince Valiant hairdo and cha-cha heels and the eyes and the teeth and the rubber gloves. And they just kind of froze, stared at me for what felt like an eternity. Then they got over it and wanted to try everything on. I was so scared when they went to see *Charlie*, so in fear that they were not going to react well to the film. My son, Jack, walked into the house and quoted Wonka and said 'You're really weird.'"[67]

Reviewers often insisted that the creepy character was based on musician Michael Jackson who at the time was involved in a trial for sexually molesting a young boy. The comments were based on Willie Wonka's appearance as a pale-faced androgynous boy-man who acted strangely. Not everyone liked Depp's interpretation and Depp commented about his performance, "I have no idea what I did," he said, which, the interviewer notes, is what he basically says about all his performances. "And I have no idea if it's anywhere near where it needs to be. I can only go by what I feel, and I feel good."[68]

In this post-*Pirates* performance, Depp apparently did not get any negative or anxious feedback from the studios, despite what seems an utterly bizarre character for Hollywood to present to a kiddie audience. Explaining how this made him question what he was doing Depp said, "Frankly, I got worried. Its like something's wrong, because they're not flipping out. I'm not doing my . . . job! But then months into it, Alan Horn, the president of Warner Bros., finally admitted to having felt a little tinge of fear over the initial dailies, and I thought, 'OK, I'm all right.'"[69]

The film was a huge success worldwide, earning $472 million, and candy metaphors filled the reviews for this satisfying treat that was called bittersweet, nutty, and tasty. But a mixed review from the *New York Times* states, "Mr. Burton's movie succeeds in doing what far too few films aimed primarily at children even know how to attempt anymore, which is to feed—even to glut—the youthful appetite for aesthetic surprise"[70] even while it has its flaws. But as Willie Wonka himself states in the movie, "Candy doesn't have to have a point. That's why it's candy."

Title: *Corpse Bride*
Release Date: 2005
Role: the voice of Victor Van Dort, a shy young man scheduled to
  marry
Director: Tim Burton (*Big Fish*, 2003; and *Charlie and the Chocolate
  Factory*, 2005)

## TAGLINES:

Loving You Is Like Loving The Dead.
Rising to the occasion.
There's been a grave misunderstanding.

## STORY:

In his first voiceover work in this stop-motion animation by Tim Burton, Depp plays Victor, a young man who is shy and nervous about his impending nuptials. When he cannot get his vows correct during the wedding rehearsal, he goes into a spooky forest to practice and mistakenly puts his wedding ring on the hand of a dead woman. The woman had been murdered on her wedding night and she claims Victor as her husband, taking him underground to a typically weird and wonderful Tim Burton-esque community of creeps and ghouls.

The puppet Victor resembles Depp, which makes his voicing more than just a disconnected job; Victor is very much like many of Depp's other memorable characters. As Depp himself explains of Victor, he is "a character who isn't so far away from characters I've played in the past for Tim. Edward Scissorhands...outsider, bumbling, deeply insecure, nervous..."[71] The film is also an awakening to the fact that Depp's deep, sexy voice is an important part of his characterizations as well as following the trend that has stars and not anonymous character actors provide the voices for today's animated features.

Was it a film for kids or adults? When Peter Travers of *Rolling Stone* says, "if younger audiences freak out when a green maggot crawls out of the Bride's eye socket, screw 'em," we are not sure of he is attributing that attitude to Tim Burton or holds it himself. He does give Burton credit for a quirky love story: "Victor is attracted to both women. In the guise of a family film, Burton evokes a darkly erotic obsession that recalls Edgar Allan Poe and Hitchcock's *Vertigo*. It would be a test for any filmmaker, and Burton aces it."[72]

Burton is interested in the folklore roots of the story and tells us that "I grew up watching monster movies, which to me are kind of like fables, and I liked how they used a certain kind of symbolism I could relate to. To me, the angry villagers always represented my neighbors. With animation and fables, you can use metaphors more literally, which I always enjoy. So in *Corpse Bride*, the land of the living represents the bureaucratic side of life and the land of the dead is more colourful, more fun, more musical."[73]

Title: *Pirates of the Caribbean: Dead Man's Chest*
Release Date: 2006
Role: Jack Sparrow
Director: Gore Verbinski (*Pirates of the Caribbean: The Curse of the Black Pearl*, 2003)

**TAGLINES:**
Yo Ho, Yo Ho

**STORY:**
It is very likely that never in the history of the cinema has a movie been so harshly raked over the coals by critics even as it raked in the big bucks at the box office. As the *Village Voice* complained, "Of course it's only a summertime sequel, an overinflated, plot-contrivance-by-committee, cheap-shot leviathan, big and graceless as a rusting luxury liner, referencing its hit source movie as if it were a holy gospel, distending gag routines that flopped like a snapper on the dock the first time around. But you were expecting...?"[74] Another characterized it as "pure cinematic junk food, a big, silly summer blockbuster whipped up from virtually nothing."[75]

Yet in its first (4-day) weekend, *Dead Man's Chest* made box office history by taking in $153.8 million in domestic receipts. It became the highest grossing film of 2006 in just two weeks. And it had the single largest one-day box office at $55.5 million. While critics were squabbling over how disappointing the second *Pirates* was, audiences were returning several times to make sense of the complex plot. They did this to the tune of $423 million in the United States and over a billion dollars worldwide by the end of 2006.

The negative attitudes towards the second *Pirates* movie can be partly attributed to the success of the first. One reviewer said, "But, arrrgh, matey, the second installment of what has become a blockbuster franchise," as if that by itself guaranteed it would be unacceptable. The same reviewer continued, "'Dead Man's Chest' has traded spontaneity for spectacle.

Everything in the film is inflated, leaving little room for the fight wit that enlivened its predecessor. . . . The latest Pirates delivers doubloons of adventure and special effects, but we miss the insouciance of the original."[76]

The screenwriters questioned why there were such negative comments on the film even as the audiences filled the theatres: "We try to figure out what the deal is. We made a smart, ambitious film that was not formula. We used literary techniques such as foreshadowing, thematic unity, dramatic irony, etc. We made a payoff line of 'the dichotomy of good and evil.' Our film is visually spectacular and funny. We invented distinctive characters, Davy Jones, Tia Dalma, Bootstrap Bill, and Lord Cutler Beckett, adding them to our pirates universe. This is all stuff the critics would usually love. And they're mauling us."[77]

When Johnny Depp was asked, "Why is this character one you can revisit over and over?" he replied, "I just feel like I'm not done. I just feel like there are more things you could do. Because, I suppose, with a character like this, the parameters are a little broader, so there are more possibilities I think. And he's a fun character to play. I was really not looking forward to saying goodbye to him."[78] And he did not have to, as the third *Pirates* movie came out a year later.

Title: *Pirates of the Caribbean: At World's End*
Release Date: 2007
Role: Jack Sparrow
Director: Gore Verbinski (*Pirates of the Caribbean: Dead Man's Chest*, 2006)

## TAGLINES:
At the End of the World, the Adventure Begins.

## STORY:
Critics were dumbfounded at what they thought was the lack of a plot and a complete loss of narrative coherence in this closer to the *Pirates* trilogy. Christopher Lloyd of the *Indianapolis Star* explained, "I do require a semblance of narrative continuity. You can't get from point A to D in the story without at least touching down on B and C. 'At World's End' jumps ahead to W, backtracks to H, skips L through P and ignores the fact that Q directly contradicts J."[79]

This is the movie critics just loved to hate. Richard Roeper thought, "Not that there's much in the way of actual pirating going on in 'Pirates of the Caribbean: At World's End.' Everyone's too busy restoring life to dead creatures, cracking jokes, debating pirate law (who knew?), lifting curses, switching allegiances and coping with hallucinations, among other problems, to engage in anything so mundane as storming a ship and making off with the loot."[80]

The critics were positively obsessed with the running time of the movie, complaining and even despairing that they had to sit through 168 minutes of pirate action. Many of the complaints came even before the movie came out, with critics just dreading their task ahead, unsure that they could endure the chore, warning that it was ridiculous for director Gore Verbinski to think he needed so much time to wrap up the story. Others just wanted more of Jack Sparrow and they wanted him earlier, as if that would have eased their dread.

*Pirates of the Caribbean: At World's End* began on a Thursday evening in theaters around the world in May 2007. The next day began the big Memorial Day holiday weekend and the movie, opening in a record 4,362 theatres, was expected to bypass the recently set record of *Spiderman 3* for an opening weekend: $151.1 million in North America. But it missed the mark, most likely because of critical early previews and competition from both *Spiderman 3* and *Shrek 3*. But by the end of the weekend, *At World's End* had a North American box office of $139.8 million for the four-day period. After four weeks, its figures were $274 million domestic and $821 million worldwide.

Will there be a sequel? If you stay for the credits you are rewarded with a scene afterwards of Will Turner returning with the *Flying Dutchman* and Elizabeth waiting to greet him along with their 10-year-old son. It looks like the pirate tradition will be passed on.

Ultimately the *Pirates* movies do perfectly what movies are supposed to do. They take us to worlds we ourselves cannot encounter; they show us people and incidents we could not have imagined; and they present actions that, while not in any way resembling those in our everyday live, are abstract models of how to behave, think, and react under particular circumstances. What is interesting about the entire *Pirates* franchise, but especially this final episode, is that there is a relentless challenge of the everyday. Not only are pirates inherently a challenge to the status quo, but *At World's End* has a touch of old-fashioned surrealism with multiple Jacks appearing throughout the movie and in various forms. And as Jack points out in this story, Up is Down, and as a result we need to read our maps differently if we are to make our way in the world.

## NOTES

1. John H. Richardson, "The Unprocessed Johnny Depp," *Esquire* 141, no 5 (May 2004).

2. Chris Nashawaty, "Johnny Depp," *Entertainment Weekly* 1, no. 729 (September 19, 2003).

3. Chris Heath, "Johnny Depp: Portrait of the Oddest as a Young Man," *Details*, May, 1993, http://www.johnnydeppfan.com/interviews/details.htm (accessed August 15, 2007).

4. "Johnny Depp interview," YOUTUBE.com, http://www.youtube.com/watch?v=V2E43RbVoI4&mode, (accessed August 15, 2007).

5. Chris Willman, "From Baby Face to 'Cry-Baby' Profile: Johnny Depp of Fox's '21 Jump Street' Plays a Juvenile Delinquent in His First Starring Film Role. The Teen Idol Insists He'll Never Do Another TV Series Again," *Los Angeles Times*, April 4, 1990, F1, http://www.johnnydeppfan.com/interviews/latimes90.htm (accessed August 15, 2007).

6. Bill Zehme, "Sweet Sensation: On the Cutting Edge with Johnny Depp, the Offbeat Hero of *Edward Scissorhands*," *Rolling Stone*, January 10, 1991, http://www.johnnydeppfan.com/interviews/rolstone.htm (accessed August 15, 2007).

7. Johnny Depp, interview with John Waters, *Interview*, April 1999, http://www.johnnydeppfan.com/interviews/interviewmagapril90.htm (accessed August 15, 2007).

8. Christophe d'Yvoire, "Johnny Depp by Johnny Depp," *Studio Magazine*, February 2000, http://www.johnnydeppfan.com/interviews/studio00b.htm (accessed August 15, 2007).

9. *Life Story*, 40.

10. Chris Heath, "Johnny Depp: Portrait of the Oddest as a Young Man," *Details*, May, 1993, http://www.johnnydeppfan.com/interviews/details.htm (accessed August 15, 2007).

11. Peter Travers, "Benny and Joon," *Rolling Stone*, no. 656 (May 13, 1993), http://www.rollingstone.com/reviews/movie/5948331/review/5948332/benny_and_joon (accessed August 15, 2007).

12. Chris Heath, "Johnny Depp: Portrait of the Oddest as a Young Man," *Details*, May, 1993, http://www.johnnydeppfan.com/interviews/details.htm (accessed August 15, 2007).

13. Quoted in Meikle, 117.

14. All quotes from *The Haunted World of Edward D. Wood, Jr.*, a film by Brett Thompson, Image Entertainment, 1996.

15. John H. Richardson, "The Unprocessed Johnny Depp," *Esquire* 141, no 5 (May 2004).

16. Roger Ebert, "Don Juan DeMarco," *Chicago Sun-Times*, April 7, 1995, http://rogerebert.suntimes.com/apps/pbcs.dll/article?AID=/19950407/REVIEWS/504070304/1023 (accessed August 15, 2007).

17. Gary Sussman, *"Dead Man Talking,"* http://72.166.46.24/alt1/archive/movies/reviews/05-09-96/DEAD_BAR.html (accessed January 19, 2007).

18. Kevin Sessums, "Johnny Be Good," *Vanity Fair,* February 1997, http://interview.johnnydepp-zone2.com/1997_02VanityFair.html (accessed August 15, 2007).

19. d'Yvoire, "Johnny Depp by Johnny Depp," February 2000.

20. "Cherokee should decide who is Cherokee, not Congress," Cherokee Nation, June 21, 2007, http://www.cherokee.org/PressRoom/story.aspx?id=lmJYbKQs8Fk= (accessed August 15, 2007); also see the work of anthropologist Circe Sturm on Cherokee identity: Circe Sturm, *Blood Politics: Race, Culture and Identity in the Cherokee Nation of Oklahoma* (University of California Press, Berkeley: 2002), pp. 2–4; also see Evelyn Nieves, "Putting to a Vote the Question, 'Who Is Cherokee?'" *New York Times,* March 3, 2007, p. A9.

21. "The Gypsy," The Johnny Depp Zone Interview Archive, http://interview.johnnydepp-zone2.com/1998.html (accessed August 15, 2007).

22. Jaques-Andre Bondy, "Johnny Goes to Cannes," *Premiere,* http://jabondy.free.fr/255Depp/3UK.html (accessed August 15, 2007).

23. Johanna Schneller, "Where's Johnny?" *Premiere,* December 1999, http://interview.johnnydepp-zone2.com/1999_12Premiere.html (accessed August 15, 2007).

24. Roger Ebert, "Fear and Loathing in Las Vegas," *Chicago Sun Times,* May 22, 1998, http://rogerebert.suntimes.com/apps/pbcs.dll/article?AID=/19980522/REVIEWS/805220303/1023 (accessed August 15, 2007).

25. John H. Richardson, "The Unprocessed Johnny Depp," *Esquire* 141, no 5 (May 2004).

26. Carrie Rickey, "Polanski Would-Be Thriller 'Ninth Gate': Devil Without A Cause," *Philadelphia Inquirer,* March 10, 2000, 3.

27. Cintra Wilson, "Viva Las Vegas," Salon.com, May 22, 1998, http://archive.salon.com/ent/movies/review/2000/03/10/ninth_gate/index.html?CP=SAL&DN=110 (accessed August 15, 2007).

28. IMDb user comments for *The Astronaut's Wife,* http://www.imdb.com/title/tt0138304/usercomments?filter=chrono;start=150 (accessed August 15, 2007).

29. Michael Sragow, "Depp Delves into the Stories behind His Characters," *Baltimore Sun,* July 14, 2006.

30. Steve Rea, "Depp Perception," *Philadelphia Inquirer,* November 21, 1999, Section I, 1.

31. Elvis Mitchell, " 'The Man Who Cried': Big Moments, Beautiful but Mysterious," *New York Times,* May 25, 2001, 14.

32. Christophe d'Yvoire, "Johnny Depp by Johnny Depp," *Studio Magazine,* February 2000, http://www.johnnydeppfan.com/interviews/studio00b.htm (accessed August 15, 2007).

33. David Rooney, "Before Night Falls," *Variety,* September 5, 2000, http://www.variety.com/review/VE1117788012.html?categoryid=31&cs=1&p=0 (accessed August 15, 2007).

34. Charles Taylor, "Chocolat," December 15, 2000, Salon.com, http://archive. salon.com/ent/movies/review/2000/12/15/chocolat/index.html (accessed August 15, 2007).

35. "When the Road Bends: Tales of a Gypsy Caravan," gypsycaravanmovie. com, http://www.whentheroadbends.com/ (accessed August 15, 2007).

36. J. Hoberman, "Social Aspirations," *Village Voice,* April 2, 2001, http:// www.villagevoice.com/film/0114,hoberman,23550,20.html (accessed August 15, 2007).

37. A. O. Scott, "'Blow': Under the Influence, a Drug Dealer Gets His Due," *New York Times,* April 6, 2001, http://www.nytimes.com/2001/04/06/ arts/06BLOW.html?ex=1187409600&en=1abd1cffd520123f&ei=5070 (accessed August 15, 2007).

38. Stephen Hunter, " 'From Hell': Gripper On Jack the Ripper," *Washington Post,* October 19, 2001, http://www.washingtonpost.com/ac2/wp-dyn/A18750-2001Oct18 (accessed August 15, 2007).

39. Elvis Mitchell, "A Conspiracy Shrouded in London Fog," *New York Times,* October 19, 2001.

40. IMDb, User comments for *From Hell,* http://pro.imdb.com/title/tt0120681/ usercomments (accessed August 15, 2007).

41. Pirates of the Caribbean: Curse of the Black Pearl screenplay, wordplayer. com, http://www.wordplayer.com/archives/PIRATES.intro.html (accessed August 15, 2007).

42. John H. Richardson, "The Unprocessed Johnny Depp," *Esquire* 141, no 5 (May 2004).

43. Mark Binelli, "The Last Buccaneer," *Rolling Stone,* July 13, 2006, http:// www.rollingstone.com/news/story/10714717/the_last_buccaneer (accessed August 15, 2007).

44. Ibid.

45. Gregory Katz, "An American in Paris," *USA Weekend,* July 6, 2003, http://www. usaweekend.com/03_issues/030706/030706johnny_depp.html (accessed August 15, 2007).

46. Paul Fischer, "Johnny Depp, Pirates of the Caribbean: Dead Man's Chest Interview," girl.com.au, http://www.girl.com.au/johnny-depp-pirates-of-the-caribbean-interview.htm (accessed August 15, 2007).

47. Peter Travers, "Pirates of the Caribbean: The Curse of the Black Pearl," *Rolling Stone,* February 2, 2004, http://www.rollingstone.com/reviews/ movie/6162831/review/5989931/pirates_of_the_caribbean_the_curse_of_the_ black_pearl (accessed August 15, 2007).

48. Stephanie Zacharek, "Pirates of the Caribbean: Curse of the Black Pearl," *Salon.com,* July 9, 2003, http://dir.salon.com/story/ent/movies/review/2003/07/09/ pirates/index.html?CP=IMD&DN=110 (accessed August 15, 2007).

49. Kevin Lally, "Pirates of the Caribbean: Curse of the Black Pearl," *Film Journal International* 106, no. 8 (August 2003).

50. Mike LaSalle, "Treasure Chest of Effects Can't Save 'Pirates" Two-Bit Story," *San Francisco Chronicle*, July 9, 2003, D-1, http://www.sfgate.com/cgi-bin/ article.cgi?f=/c/a/2003/07/09/DD285630.DTL (accessed August 16, 2007).

51. Dawn Taylor, "Come Aboard for High Jinks on High Seas: Johnny Depp Shines Amid Swashbuckling Fun," *The Portland Tribune*, July 11, 2003, http:// www.portlandtribune.com/features/story.php?story_id=19096 (accessed August 16, 2007).

52. See the official *Once Upon A Time In Mexico* website, http://www.sonypic tures.com/movies/onceuponatimeinmexico/site/mexico.html (accessed August 16, 2007).

53. Peter Travers, "Once Upon a Time in Mexico," *Rolling Stone*, September 8, 2003, http://www.rollingstone.com/reviews/movie/5949515/review/5949516/once_ upon_a_time_in_mexico (accessed August 16, 2007).

54. Dennis Lin, "Despite Star's Best Efforts, Corny Thriller Goes off the Depp End: *Secret Window*," *Village Voice*, March 17–23, 2004, http://www.villagevoice. com/film/0411,lim2,51871,20.html (accessed August 16, 2007).

55. "An interview with Johnny Depp," handbag.com, http://www.handbag. com/gossip/celebrityinterviews/johnnydepp04/ (accessed August 16, 2007).

56. Dennis Lin, "Despite Star's Best Efforts, Corny Thriller Goes off the Depp End: *Secret Window*," *Village Voice*, March 17–23, 2004, http://www.villagevoice. com/film/0411,lim2,51871,20.html (accessed August 16, 2007).

57. Manohla Dargis, "Secret Window: 'Secret Window' Takes a Stab at Both. But It Misses, Even with Johnny Depp Delivering a Performance that Tickles the Funny Bone," *Los Angeles Times*, March 12, 2004, http://www.calendarlive. com/movies/dargis/cl-et-dargis12mar12,0,6661709.story (accessed August 16, 2007).

58. Roger Ebert, "Happily Ever After," *Chicago Sun-Times*, July 29, 2005, http:// rogerebert.suntimes.com/apps/pbcs.dll/article?AID=/20050728/REVIEWS/ 50713004/1023 (accessed August 16, 2007).

59. The same information is at "Finding Neverland," RottenTomatoes.com, http://www.rottentomatoes.com/m/finding_neverland/about.php (accessed August 16, 2007).

60. Steve Davis, "Finding Neverland," *The Austin Chronicle*, December 10, 2004, http://www.austinchronicle.com/gyrobase/Calendar/Film?Film=oid% 3A240860 (accessed August 16, 2007).

61. Manohla Dargis, "A Never-Impolite Land Where One Never Grows Up," *New York Times*, November 12, 2004, http://movies2.nytimes.com/2004/11/12/ movies/12neve.html?ex=1182398400&en=7e9408ff2e8a85bb&ei=5070 (accessed August 16, 2007).

62. Carina Chocano, "Finding Neverland: One Man's Escape from the Darkness of Adulthood," *Los Angeles Times*, November 12, 2004, http://www.calendar live.com/movies/chocano/cl-et-neverland12nov12,0,1509829.story (accessed August 16, 2007).

63. Owen Gleiberman, "The Libertine," *Entertainment Weekly*, November 22, 2005, http://www.ew.com/ew/article/0,,1133613,00.html (accessed August 16, 2007).

64. Manohla Dargis, "A Noble With Big, and Fatal, Appetites," *New York Times*, November 25, 2005, http://movies2.nytimes.com/2005/11/25/movies/25libe.html?ei=5070&en=e20e7f1d8e17b1f0&ex=1181188800&adxnnl=1&adxnnlx=11810 56256–9RNHHJz301RNYePnyPyHXg (accessed August 16, 2007).

65. Michael Sragow, "Depp Delves into the Stories behind His Characters," *Baltimore Sun*, July 14, 2006.

66. Rob Alicea, "Johnny Depp," TheCinemaSource.com, http://www.thecine masource.com/v3/spotlight.php?id=153&wordcount=0 (accessed August 16, 2007).

67. Ray Dademo, "Johnny Depp," TheCinemaSource.com, http://www.thecinemasource.com/v3/spotlight.php?id=192&wordcount=0 (accessed August 16, 2007).

68. Erik Hedegaard, "Johnny Depp: He's Found Neverland with The Woman He Loves and Their Kids, but 'Rage Is Still Never Far Away,' " *Rolling Stone*, no. 967 (February 10, 2005), http://www.rollingstone.com/news/coverstory/johnny_depp_found_neverland (accessed August 16, 2007).

69. Ibid.

70. A. O. Scott, "Looking for the Candy, Finding a Back Story," *New York Times*, July 15, 2005, http://movies2.nytimes.com/2005/07/15/movies/15char.html?ex=1 181188800&en=b49a1640282d7f00&ei=5070 (accessed August 16, 2007).

71. Ray Dademo, "Johnny Depp," TheCinemaSource.com, http://www.thecinemasource.com/v3/spotlight.php?id=192&wordcount=0 (accessed August 16, 2007).

72. Peter Travers, "Tim Burton's *Corpse Bride*" *Rolling Stone*, September.

73. Tim Burton, "Corpse Bride? It's Just a Love Story with Skeletons," *The Guardian*, October 14, 2005, http://arts.guardian.co.uk/filmandmusic/story/0,,1591186,00.html (accessed August 16, 2007).

74. Michael Atkinson, "Treasure Chest: Well-Oiled Assembly-Line Sequel is Pure Make-Believe," *Village Voice*, July 5, 2006, http://www.villagevoice.com/film/0627,atkinson,73745,20.html (accessed August 16, 2007).

75. Sean Axmaker, "Johnny Depp and the 'Pirates 2' Crew Invite You Aboard," *Seattle Post-Intelligencer*, July 5, 2006, http://seattlepi.nwsource.com/movies/276531_pirates06q.html (accessed August 16, 2007).

76. Rex Roberts, "Pirates of the Caribbean: Dead Man's Chest," *Film Journal International* 109, no. 8 (August 2006).

77. Terry Rossio, "Nine Pieces of Eight-2006," WordplayArchives, wordplayer.com, http://www.wordplayer.com/archives/rossio08.Nine.Pieces.html (accessed August 16, 2007).

78. Paul Fischer, "Johnny Depp, Pirates of the Caribbean: Dead Man's Chest Interview," http://www.girl.com.au/johnny-depp-pirates-of-the-caribbean-interview.htm (accessed August 16, 2007).

79. Christopher Lloyd, "Arrrrgh! 'Pirates 3' is a chaotic, confusing mess," IndyStar.com, May 25, 2007, (accessed May 25, 2007; no longer online).

80. Richard Roeper, "Techno World: Visual Effects, Cinematic Mastery Saves Illogical Third 'Pirates,' " *Albany Times Union*, May 24, 2007.

# Chapter 11

# "JOHNNY ARE YOU QUEER?":
# A PIRATE'S LIFE FOR US

At 4 A.M. on an early summer's day in 2006, dozens of females (and a smattering of males), dressed in an indefinable style somewhere between old-fashioned goth and new-fangled pirate, lined up to enter Disneyland, The Happiest Place on Earth as one entrance sign proclaims. Their happiness hinged on getting in early in order to find a spot along Main Street USA, Walt Disney's homage to middle America and simpler American times. When the gates of the Anaheim, California, park opened unusually early at 6:30 A.M., the teens and 20-somethings rushed in to stake out their territories in front of the clothing shops and souvenir emporiums that lined the main entrance to the Magic Kingdom. Throughout the day the crowd grew, taking the places on the curb usually reserved for kids and families waiting for a Disney parade about dreams that come true.

That day, instead of the usual array of princesses and Goofy imitators, Disneyland belonged to pirates—fans of the Pirates of the Caribbean film franchise. That day was the world premiere of the second film in the series, *Pirates of the Caribbean: Dead Man's Chest,* and all three of the wildly adored stars—Keira Knightly, Orlando Bloom, and Johnny Depp—were scheduled to appear that evening on the red carpet, which by show time extended from the park entrance to the giant screen erected near the original Pirates of the Caribbean ride. The park closed the rides early but stayed open for those wanting a glimpse of some of the most famous stars and celebrities around. The first *Pirates* movie had also premiered at Disneyland in a similar scenario although not as large. By the time the third movie premiered, in May of 2007, the event was enormous and had a new twist: guests not associated with the movie could buy tickets to walk the red carpet and see the first showing of the movie, all for $1,500 a ticket. The tickets easily sold out, with most of the proceeds going to the Make-A-Wish Foundation.[1]

Throughout the day of the second premiere, pirates were everywhere. It was like stepping back into the past, like being transported to a clean and safe version of the Island of Tortuga. Adults and kids were decked out in an array of costume parts that suggested an alliance with the pirate lifestyle: dreadlocks and swords and flashy rings and three-cornered hats mixed with strollers and digital cameras and souvenir autograph books with Minnie and Mickey signatures. A spectacular entrance was erected during the day, featuring a huge pirate sign arching over the street.

The park closed early and all the guests who were staying crammed onto Main Street, behind the loyal fans who had waited all day for a front-row seat to the Hollywood event. The famous included an amazing range of those we elevate to star status: sports greats Kareem Abdul-Jabbar and Pat Riley, the Miami Heat coach; actors Jennifer Love Hewitt, Helen Mirren, and Martin Landau, as well as Ashley Tisdale of *High School Musical*; musician and Depp-pal Marilyn Manson and *American Idol* runner-up Ace Young; and *Titanic* and *Terminator* director James Cameron. *Pirates* director Gore Verbinski was there as was Jerry Bruckheimer, famed producer of blockbusters, including the *Pirates* movies. Anybody with kids or clout showed up. Mickey was dressed as a pirate too. California Governor and former superstar Arnold Schwarzenegger got perhaps the most crowd and media attention until Keira Knightly, then Orlando Bloom, then Johnny Depp touched the red carpet. When they did, the crowd exploded and the frenzy was stunning, even in comparison to other star-studded movie premieres.

Knightly was ethereal in a white gown and styled hair and came earlier than her male costars, working her way fairly quickly along Main Street. Bloom and Depp went casual, Depp sporting a fedora that made it easy to spot his slow progress through the crowd. Along the way the three *Pirates* stars stopped to sign autographs and take pictures with fans.[2] But after some minutes of working with the fans, and with the movie showing at least an hour behind schedule, Johnny Depp and Orlando Bloom suddenly took a right off of Main Street and disappeared into some of the faux-Victorian buildings. The crowd was stunned as the frenzy suddenly died, and many disappointed fans could be heard complaining that they had waited hours only to be abandoned. All the television interviewers, set up on brightly lit platforms past the turnoff point, were as confused as the fans. Disney "cast members" finally reported that the stars were just taking a break and soon they returned to the endless interviews, signings, and photos. As the invitation-only movie premiere started, fans were required to leave the park.

The pirate frenzy continued the next day when Disneyland reopened the Pirates of the Caribbean attraction after a 4-month refurbishment. A Disney map to the park had a full-page spread of Jack Sparrow swinging near the Magic Kingdom castle with a tagline that read: "Dead Men Tell New Tales." It continued, "On June 26th, Captain Jack comes aboard the classic attraction." Disney hotel guests lined up for the early morning opening and were entertained by singing and joking pirates. By the time the park opened for the public, the line was all the way down Main Street and took over an hour to get through. The ride was crowded for weeks afterwards. Even the Star Wars fans, there for an unofficial gathering, were overwhelmed by the pirate atmosphere.

The Pirates of the Caribbean attraction (commonly called POTC, as is the movie franchise) was designed in part by Walt Disney and opened in March 1967, a few months after Disney's death. It was placed in New Orleans Square, the first entire land added to the original Disneyland, which opened in 1955. The pirate attraction was originally designed as a wax museum but after the New York World's Fair (1964–1965) and the Disney work shown there with the animated statues known as Audio-Animatronics®, the pirates came alive in the attraction.[3] There is also a Pirates of the Caribbean attraction at Walt Disney World in Florida, at Tokyo Disney, and at Disneyland Paris. While adding the movie elements to the California version, Disney also updated the attraction with new sound and visual effects and improved the look of several treasure scenes.[4]

The POTC ride takes passengers who have boarded a boat down a waterfall, past scenes of pirate booty and long dead skeleton pirates, through a battle between a pirate ship and a fort, and through a burning looted town which features drunken pirates who auction off the local women, torture the mayor by dunking, and steal rum and treasures. Some fans of the ride find it an open narrative, ready for their personal interpretation. One fan said, "'I've never been able to figure out if the ride tells a real story. It's really just a vignette of images without any underlying narrative. It's like a Latin Mass. Not understanding it means you'll project more personal meaning into it."[5] Objections to the depiction of pirates chasing and auctioning women resulted in a brief revamping of the ride for political correctness in the 1990s, but calls of "We wants the redhead" are again audible and the pirates once again chase women for their bodies and not the food they were carrying in the PC days.

The refurbished ride did not eliminate many of the traditional elements but added the movie characters to the scenes. Jack Sparrow appeared twice hiding in the town and the audio now advises that town officials are searching for him. He also appears at the end of the ride as the boats go up a waterfall. He is sitting in a chair surrounded by treasures and drinking rum. The ride's Jack Sparrow is eerie, imitating perfectly the jerky movements and strange head turns that Depp gave to the screen version. Depp is shown in several television specials about the reopened ride looking at his character close up and saying, "That's insane" and "Absolutely amazing." "The gestures and the movement of the eyes," he says of his replica, "is staggering."[6]

The reopened attraction also features an animatronics appearance by Captain Barbossa on the battling pirate ship, and a projection of the image of Davy Jones on a misty screen that the ride boats float through. The last effect is impressive and captures the creepiness of the legendary squid-faced captain. Animatronic additions of Will Turner and Elizabeth Swann (Orlando Bloom and Keira Knightly) to either the Pirates ride or a related attraction have also been speculated.[7] The first *Pirates* movie makes many references to the ride including using the "Yo Ho, Yo Ho, A Pirate's Life for Me" song and having a mongrel dog refuse to give prisoners the jail door key. The same elements reappear in the third movie, *At World's End* (2007), and at one point in the movie, when the pirates fall down a waterfall, sounds from the Disneyland ride can be heard during a darkened screen.

Universal Studios and MGM Studios are theme parks entirely based on movies and television programs so the idea is not an unusual one. Making a movie based on a Disneyland park attraction was nevertheless treated as an odd idea when the *Pirates* movie was first announced and again when it came out. The *New York Times* snidely asked, "The action comedy 'Pirates of the Caribbean: Curse of the Black Pearl' raises one of the most overlooked and important cinematic questions of our time: Can a movie maintain the dramatic integrity of a theme park ride?"[8] What they did not understand is that Disney always designed its rides with a strong narrative element and translating that to a movie narrative strengthened both theme park source and the motion picture offspring.

Nevertheless, critics still blamed the connection to the theme ride for their disappointment with the films, a blame game still being played out with the third movie, *At World's End*. As one major newspaper reviewed it, "Look, I realize this isn't Ingmar Bergman here. Big-budget summer movies are supposed to be flashy and fun. These flicks are based on a theme park ride, for Pete's sake,"[9] as if that connection automatically determines the quality of the storytelling. The *Associated Press* continued the analogy: "For better and for worse, the latest "Pirates of the Caribbean" actually resembles the Disney amusement park ride that inspired the series more than its predecessors (with traces of the "It's a Small World" ride thrown in for good measure)."[10] *The Arizona Republic* explained, "The movie is always fun to look at, and even after three, the filmmakers manage to capture the feel of the Disneyland ride. The movie gives us a ride as well. Just one that goes around a few too many corners."[11] In the *Baltimore Sun*, the problem was that the third film was not close to its theme park roots and so it rated the movie a D+: "The first Pirates of the Caribbean turned a Disneyland attraction into a ripsnorting movie. The second took the franchise back to its carnival roots, with its clawed and tentacled Davy Jones and his humanoid aquarium of a crew. But theme-park rides do a better job of spacing out peak thrills than *Pirates of the Caribbean: At World's End*."[12]

The move back and forth between movies and their theme park manifestations was common for Disney. Many of the early Fantasyland rides at Disneyland came from animated classics like *Dumbo* (1941), *Peter Pan* (1953), *Snow White and the Seven Dwarfs* (1937), and *Pinocchio* (1940). In 2002, Disney released *The Country Bears* which was based on the Country Bears Jamboree Audio-Animatronics® show which oddly was removed from Disneyland before the movie came out (the attraction still exists at Tokyo Disney and Walt Disney World). The movie was unpopular. The popular Tower of Terror ride was based on a 1997 mediocre television movie. And after the first *Pirates* was released, the movie *Haunted Mansion* with Eddie Murphy did well at the box office. Every October until January, Disneyland makes its Haunted Mansion over into a redecorated *The Nightmare Before Christmas* (1993) themed ride, celebrating the spooky world of Tim Burton's animated movie. Disneyland is also preparing a *Finding Nemo* (2003) ride for opening in 2007.

Pirate movies in film history have had a mixed reception. Some are considered movie classics: *Captain Blood* (1935, with Errol Flynn), *Crimson Pirate* (1952, with Burt Lancaster), and Disney's own *Treasure Island* (1950). Others like Steven Spielberg's *Hook* (1991) were box office successes but had mixed critical reception (the *Los Angeles Reader* titled its negative review, "Pan Ick"[13]). Many pirate movies have been real stinkers; 1995's *Cutthroat Island*, starring Geena Davis and directed by her boyfriend Renny Harlin, is considered the biggest box office flop of all history. The movie cost approximately $100 million to make and garnered only $11 million or so at the box office. As one review explained it, "It takes a two-hour act of will to keep facing the screen during this moribund movie. Every cliffhanger is enough to make you a cliff jumper."[14] Pirates have appeared regularly in other Disney animations and live action films including in *Peter Pan* (1953), *Treasure Planet* (2002), *Return to Never Land* (2002), *Muppet Treasure Island* (1996), *Swiss Family Robinson* (1960), *The Little Mermaid* (1989), and *Shipwrecked* (1990).

Pirates have stormed American popular culture since the opening of the first *Pirates of the Caribbean* movie. Pirate books, including classics like *Treasure Island* by Robert Louis Stevenson (written in 1883), have shown up on middle school summer reading lists, and pirate literature for both kids and adults is expanding. An amazing array of pirate encyclopedias like *Pirateology*,[15] along with novels, pop-up books, non-fiction accounts of real pirates, and fictional accounts for all ages now overflow in bookstores. Merchandise and tie-ins abound: you can wear a pirate t-shirt sitting in your pirate-themed bedroom,[16] painted with *Pirates* paint colors from The Home Depot,[17] sporting a Jack Sparrow ring, and watching television documentaries about real pirates[18] as you sip your pirate-themed Coke and eat your pirate themed snack bars, cereal, chocolate bars or M&Ms. You can play pirate poker and fly a pirate kite or read a pirate fan magazine[19] and play with your pirate action figures, board games, pinball machine, or video games. There are pirate windsocks and shot glasses, dolls and mouse pads, underwear, Band-Aids, and toilet paper. A kite and toy store (Air Circus) on the boardwalk in Ocean City, New Jersey, now carries so much pirate stuff that people commonly call it "the pirate store" and new business cards sport the name "Pirates Arrrgh Us."

Legoland, an amusement park in southern California that is based on the LEGO building toy, has developed an entire pirate experience called Pirate Shores as well as a line of *Pirates* building sets.[20] In 2007, Disneyland changed its venerable Tom Sawyer Island into a Pirate's Lair, inhabited by wenches and pirates and objects from the movies.[21] For those wishing to investigate the pirate life even more, the 2006 Renaissance Faire in Pennsylvania featured a pirate's weekend that was attended by thousands of people, many in pirate gear. For 2007, the Invasion of the Pirates weekend promises more of the same exciting excess of swaggering Jack Sparrow clones, exquisitely costumed adults, and pirate-themed activities.[22] And once an activity goes mainstream, it has a convention: for pirates there is PyrateCon, a conference to celebrate pirates, buccaneers, and privateers held in New Orleans in April, 2007. The description reads, "Aye, three days of gallivantin' with scallywags in the Tortuga of the South, dancin' the jig to piratical bands, swaggerin' through the historic French Quarter in a pirate parade, crowning the Pirate King and Queen and their court!! How can ye resist, mate?"[23] Pirate fairs and events were scheduled throughout the country the summer that the second and third pirate movies opened.

September 19th is the International Talk Like A Pirate Day.[24] Dave Barry, in his blog for the *Miami Herald,* joked, "This blog has no doubt that this event will some day be considered the high-water mark of Western civilization."[25] A spoof of language instruction videos that teaches piratespeak can prepare landlubbers of the event.[26]

A reality-based television program called *Pirate Master* began the week after the third installment of the Disney *Pirates* franchise opened and was a direct spawn of their popularity. *Pirate Master's* description reads, "Sixteen modern-day pirates embark on a high seas adventure around the Caribbean island of Dominica in search of hidden treasure that will total $1 million. Only one pirate will win the largest booty and claim the title of 'Pirate Master.'"[27] They will live for 33 days aboard a 179-foot boat and engage in machinations similar to those on the long-running television series *Survivor* (they have the same creator and executive producer, Mark Burnett). As with all pirate adventures, law and order will battle with greed, betrayal and sabotage. As Burnett explains on the show's website, "Pirate Master breaks new ground in that it's the collision of fantasy and reality. This is a show where, in true pirate fashion, anything can happen with a group of people that live by their own set of rules and usually break them. It's adventure, excitement and loads of treasure. Anyone who ever wanted to be a pirate will love this show!"[28]

And that might just be a lot of people. Ah, pirates. For ages, and in many regions around the world, pirates have been nearly mythological characters, figures that appear in both real histories and fabulously constructed fictions. In a 1992 exhibit at the National Maritime Museum in London called *Pirates: Fact and Fiction,* these stories were sorted out but pirates were no less wonderful in light of the clarifications. The exhibit was so popular it was kept up for three years instead of the originally planned three months. Pirates have existed since ancient times, wherever and whenever merchants moved materials over the seas and oceans. A pirate is defined as someone who "robs and plunders on the sea" and there are records of pirates from the Greek and Roman periods, among the Vikings, in the Netherlands, on the Mediterranean, in the English Channel, the Red Sea and the Persian Gulf, and the coast of India and the South China Sea.[29]

Pirates still exist today, especially in the South China Sea and the Indian Ocean. One of the most infamous recent acts of piracy, which today is labeled "terrorism," was the 1985 *Achille Lauro* incident during which four men from the Palestine Liberation Front boarded the cruise ship and murdered an American named Leon Klinghoffer. The story was compelling enough to be made into a movie and an opera.[30]

In the Western world, especially the New World, piracy reached its Golden Age in a time period generally accepted to range from 1650 to 1725, and peaking around 1720 when there were about 2,000 pirates in the Atlantic.[31] Gold and silver from the Americas were sent back to Europe and the ships carrying them were less armed and had smaller crews than the pirate ships.[32] It is from tales and factual reports from this period, later translated into plays, novels, poems, musicals, illustrated books, and movies, that we get our current image of the pirate. The pirates depicted in *Pirates of the Caribbean* are working at the tail end of this golden age. As the third movie makes clear, piracy was dying in the 1720s and the last stand against the commercialization of piracy into a form called privateering would signal the end of the romantic pirate period.

All these pirate stories from fact and fiction present us with characters who live by a simple rule: defy the conventions and laws of regular society and do whatever you want whenever you want. This is the essence of a pirate. In *Pirates of the Caribbean: Dead Man's Chest*, Jack Sparrow confronts Elizabeth Swann about her own pirate-like actions, which she denies define her as a pirate. Jack suggests the two are alike because they both act like pirates: "We are very much alike, you and I, I and you, us," says Jack. Elizabeth replies, "Except for a sense of honor and decency and a moral center...and personal hygiene." Jack teases, "You will come over to my side, I know it....One word, love: curiosity. You long for freedom. You long to do what you want to do because you want it, to act on selfish impulse. You want to see what it's like. One day, you won't be able to resist."

That day comes near the end of the movie. As the mythological sea creature, the kraken, threatens to take down their vessel, Elizabeth boldly kisses Jack as the crew abandons ship. But this is no ordinary kiss as Elizabeth deftly chains Jack's hand to the ship even as she breathlessly locks lips with him. "It's after you, not the ship," she says, desperately trying to explain why she both passionately kissed the man and condemned him to die by attaching him to the ship he has loved as much as any woman. "It's not us," she continues but we do not know if the "us" is her and Jack or her and the rest of the crew, including her lover, Will, who is already in the longboat. "This is the only way, don't you see?" she continues as she keeps her lips inches from Jack's, ready to indulge her passions again. She moves towards him and then gritting her teeth pulls back and says, "I'm not sorry." She leaves and the kraken takes Jack and the ship down to Davy Jones's locker.

Elizabeth had previously been horrified at the idea of consorting with pirates. In the first movie, she secretly stole a pirate's medallion from Will

Turner when he was a boy, fearing it would have marked him as a pirate. When they talk about it years later, she said she took it "because I was afraid that you were a pirate," and in fact he is, by blood from a pirate family. So when Elizabeth kisses Jack before the kraken takes him, he grins at her and utters only one word to prove he was right: "Pirate."

Perhaps it is true what Johnny Depp is quoted as saying in a film magazine geared for teens and tweens: "Isn't it every boy's dream to be a pirate and get away with basically anything? Who wouldn't want to play—or watch—a pirate?"[33] *Pirates* director Gore Verbinski sees pirate stories as a basic form of storytelling: "There's something primal about pirates. For me, pirate movies have always been about characters obtaining their desires—ultimately through piracy—and the good and bad that comes with it."[34] He also advised, "I love pirates. There's a nine-year-old inside us all that just loves pirates."[35]

So why are we so interested in pirates and just what do they do for us? Do we have Jack Sparrow to thank for reinvigorating pirate lore or should we blame him for our plunging into the depths of pirate-like behavior that is rude, crude, and unacceptable? Should we really celebrate pirates and act like them? The clothing and the food and the toys are ways for all of us to participate in the pirate culture. The earrings and headscarves and pirate jargon—Arrrgh, matey!—are ways of taking the stories into our everyday lives and acting out small bits of the movies, often with unexpected results. For example, on opening day for the third *Pirates* movie, the suburban crowd outside Philadelphia filled the theater an hour ahead of the start of the movie. The crowd was festive; many (adults even more than kids) dressed in pirate gear. One group played Pirate's Dice—a.k.a. Liar's Dice, a game shown in the second movie—at the front of the theatre, beneath the screen.

About five minutes before the movie was to begin, four adults dressed in elaborate pirate costumes and reeking of alcohol came into the theater and, standing at the back, discussed in loud and expletive-laden voices how they were going to move people, just like a pirate would do, so that they could sit together. One man went down to several rows of people but they pointed out that all the seats were taken (and in fact had been saved for over an hour). Complaining loudly, they all left to tell the manager there were no real seats left!

Pirate behavior in real life may not really be acceptable but the promise of pirates, the idea that there exists a way of living in the world that boldly overturns normal rules and allows one to live by a different code, is very appealing. In an interview for *Rolling Stone*, both Johnny Depp and guitarist Keith Richards, who plays Jack Sparrow's father in *Pirates 3*, see rock stars as having the same appeal as pirates. Richards describes Captain Jack's appeal: "He represents potential freedom, to break out of the bounds."[36]

Depp said in another interview, "Being a pirate is a state of mind. You don't need a sword or a bandanna. You don't even need rum to get there. You just need to look at things from outside the norm. Do that and you're a pirate."[37] Bill Nighy, who plays Davy Jones in the *Pirates* movies, explained about pirates, "A lot of grog, a lot of sex, it's a great daydream. Of course, nobody wants to really live the life of the pirate, but the idea of a pirate might take you out of the cubicle for a while."[38]

Pirates are attractive because they are the quintessential liminal beings. Liminality is the state of being between two worlds, a position one occupies when in transition or unable to get firmly rooted in two contradictory worlds. Being engaged to be married, as Elizabeth and Will discover through three *Pirates* movies, is a liminal state between the total freedom of being single and the rule-driven world of marriage. Becoming a teenager is a form of liminality: 12-year-olds are familiar with this state because they are not considered young children anymore but they are also not teenagers yet so we call them "tweens" or "tweeners." This is the age also marked by rituals that mark the symbolic transition to adulthood out of childhood, so a Jewish child will participate in their Bat Mitzvah or Bar Mitzvah and a Catholic child might participate in the sacrament of Confirmation.

Liminality is a word used often in the work of anthropologist Victor Turner in the middle of the twentieth century. Turner studied rituals and laid out a three-part structure of rituals that still is significant today. Rituals are ceremonies that mark a change of life or identity (rites of passage) or that try to bring about a change, such as a curing ritual or a political rally to affect people's votes. Rituals, especially rites of passage, have three parts: they start with a separation of the initiate from normal life either physically or symbolically. Then the initiate enters the liminal stage, the "betwixt-and-between" phase[39] where normal life is suspended and the rules are different. The purpose of most rituals is to reach the third phase, reintegration and the restoration of the social order, the return to normal.

Liminality is appealing not because it means we can live without rule and order; liminality is important because it shows how society is put together and what can make it fall apart. Think of Halloween, one of our most important liminal rituals. On Halloween night, darkness invites the most bizarre transformations: burly men become large-breasted women, common women become famous movie stars, objects get animated and walk and talk, and animals dress like people. In the costumes that we chose and the characters they represent, we mix up genders, the living and the dead, the outlaw and the law enforcer. We are shown that these things that cross boundaries can make society too confusing to live in and for one night, Halloween, we revel in this confusion and the shattering of boundaries. One of the most popular costumes for the past few Halloweens has been the pirate, one of the best liminal characters we have and one everyone understands as a "betwixt-and-between" entity.[40]

The pirate's world is said, in its heyday, to have had a pirate's code that defined the limits of behavior for these hooligans. The code was popularized in a book called *A General History of the Robberies & Murders of the Most Notorious Pirates*[41] that was first published in 1724 by an unknown author, Captain Charles Johnson. Although the real author is unknown (and for a while had been attributed to Daniel DeFoe), the book set the standard for how pirates were to be understood. The pirate code laid out in Johnson's book—payment for lost limbs, equal shares of the booty, requirements to keep their weapons clean—got repeated in other novels, poems, plays, songs, and movies.[42]

Jack Sparrow joins the ranks of the pirate elite, those characters real and fictionalized whose exploits have been widely celebrated and discussed and imitated. Why would we do this, celebrate these scoundrels and lawbreakers and pillagers and rapists who wreak havoc on all they encounter? If we are trying to make sense of the world we live in, and are using movies as part of that sense-making, then the *Pirates* movies, and the work done by Johnny Depp to create a memorable and complex pirate in Jack Sparrow, is a fine contribution to this most human of activities. Pirates keep alive the hope that there are those adventurous enough and brave enough and clever enough to constantly challenge the status quo. They also point out in very obvious ways that "keeping to the code," whether a pirate code or the rules and laws of everyday society, is always an ambiguous activity and not a simple black-and-white affair.

Pirates have been a part of American lore and American culture for centuries and the pirate in many ways is the essence of an American hero. The delicious irony, of course, is that although pirates are supposed to be inherent critics of the established system of the laws protecting merchandise, the *Pirates* franchise is one of the best recent examples of the merchandizing system working its magic. Johnny Depp, who before *Pirates* had a reputation for resisting the selling of his persona as a product, seems to have made peace with Jack Sparrow's commercialization. When asked about the *Pirates* merchandizing in an interview for *Entertainment Weekly* before the third movie was released, Depp declared, "You can only do your work, and your work represents whatever you want it to represent. I've arrived at a certain place where I just go: You know what? I don't care. It's freeing."[43] A year earlier he elaborated for the same magazine, "It's fascinating to witness the machine at work, watch it hum and scream and howl. To see these products, like cereal boxes and fruit chews and action figures and sheets and towels and pillows…I mean, we've entered the arena where Marcel Duchamp and Andy Warhol are Snoopy-dancing in the nude. It's so absurd and so surreal and so irreverent that I love it."[44]

Depp has spoken often of the difficulty of saying goodbye to the character of Jack Sparrow and this may be a good indication that he had created a most precise match between his own life and that of his most famous character.[45] As he described to CBS News, "It sounds ludicrous because you're talking about an imaginary being, in a way. But having been that character for a good number of years—for 12 to 14 to 15 hours a day, for months on end or years on end—it's like saying goodbye to a person. I mean, to a living, breathing thing. So, it's very emotional."[46]

And this is why Johnny Depp's story is so perfectly American. For all its French attachments and oddball characteristics, his is the story of the pirate, the lone heroic yet dubious character who knows the code he should live by, abides by it when necessary, flaunts his transgressions without regret or shame, and ultimately seems honorable enough to earn our respect.

## NOTES

1. C.E. Smith, "PyrateCon 07- A Look Back," Keep to the Code, http://www.keeptothecode.com/01news.html (accessed August 16, 2007).

2. See some of the photos at MSN.com, "Pirates of the Caribbean": Dead Man's Chest: Photos, http://movies.msn.com/movies/movie.aspx?m=580632&mp=p&vpid=688023 (accessed August 16, 2007).

3. Bruce Gordon, and Tim O'Day, *Disneyland Then, Now, and Forever* (Disney Enterprises, Inc: 2005), 146.

4. "Disney Adds More Depp," Yahoo Entertainment, http://entertainment.tv.yahoo.com/entnews/eo/20060623/115112652000.html (accessed August 16, 2007).

5. Finn-Olaf Jones, "Not for Kids Only: Seeking Buccaneer Bliss," *New York Times*, May 18, 2007.

6. "Pirates of the Caribbean Ride," YouTube.com, see one version at http://www.youtube.com/watch?v=bTQ5eWBlApY (accessed August 16, 2007).

7. "So Long, Tom Sawyer. Hellooo, Keira Knightley," In the Zone, TMZ.com, http://www.tmz.com/2006/10/03/so-long-tom-sawyer-hellooo-keira-knightley/ (accessed August 16, 2007).

8. Elvis Mitchell, "Mascara As Black As a Jolly Roger," *New York Times*, July 9, 2003.

9. Christopher Lloyd, "Arrrrgh! 'Pirates 3' Is a Chaotic, Confusing Mess," *Indianapolis Star*, May 25, 2007.

10. Lacey Rose, "Yar! Disney Banks on Box Office Booty," Forbes.com, http://www.forbes.com/media/2007/05/24/hollywood-disney-pirates-biz-media_cx_lr_0524pirates.html (accessed August 16, 2007).

11. Bill Muller, "Pirates of the Caribbean: At World's End," *Arizona Republic*, May 25, 2007, http://www.azcentral.com/ent/movies/articles/0522pirates0525.html (may require registration; accessed August 16, 2007).

12. Michael Sragow, "Sea of Confusion," *Baltimore Sun*, May 24, 2007.

13. Andy Klein, "Pan Ick: A Funny Thing Happened on the Way to the Slam-Dunk, Feel-Good Movie," *Los Angeles Reader*, December 13, 1991, 27.

14. Desson Howe, "*Cutthroat Island*," *Washington Post*, December 22, 1995, http://www.washingtonpost.com/wp-srv/style/longterm/movies/videos/cutthroatislandpg13howe_b003a7.htm (accessed August 16, 2007).

15. Captain William Lubber, *Pirateology: The Pirate Hunter's Companion* (Cambridge, MA: Candlewick, 2006); and Alisha Niehaus and Alan Hecker, *Piratepedia* (New York: DK Pub, 2007).

16. Room for Kids catalog, May 2007, 9; also Sears catalog online, http://roomforkidscatalog.com/ (search for "pirates").

17. "Paint and Wall Décor," Disney.go.com, http://disney.go.com/disneyhome/pirates/paint.html (accessed August 16, 2007).

18. See "True Caribbean Pirates,"History.com, http://www.history.com/marquees/pirates (accessed August 16, 2007).

19. Such as *Disney Adventures*, June/July 2007, which had an "ultimate Pirates fan guide."

20. See "Pirate Shores" at http://www.legoland.com/park/parkoverview/pirateshores.htm. The *Pirates* line can be found at http://search2.lego.com/?cc=US&d=DUPLO%C2%AE+%3E+Pirates&i=1&l=2057&pt=initial&q=pirates&u=&u1=q&u2=d (accessed August 16, 2007).

21. See photos at "Disneyland Resort," MiceChat.com, http://www.micechat.com/forums/showthread.php?t=65549 (accessed August 16, 2007).

22. "Pennsylvania Renaissance Faire 2007," http://www.parenfaire.com/ (accessed August 16, 2007).

23. "Latest news: PyrateCon," April 22, 2007, http://www.keeptothecode.com/events/index.html (accessed August 16, 2007).

24. "Talk Like a Pirate Day," talklikeapirate.com, http://www.talklikeapirate.com/piratehome.html (accessed August 16, 2007).

25. September 18, 2006, DaveBarry.com, http://blogs.herald.com/dave_barrys_blog/2006/09/arrrrrrrrrrrrrr.html (accessed August 16, 2007).

26. "How to talk like a Pirate," loadingreadyrun.com, http://loadingready-run.com/videos/view/49/How+to+Talk+like+a+Pirate/QT (accessed August 16, 2007).

27. "Pirate Master," cbs.com, http://www.cbs.com/primetime/pirate_master/ (accessed August 16, 2007); show was cancelled mid-season after one departed contestant committed suicide.

28. "Pirate Master," cbs.com, http://piratemasterwiki.cbs.com/page/Pirate+ Master%3A+The+Show (accessed August 16, 2007).

29. David Cordingly, *Under the Black Flag: The Romance and the Reality of Life Among the Pirates* (New York: Random House Trade Paperbacks, 2006), xvii.

30. "Achille Lauro Hijacking," SpecialOperations.com, http://www.special operations.com/Images_Folder/library2/achille.html (accessed August 16, 2007).

31. David Cordingly, *Under the Black Flag: The Romance and the Reality of Life Among the Pirates* (New York: Random House Trade Paperbacks, 2006), xvi.

32. Ibid., 34–39.

33. From Bauer Publishing, "Pirates of the Caribbean—An Overview," *Life Story: Film Fantasy: Pirates of the Caribbean At World's End*, 2007, 9; the publisher's description of the magazine reads: "Published 11 times a year, LIFE STORY is a newsstand-only special issue designed for teens and tweens. Each issue is devoted to one musical group or individual celebrity and features in-depth biographical information and TONS of up-close photographs. Occasionally, Bauer publishes a version of LIFE STORY sub-titled Movie Magic or Film Fantasy, which focuses on specific genres of films," from their website at http://www.bauerpublishing. com/LIFE/LIFE_mission/LIFE_mission.html (accessed August 16, 2007).

34. Michael Singer, *Bring Me That Horizon: The Making of Pirates of the Caribbean* (New York: Disney Enterprises, Inc., 2007), 29.

35. Kevin Lally, "See Worthy," *Film Journal International* 106, no. 6 (June 2003).

36. David Wild, "Johnny Depp & Keith Richards: Pirates of the Caribbean's Blood Brothers," *Rolling Stone*, no. 1027 (May 31, 2007), http://www.rollingstone. com/news/coverstory/johnny_depp__keith_richards_ipirates_of_the_caribbeanis_ blood_brothers/page/3.

37. Glenn Whipp, "Sex 'n' Swagger a Pirate's Booty," *Los Angeles Daily News*, May 19, 2007, http://www.dailynews.com/search/ci_5930343.

38. Ibid.

39. Victor W. Turner, "Passages, Margins, and Poverty: Religious Symbols of Communitas," in *High Points In Anthropology*, 2nd edition, ed. P. Bohannan, and Mark Glazer (New York, McGraw-Hill, 1988), 504.

40. Olivia Barker, "What Will You Be for Halloween?" *USA Today*, October 5, 2006, http://www.usatoday.com/life/2006-10-04-halloween-costumes_x.htm.

41. Captain Charles Johnson, *A General History of the Robberies & Murders of the Most Notorious Pirates* (Guilford, CT: The Lyons Press, 2002).

42. David Cordingly, *Under the Black Flag: The Romance and the Reality of Life Among the Pirates* (New York: Random House Trade Paperbacks, 2006), xvii.

43. Josh Rottenberg, "The Captain at Ease," *Entertainment Weekly*, May 18, 2007, 33, http://www.ew.com/ew/article/0,,20035285_20035331_20038360,00. html (accessed August 16, 2007).

44. "JohnnyDeppOn…,"EW.com,http://www.ew.com/ew/gallery/0,,20037288_ 20037289_20039648,00.html (accessed August 16, 2007).

45. Josh Rottenberg, "The Captain at Ease," *Entertainment Weekly*, May 18, 2007, 33, http://www.ew.com/ew/article/0,,20035285_20035331_20038360,00.html (accessed August 16, 2007).

46. "Depp: Tough To Say 'So Long' To Capt. Jack," CBS/The Early Show, May 25, 2007, http://www.cbsnews.com/stories/2007/05/25/earlyshow/leisure/celebspot/main2851958.shtml?source=mostpop_story (accessed August 16, 2007).

# Appendix A

# THE JOHNNY DEPP OF . . .

If you and your friends all owned mp3 players, but you just know that yours was the best of the lot, you might say something like, "My iPod is the BMW of mp3 players." Just about everyone would know what you meant. You would be saying that your player was superbly designed, stylish, reliable, luxurious—a status symbol. It probably would not be as effective to say, "My iPod is the Levenger of mp3 players." Although Levenger is a top-quality brand and a designer name in the world of fountain pens, somehow the name does not bring much to mind for the general population, and even if you knew what a Levenger pen was, you might have to strain your brain to figure out how to make the analogy between a fountain pen and an iPod work.

Fortunately, American popular culture has no shortage of better-known terms, many derived from the world of entertainment, that we can use to create analogies: for the best of we can say "the Cadillac of Cookbooks;"[1] the scariest can be "the Hannibal Lecter of Hip Hop;"[2] the strongest "the Schwarzenegger of all Metaphors;"[3] or even the wimpiest as in Kenny G is "the David Blaine of elevator music."[4]

So what would it mean to say that something or someone is "the Johnny Depp of...?" What qualities would we be connecting between the Hollywood actor and the person or object in question? What would the Johnny Depp of mp3 players be like, for instance? A player able to perform in multiple genres? A device that is universally enjoyed and, at the same time, enigmatic and eccentric in appearance? An mp3 that is flat-out fascinating to look at?

The analogies below are not necessarily consistent but they do suggest the wide range of ways we incorporate Johnny Depp into our daily lives and thoughts. Here, then, are examples of the ways in which people have used "Johnny Depp" to describe someone, to define something, or to direct our attention to the important Depp-like qualities that a person, place, or thing is thought to possess.

1. A Cornell University student writes about one of his alumni-mentors, "I even dreamed that she would discover my talent in performance and help me to become the Tom Hanks or, better yet, the Johnny Depp of China."[5]
2. Shine Media is the Johnny Depp of graphic design.[6]
3. Jensen Ackles (star of the television show *Supernatural*) is "the Johnny Depp of TV."[7]
4. "A 20-something guy who apparently fancies himself the Johnny Depp of Mexico is leading me...straight out the front door of the spa and down the never-ending levels that lead to the resort beach at Westin Los Cabos."[8]
5. A dropped lollipop that symbolizes the desirable-but-unattainable is called the "Johnny Depp of Suckers."[9]
6. A writer who wanted her dog to appear in the author photograph in her book referred to her pet as the "Johnny Depp of Dogdom."[10]
7. About Phil Elvrum's recent music CD, one Amazon.com reviewer wrote that the artist "seems like one twisted soul, the Johnny Depp of music."[11]
8. In an Indiana University/Kelly School of Business review of Depp's film *The Secret Window*, the writer refers to "the ultra-hip Hotel Nelligan (a place that is the Johnny Depp of hotels itself) in Old Montreal."[12]
9. "There was my roommate, the Peaceful Pastor's son, Life from Nowhere, who became my closest spiritual brother. We would talk and drink beer right through the night. This musician is the Johnny Depp of the Christian faith. Guys wanted to be like him and girls wanted to be with him."[13]
10. Mauro Polawski is "the Johnny Depp of Wahloon rock."[14]
11. The Canadian band The Hip is "the Johnny Depp of Canadian rock."[15]
12. Tadanobu Asano has been referred to as "the Johnny Depp of Japan."[16]
13. "[Sean] Connery was sort of the Johnny Depp of the Sixties/Seventies..."[17]

14. A small "DeviantArt" web-drawn figure is "the Johnny Depp of olives."[18]
15. French actor Gerard Philipe "was the Johnny Depp of his time."[19]
16. Handsome Hook, a curious and gentle horse, is known as "the Johnny Depp of the Horse Sense farm" of the Carolinas.[20]
17. Kudo Tsunoda "is recognized industry wide as the Johnny Depp of the video game development community."[21]
18. Actor Wil Wheaton is referred to, on a video gamer's blog, as "the Johnny Depp of geeks."[22]
19. Aaron is told he is "like the Johnny Depp of myspace."[23]
20. Al-Qaeda "Boogieman" Abu al-Masri is "the Johnny Depp of terrorwood."[24]
21. Deceased comedian Mitch Hedberg, with "his shaggy hair," looked like "the Johnny Depp of standup."[25]
22. A college drama major is "smart and nice enough to realize that he's the Johnny Depp of musical theater, and very much like Captain Jack Sparrow."[26]
23. Producer Danny Elfman "is so eclectic; so bizarre....He's like the Johnny Depp of film composition; the guy can do everything!"[27]
24. A New Zealand athlete is referred to as the "Johnny Depp of cricket."[28]
25. Takeshi Kaneshiro is "the Johnny Depp of Asian cinema."[29]
26. Coppermine (dog) Shelby is "the Johnny Depp of the canine world."[30]
27. Stevie the Boxer is "the Johnny Depp of dogs."[31]
28. Zappa is "the Johnny Depp of Labradoodles."[32]
29. Singer So Ji Sub is the "Johnny Depp of Korea."[33]
30. Chris Cornell is "the Johnny Depp of music."[34]
31. Actor Donald Sutherland "was the Johnny Depp of his era."[35]
32. Gael Garcia Bernal is "the Johnny Depp of Latin cinema."[36]
33. Australian actor Nicholas Rogers is "the Johnny Depp of Cave of the Golden Rose."[37]
34. An animated goat in a video game is "the Johnny Depp of the animal kingdom."[38]
35. "Rosie, our Welsh pony is in foal. The stallion is a local lad. In looks he is the 'Johnny Depp' of the horse world."[39]
36. *New Left Review* editor and author of *Pirates of the Caribbean: Axis of Hope* (a 2006 book about Hugo Chavez's political rise in Venezuela) is "the Johnny Depp of international comment."[40]
37. "I consider The Flaming Lips the Johnny Depp of music."[41]

38. Actor Leslie Cheung is "the Johnny Depp of HK [Hong Kong]."[42]

39. Charlie White, of Spokane, Washington, is "the Johnny Depp of skating, or at least ice dancing."[43]

40. New Zealand cricket-player Jason Gillespie is "the Johnny Depp of cricket."[44]

41. Dinah Faber of the Historical Society of Hartford County calls Edwin Booth, brother of Lincoln assassin John Wilkes Booth, "the Johnny Depp of his day."[45]

42. Ollie, a German wirehaired pointer, is "the Johnny Depp of the dog world."[46]

43. Hollywood composer Mark Mothersbaugh is "the Johnny Depp of New Wave."[47]

45. 71-year-old folk singer Utah Phillips is introduced as "the Johnny Depp of his age group" at the University of Rhode Island Songs of the Union Movement concert in 2006.[48]

# NOTES

1. https://www.tasteofhomebooks.com/TOHCookbook/AdOffer.aspx?KeyCode=TT691VO04M (accessed August 17, 2007).

2. http://www.sacbee.com/macias/story/191646.html (accessed May 5, 2007).

3. Michael Blitz and Louise Krasniewicz, *Why Arnold Matters: the Rise of a Cultural Icon.* (New York: Basic Books), 2004, 69.

4. http://www.blender.com/guide/articles.aspx?ID=1990 (accessed May 5, 2007).

5. Mao Ye, "Remembrance of Thing Past," *Cornell Daily Sun*, March 13, 2007, http://cornellsun.com/node/22068 (accessed April 1, 2007).

6. http://www.shinemedia.com.au/our_work/case_studies/soasiandvd_casestudy.html (accessed August 17, 2007).

7. http://www.people.com/people/article/0,26334,1539873,00.html (accessed June 2, 2007).

8. Chris Baldwin, "Beware the Beach Massage: A Hard-Core Golfer Gets a Lesson in Spa Etiquette," December 6, 2006, http://www.msnbc.msn.com/id/16075016/ (accessed April 1, 2007).

9. http://laurayoung.typepad.com/dragonslaying/funny_stories_from_my_life/index.html (accessed August 17, 2007).

10. http://www.sharonkaypenman.com/penmanchronicles.htm (accessed August 17, 2007).

11. http://www.amazon.ca/Pt2-Glow-Microphones/dp/B00005NB2Q (accessed August 17, 2007).

12. http://www.thegate.ca/interviews/secret-window.php (accessed August 17, 2007).

13. feed://countryofmyskull.blogspot.com/feeds/posts/default (accessed June 3, 2007).

14. http://bak.spc.org/cherrybomb/pop/music.html (accessed August 17, 2007).

15. http://cn.last.fm/user/Squiddles/journal/2007/02/25/353942/ (accessed April 4, 2007).

16. http://www.amazon.com/gp/cdp/member-reviews/A29TQOG3Y48T8L?ie= UTF8&sort_by=MostRecentReview (accessed August 17, 2007).

17. http://www.amazon.com/gp/product/customer-reviews/B000ERVK3K/ ref=cm_cr_dp_2_1/104-4358157-5670355?ie=UTF8&customer-reviews. sort%5Fby=-SubmissionDate&n=130 (accessed August 17, 2007).

18. http://killerguppy.deviantart.com/ (accessed May 7, 2007).

19. Desson Thomson, "'Fanfan': After 54 Years, The Swash Still Buckles," *Washington Post*, October 13, 2006, C5.

20. http://www.horsesenseotc.com/about/meet-horses (accessed August 17, 2007).

21. http://www.acm.uiuc.edu/conference/2006/speakers.php (accessed August 17, 2007).

22. http://digg.com/gaming_news/Wil_Wheaton_Gets_His_Geek_On_At_ E3 (accessed August 17, 2007).

23. http://profile.myspace.com/index.cfm?fuseaction=user.viewprofile&friend ID=48243303 (account no longer active, August 17, 2007).

24. http://www.davidcorn.com/archives/2006/06/the_bush_bounce.php (accessed March 22, 2007).

25. http://osakasteve.com/2005/04/ (accessed August 17, 2007).

26. http://www.pointsincase.com/columns/simonne/10-1-06.htm (accessed April 18, 2007).

27. http://soundtrack-central.blogspot.com/2006_06_01_soundtrack-central_ archive.html (accessed June 4, 2007).

28. http://www.cordite.org.au/ashes/?cat=1 (accessed August 17, 2007).

29. http://www.youtube.com/watch?v=0zmAMmscxMk (accessed August 17, 2007).

30. http://sophieballou.com/coppermine/displayimage.php?album=random& cat=0&pos=-165 (accessed August 17, 2007).

31. http://www.boxertown.com/rescue/happyendings2004 (accessed May 5, 2007).

32. http://www.cloudcatcherlabradoodles.com/Labradoodle_males.htm (accessed June 1, 2007).

33. http://www.youtube.com/watch?v=ahlytWW45AI (accessed August 17, 2007).

34. http://www.yelp.com/topic/ZfGYX0nCdDKn2XDrDowC7g (accessed August 17, 2007; a fellow blogger replied that "Johnny Depp is actually the Johnny Depp of music").

35. http://www.dailyrevolution.net/labels/Microsoft.html (accessed April 4, 2007).

36. http://stheoutlawtorn.com/labels/tv%20and%20film.php (accessed May 15, 2007).

37. http://dann-u.blogspot.com/2006_09_01_archive.html (accessed May 16, 2007; no longer available online).

38. http://forums.wow-europe.com/thread.html?topicId=291749802&pageNo =1&sid=1 (accessed February 12, 2007).

39. http://www.helenhollick.net/webvault.html (accessed March 3, 2007).

40. http://findarticles.com/p/articles/mi_qa3724/is_200611/ai_n17189814 (accessed June 5, 2007).

41. http://www.musicsnobbery.com/concerts/index.html (accessed December 9, 2006).

42. http://www.montrealmirror.com/ARCHIVES/1998/080698/film2.html (accessed August 17, 2007).

43. http://www.ice-dance.com/mombo9/2007/01/datebook-saturday-january-20th-2007.html (accessed February 21, 2007).

44. http://www.cordite.org.au/ashes/?m=200503 (accessed October 18, 2006).

45. http://www.examiner.com/a-210974~Harford_County_to_purchase_ the_home_of_John_Wilkes_Booth_for__810_000.html (accessed August 17, 2007).

46. http://www.klancraig.co.uk/dogs.asp (accessed March 30, 2007).

47. http://mog.com/brand_X/blog_post/40462 (accessed June 6, 2007).

48. http://mog.com/music/Devo/New_Traditionalists_%28Infinite_Zero%29 (accessed August 17, 2007).

# Appendix B

# JOHNNY DEPP IS . . .

Famous actors always carry an image that goes beyond their person. Usually it is an image that is not of their making, even though they may try to guide and form it. Throughout his career Johnny Depp fought this image production machine because he thought it turned him into a product. But actors, no matter how independent and defiant they are, are molded and shaped by writers and directors, created and recreated by camera men and women, enhanced by makeup artists, promoted by agents, studied by critics, and consumed by audiences. The resulting images are found in interviews, biographies, film reviews, blogs, fansites, songs, websites, and print material as well as the movies themselves. Then they are recycled and reproduced again and again. The actor's name comes to indicate a set of traits or values that may or may not be true but that are circulated endlessly without permission or endorsement. Once they are out there, this "product" is hard to take back and it can color the actor, and all audience perceptions of him, throughout his career.

Here then are some of the many images of Johnny Depp commonly in circulation. The list can be best appreciated by being read out loud!

**JOHNNY DEPP IS:**
The best actor of his generation[1]
The greatest actor of this generation[2]
The greatest actor of all time[3]

One of the most enigmatic and interesting actors of his generation[4]
The Marlon Brando of his generation[5]
The most absorbing actor of our time.[6]
The actor least in need of an animated alter ego[7]
King of the weirdo actors[8]
The Wade Boggs of actors[9]
The Miles Davis of acting[10]
The new Jerry Lewis[11]
The Shirley Temple of the 2000s[12]
The Vincent Price of our times[13]
The Luke Skywalker of Hollywood[14]
The true definition of "actor"[15]
The most intriguing actor of this last decade[16]
One of America's finest young character actors[17]
The most versatile actor of our time[18]
One of Hollywood's most sought-after talents[19]
A brilliant and truly unique actor[20]
One of the most versatile and compelling actors working in
    contemporary world cinema[21]
The quirkiest leading man of his time[22]
America's most eccentric movie star[23]
The king of diverse roles[24]
Iconoclastic yet eminently bankable[25]
The most talented independent actor of our century[26]
A former darling of the "art-house" minority cinema scene[27]
Like the best actor of all friggin' time[28]
The embodiment of a treat[29]
An eccentric, tattooed maverick[30]
The essence of cool[31]
The King of Cool[32]
The very definition of cool[33]
Coolest Guy on the Planet[34]
The coolest man on the face of the planet[35]
The hottest man of the day[36]
The hottest daddy[37]
Hotter than the back of a car mid-August[38]
The hottest of the stonerz[39]
The hottest of the hottest[40]
Super hot[41]
Hotter than Orlando Bloom[42]
The definition of a hottie[43]

The very essence of lovely[44]
The essence of charm[45]
The man of our dreams[46]
The dream of every teenage girl in the land[47]
The kind of guy that every girl wants but shouldn't marry![48]
An artist[49]
One of the most sensitive artists of our time[50]
A sensitive and compelling screen presence[51]
Wandering soul Johnny[52]
The master of the blank stare[53]
The definition of perfection[54]
The personification of charisma[55]
The personification of freedom[56]
The captain of my ship![57]
The modern king of slapstick[58]
The Man[59]
The bomb[60]
The best of the best[61]
The cat's meow[62]
The objective standard of masculine prettiness[63]
The Robin Hood of modern cinema[64]
The sexiest pirate I've ever seen[65]
One of the most beautiful men I've ever seen[66]
One of the best people ever[67]
Mysterious and beautiful and other-worldly and kind and
    intelligent and insightful.. .[68]
The love of my life[69]
The ultimate love of my life[70]
Both the antithesis and the apex of all I love in a man[71]
The most talented and sexiest man alive[72]
The sexiest, most talented, and eye-catching man in the universe[73]
The plastic man of entertainment[74]
The master of the message[75]
The true picture of a real pirate[76]
The life of all his movies[77]
The new golden boy of Hollywood[78]
NOT the United States of America[79]
Nobody in the wide body of relevant world events[80]
The most searched-for celeb of 2006[81]
The panacea for all of life's woes[82]
An outsider who was attracted to the strangely gothic[83]

The man-god of Hollywood[84]

Patron saint of the lost and lonely[85]

The lord saint of this religion[86]

Actually 44[87]

The second coming of Gregory Peck[88]

The meaning of life[89]

Ethereal[90]

A true original[91]

The closest thing to a perfect human being[92]

A magnificent actor with such good looks that he could make a straight man turn gay[93]

A constant reminder of the joys and perils of being a critic[94]

## NOTES

1. http://www.bbc.co.uk/films/2005/07/25/johnny_depp_chocolate_factory_interview.shtml (accessed August 16, 2007).

2. http://www.cinemablend.com/new/Depp-Is-In-To-XS-2585.html (accessed April 4, 2007).

3. http://fametastic.co.uk/archive/20060905/2442/orlando-bloom-mocks-johnny-depp-in-extras-skit/ (accessed April 10, 2007).

4. http://www.scifi.com/sfw/issue325/interview.html (accessed June 2, 2007)

5. http://www.roanoke.com/entertainment/insideout/movies/wb/wb/xp-72917 (accessed April 10, 2007).

6. http://www.afi.com/onscreen/AFIFEST/2005/pdf/jd.pdf (accessed May 31, 2007).

7. http://www.eye.net/eye/issue/issue_09.15.05/film/onscreen.html (accessed April 10, 2007).

8. Michael Sragow, "Depp Delves into the Stories behind His Characters," *Baltimore Sun*, July 14, 2006.

9. http://yanksfansoxfan.typepad.com/ysfs/2006/07/worst_lineup_ev.html (accessed March 30, 2007).

10. Michael Singer, *Bring Me That Horizon: Pirates of the Caribbean—the Making of the Swashbuckling Movie Trilogy* (Disney Editions, 2007), 56.

11. http://www.tmz.com/2006/07/07/france-loves-johnny-depp/ (accessed April 10, 2007).

12. http://www.rottentomatoes.com/vine/showthread.php?t=509387&page=2 (accessed April 10, 2007).

13. http://forums.superherohype.com/showthread.php?t=161915&page=2 (accessed April 10, 2007).

14. http://www.lovefilm.com/visitor/editorial.html?editorial_id=2221 (accessed April 4, 2007).

15. http://www.tmz.com/2006/08/24/everyones-favorite-pirate-is-back/2 (accessed January 13, 2007).

16. http://www.johnnydeppfan.com/interviews/studio00.htm (accessed April 10, 2007).

17. http://www.bbc.co.uk/films/2003/07/29/johnny_depp_pirates_of_the_caribbean_interview.shtml (accessed August 16, 2007)..

18. http://www.bigpondmovies.com/user/movieDisplay.php?movie_id=15182 (accessed April 10, 2007).

19. http://www.girl.com.au/johnny-depp-willy-wonka.htm (accessed June 2, 2007).

20. http://www.afi.com/onscreen/AFIFEST/2005/pdf/jd.pdf (accessed May 31, 2007).

21. http://www.afi.com/onscreen/AFIFEST/2005/pdf/jd.pdf (accessed April 10, 2007).

22. http://horoscopes.aol.com/astrology/zodiac-central/gemini/johnny-depp (accessed April 4, 2007).

23. John H. Richardson, "The Unprocessed Johnny Depp," *Esquire* 141, no. 5 (May 2004).

24. http://www.bloggerman.com/articles/2004/January/toptenactors (accessed April 10, 2007).

25. http://www.afi.com/onscreen/AFIFEST/2005/pdf/jd.pdf (accessed May 31, 2007).

26. http://www.rottentomatoes.com/vine/journal_view.php?username=iskia (accessed April 10, 2007).

27. Emily Smith, "I Adore Playing Captain Jack…Roll on Pirates VIII," *The Sun*, July 5, 2006.

28. http://forum.cncreneclips.com/index.php?s=d481d0a392e625a795c301ff99bd4c2d&showtopic=2105&pid=253586&st=275&#entry253586 (accessed April 10, 2007).

29. http://www.matchflick.com/movie-review/13401–3195 (accessed February 20, 2007).

30. http://www.calgarysun.com/cgi-bin/publish.cgi?p=144830&x=articles&s=showbiz .(accessed August 16, 2007).

31. http://www.reelmoviecritic.com/movies20034q/id1891.htm (accessed January 19, 2007).

32. http://www.johnnydeppfan.com/interviews/8809splice.htm (accessed January 19, 2007).

33. http://interview.johnnydepp-zone2.com/1989_0528SunHerald.html (accessed May 1, 2007).

34. http://www.urbandictionary.com/define.php?term=johnny+depp (accessed August 16, 2007).

35. http://mobile.channel4.com/mobile-portal/film/july_2006/johnny_depp_cool_as.xml (accessed April 10, 2007).

36. http://www.celebrific.com/you-tell-me-how-are-we-going-to-seduce-johnny-depp/ (accessed April 10, 2007).

37. http://x17online.com/celebrities/brad_pitt/hollywoods_hottest_dads.php (accessed April 10, 2007).

38. http://www.citypaper.com/printReview.asp?rid=6373 (accessed April 10, 2007).).

39. http://www.hightimes.com/ht/entertainment/content.php?bid=215&aid=24 (accessed April 10, 2007).

40. http://answers.yahoo.com/question/index?qid=20060623132633AAw2bb5 (accessed March 3, 2007).

41. http://www.urbandictionary.com/define.php?term=johnny+depp (accessed August 17, 2007).

42. http://www.urbandictionary.com/define.php?term=johnny+depp (accessed August 17, 2007).

43. http://www.urbandictionary.com/define.php?term=o.c.d. (accessed April 4, 2007).

44. http://profile.myspace.com/index.cfm?fuseaction=user.viewprofile&friendid=41701735 (accessed December 1, 2006).

45. http://www.tollbooth.org/2004/movies/fn.html (accessed December 1, 2006).

46. http://www.ohjohnny.net/newsdec04.html (accessed December 1, 2006).

47. http://archive.worcesternews.co.uk/2004/4/28/(accessed April 10, 2007).

48. http://cgi.ebay.com/CRY-BABY-JOHNNY-DEPP-movie-sexy-juniors-t-shirt-XL_W0QQitemZ120104496873QQihZ002QQcategoryZ63869QQcmdZViewItem (accessed April 10, 2007).

49. http://www.afi.com/onscreen/AFIFEST/2005/pdf/jd.pdf (accessed May 31, 2007).

50. http://blog.360.yahoo.com/blog-UGcxq2Uyaa_5LcMBHjBD5SV.Cdub HWA-?cq01&tag=vanityfair (accessed November 11, 2006).

51. David Blum, "The Buzz on Johnny Depp," *Esquire* 123, no. 4 (April, 1995), http://www.johnnydeppfan.com/interviews/esquire.htm.

52. Emily Smith, "I Adore Playing Captain Jack...Roll on Pirates VIII," *The Sun*, July 5, 2006.

53. http://www.patrickkellogg.com/hobbies/45stars.htm (accessed April 4, 2007).

54. http://breathinmusic.mydeardiary.com/notes.html (accessed April 4, 2007).

55. http://www.sfgate.com/cgi-bin/article.cgi?f=/e/a/1998/06/05/WEEKEND8781.dtl (accessed April 4, 2007).

56. http://www.efilmcritic.com/review.php?movie=7895 (accessed April 4, 2007).

57. http://profile.myspace.com/index.cfm?fuseaction=user.viewprofile&friendid=41701735 (accessed April 4, 2007).

58. http://www.hit-n-run.com/cgi/read_review.cgi?review=53630_mccartney (accessed April 4, 2007).

59. http://www.moviecynics.com/item/162 (accessed August 16, 2007).

60. http://www.metacafe.com/watch/188432/pirates_of_the_carribbean_2_dead_mans_chest_water_wheel/ (accessed April 10, 2007).

61. http://groups.msn.com/LaurekeMcFly/links.msnw (accessed January 21, 2007).

62. http://blog.360.yahoo.com/blog-UGcxq2Uyaa_5LcMBHjBD5SV.Cdub HWA-?cq=1&tag=vanityfair (accessed April 1, 2007).

63. http://www.unfogged.com/archives/comments_5377.html (accessed January 13, 2007).

64. http://www.deppimpact.com/mags/transcripts/timeout_06apr05.html (accessed January 13, 2007).

65. http://www.urbandictionary.com/define.php?term=johnny+depp (accessed August 16, 2007).

66. http://interview.johnnydepp-zone2.com/1990_06Sky.html (accessed December 12, 2006).

67. http://www.joep.org.uk/2006/07/goats-on-radio.html (accessed February 26, 2007).

68. John H. Richardson, "The Unprocessed Johnny Depp," *Esquire* 141, no. 5 (May 2004).

69. http://www.dtheatre.com/read.php?sid=2778 (accessed April 10, 2007).

70. http://universalrandomness.blogspot.com/2005_06_01_archive.html (accessed April 1, 2007).

71. http://ubersite.com/m/78700 (accessed April 10, 2007).

72. http://www.johnnydeppfever.net/ (accessed June 1, 2007).

73. http://www.urbandictionary.com/define.php?term=johnny+depp (accessed August 16, 2007).

74. http://community.livejournal.com/ohnotheydidnt/11761203.html (accessed April 10, 2007).

75. http://variagate.com/charlief.htm (accessed March 10, 2007).

76. http://www.texasescapes.com/Peary-Perry/Cowboys-Pirates-and-Robin-Hood.htm (accessed April 10, 2007).

77. http://blogcritics.org/archives/2005/07/28/195447.php (accessed April 10, 2007).

78. http://moviematt.blogspot.com/2005/07/july-15-charlie-and-chocolate-factory.html (accessed April 10, 2007).

79. http://www.cnczone.com/forums/archive/index.php/t-34381.html (accessed March 30, 2007).

80. http://martyk.blogspot.com/2003_09_01_martyk_archive.html (accessed April 10, 2007).

81. http://keiraknightly.celebden.com/?cat=5 (accessed March 27, 2007).

82. http://smallforcefield.little-wonder.net/oldposts/2005_08_01_archive.html (accessed April 10, 2007).

83. http://tob.hollywood.com/2007/05/18/johnny-depp-explains-how-his-family-is-his-real-treasure/.

84. http://similarminds.com/forums/viewtopic.php?t=1190&start=15&sid=f2da54b21eb7f27cd95289ee2826eda2 (accessed April 10, 2007).

85. John H. Richardson, "The Unprocessed Johnny Depp," *Esquire* 141, no. 5 (May 2004).

86. http://www.womanhonorthyself.com/?p=2941 (accessed January 1, 2007).

87. http://forums.ytv.com/boards/index.php?showtopic=311530 (accessed April 10, 2007).

88. http://www.commonsensetx.com/2006/07/09/pirates-of-the-caribbean-dead-movie-blogs-chest/ (accessed April 10, 2007).

89. http://www.angelfire.com/nc2/plexie/ (accessed November 19, 2006).

90. http://www.urbandictionary.com/define.php?term=johnny+depp (accessed August 16, 2007).

91. http://www.afi.com/onscreen/AFIFEST/2005/pdf/jd.pdf (accessed March 31, 2007).

92. http://www.urbandictionary.com/define.php?term=johnny+depp (accessed August 16, 2007).

93. http://www.urbandictionary.com/define.php?term=johnny+depp (accessed August 16, 2007).

94. http://johnnydeppweb.com/info/quotes.php (accessed March 30, 2007).

# Appendix C

# TATTOOS TREASURE MAP

Johnny Depp has said that his body is the place where he makes a record of his life experiences. As he explained, "Your body is like your personal diary. The others should be able to read what you've been through."[1] He has marked his body with cutting and with tattoos.

It is not unusual now for Hollywood stars to have body modifications of this sort, but when Depp began in acting, it was considered odd. He remembers, "When I did *Nightmare on Elm Street*, there was a scene where I had to take off my shirt and they saw my Indian tattoo—it was 1984, and they were like, '*He's got a tattoo! This kid's got a tattoo!*' They were really freaked out by it. They said, 'Could you lie on your other side?' It's funny now, thinking back on that, how it was a real shock to them. Now, everybody and their mother and their goldfish is inked."[2]

Depp's inking and body markings do indeed record his history and the following map lets you trace that history.

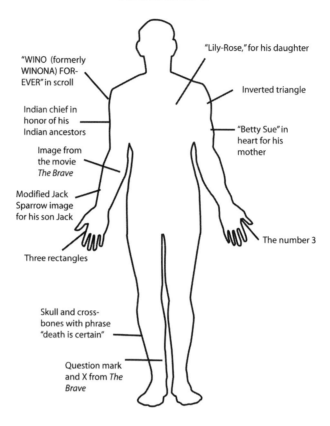

"Lily-Rose," for his daughter

"WINO (formerly WINONA) FOR-EVER" in scroll

Inverted triangle

Indian chief in honor of his Indian ancestors

"Betty Sue" in heart for his mother

Image from the movie *The Brave*

Modified Jack Sparrow image for his son Jack

The number 3

Three rectangles

Skull and cross-bones with phrase "death is certain"

Question mark and X from *The Brave*

## NOTES

1. Christophe d'Yvoire, *Studio Magazine*, February 2000, http://www.john nydeppfan.com/interviews/studio00.htm.

2. Mark Binelli, "The Last Buccaneer," *Rolling Stone*, July 13, 2006, http://www.rollingstone.com/news/story/10714717/the_last_buccaneer.

# WORKS CITED

Adler, Shelley R. "Sudden Unexpected Nocturnal Death Syndrome among Hmong Immigrants: Examining the Role of the 'Nightmare'." *Journal of American Folklore* 104 (1991): 54–71.

Aurelia. "Depp!" http://www.depp.ca/, 2000–2007.

Bennett, Trish. "Depp Impact," www.deppimpact.com, 2000–2007.

Blitz, Michael, and Louise Krasniewicz. *Why Arnold Matters: the Rise of a Cultural Icon*. New York: Basic Books, 2004.

Brozan, Nadine. "Chronicle." *The New York Times*, September 14, 1994, B-8

*Charlie Rose Show*, "A Discussion about *Fear and Loathing in Las Vegas*," aired May 11, 1998.

Cordingly, David. *Under the Black Flag: The Romance and the Reality of Life among the Pirates*. New York: Random House Trade Paperbacks, 2006.

DeAngelis, Michael. "Gender and Other Transcendences: William Blake as Johnny Depp." In *Ladies and Gentlemen, Boys and Girls: Gender in Film at the End of the Twentieth Century*, ed. Murray Pomerance. Albany, NY: Albany State University Press, 2001.

Depp, Johnny. Foreword to *Burton on Burton*, ed. Mark Salisbury. Rev ed. London: Faber and Faber, 1995.

Depp, Johnny. "Kerouac, Ginsberg, the Beats and Other Bastards Who Ruined My Life." In *The Rolling Stone Book of the Beats*, ed. Holly George-Warren. New York: Hyperion, 1999.

d'Yvoire, Christophe. "Johnny Depp by Johnny Depp," *Studio Magazine*, February 2000.

George-Warren, Holly, ed. *The Rolling Stone Book of the Beats*. New York: Hyperion, 1999.

Goodall, Nigel. *The Secret World of Johnny Depp*. London: Blake Publishing, 2006. Also published as *What's Eating Johnny Depp: An Intimate Biography*, 2004.

Gordon, Bruce, and Tim O' Day. *Disneyland Then, Now, and Forever*. New York: Disney Enterprises, 2005.

Gordon, William A. *The Ultimate Hollywood Tour Book*. 3d ed. Lake Forest, CA: North Ridge Books, 2002.

Heard, Christopher. *Depp*. Toronto: ECW Press, 2001.

Heath, Chris "Johnny Depp: Portrait of the Oddest as a Young Man." *Details*, May 1993.

Hedges, Peter. *What's Eating Gilbert Grape*. New York: Simon and Schuster, 1999.

Irving, Washington. *The Legend of Sleepy Hollow*. Rockville, MD:Wildside Press, 2004.

Jacobson, Laurie, and Marc Wanamaker. *Hollywood Haunted*. Santa Monica, CA: Angel City Press, 1994.

*Johnny Depp: The Complete Chronicle of a Hollywood Legend*. March 2007.

Johnstone, Nick. *Johnny Depp: the Illustrated Biography*. London: Carlton Books, 2006.

Kaylin, Lucy. "Johnny in Paradise." *Gentleman's Quarterly*, August, 2003, 92–98.

Lubber, Captain William. *Pirateology: The Pirate Hunter's Companion*. Cambridge, MA: Candlewick, 2006.

MacDonald, Gregory. *The Brave*. Fort Lee, NJ: Barricade Books, 1991.

Meikle, Denis. *Johnny Depp: A Kind of Illusion*. Rev. ed. Surrey, England: Reynolds & Hearn, 2007.

Niehaus, Alisha, and Alan Hecker. *Piratepedia*. New York: DK, 2007.

Pela, Robert. *Filthy: The Weird World of John Waters*. Los Angeles, CA: Alyson Books, 2002.

Pomerance, Murray. *Johnny Depp Starts Here*. New Brunswick, NJ: Rutgers University Press, 2005.

Rebello, Steven. "Johnny Handsome." *Movieline*, May 1990.

Richardson, John H. "The Unprocessed Johnny Depp." *Esquire* 141, no. 5 (May 2004).

Rottenberg, Josh. "The Captain at Ease." *Entertainment Weekly*, May 18, 2007.

Ryan, James. "Depp Gets Deeper." *Vogue Magazine*, September 1994.

Sacks, Ethan. "Job Was Killing Them: Actors Made a Living Dying in Horror Flix." *New York Daily News*, October 29, 2006, 27.

Schneller, Johanna. "Johnny Angel." *GQ: Gentlemen's Quarterly* 63, no. 10 (October 1993).

Sessums, Kevin. "Johnny Be Good." *Vanity Fair*, February 1997.

Singer, Michael. *Bring Me That Horizon: The Making of Pirates of the Caribbean.*
    New York: Disney Enterprises, 2007.

Sturm, Circe. *Blood Politics: Race, Culture and Identity in the Cherokee Nation of
    Oklahoma.* University of California Press, Berkeley: 2002.

Thompson, Hunter S. *Fear and Loathing in Las Vegas: A Savage Journey to the
    Heart of the American Dream.* New York: Vintage, 1988.

Turner, Victor. "Passages, Margins, and Poverty: Religious Symbols of Commun-
    itas." In *High Points In Anthropology,* ed. P. Bohannan, and Mark Glazer. 2d
    ed. New York: McGraw-Hill, 1988.

Vancheri, Barbara. "Depp's Nightmare Returns," *Pittsburgh Post Gazette,* September 1,
    2006, C-4.

Wallace, Stone. *Johnny Depp: The Passionate Rebel.* Alberta, Canada: Icon Press),
    2004.

Wild, David. "Blood Brothers: Johnny Depp and Keith Richards Tell Why They're
    Pirates Onscreen and Off," *Rolling Stone,* May 31, 2007, 52–56.

# INDEX

# ABOUT THE AUTHORS

MICHAEL BLITZ is Professor of English and Chair of Interdisciplinary Studies at John Jay College of Criminal Justice of the City University of New York. He is the co-author of *Arnold Schwarzenegger: A Biography* (2006).

LOUISE KRASNIEWICZ is a senior research scientist in the American Section at the University of Pennsylvania Museum of Archeology and Anthropology. She is the co-author of *Arnold Schwarzenegger: A Biography* (2006).